I0823002

Honest Motherhood

On Losing My Mind and Finding Myself

Libby Ward

CROWN
NEW YORK

CROWN
An imprint of the Crown Publishing Group
A division of Penguin Random House LLC
1745 Broadway
New York, NY 10019
crownpublishing.com
penguinrandomhouse.com

Library of Congress Cataloging-in-Publication Data has been applied for.

Hardcover ISBN 978-0-593-73521-3
Ebook ISBN 978-0-593-73522-0

Editor: Aubrey Martinson
Production editor: Joyce Wong
Text designer: Andrea Lau
Production: Christopher Andrus
Copy editor: Eldes Tran
Proofreaders: Sigi Nacson, Rachel Markowitz, Hope Clarke
Publicist: Tammy Blake
Marketer: Chantelle Walker

Manufactured in the United States of America

1st Printing

First Edition

The authorized representative in the EU for product safety and compliance is Penguin Random House Ireland, Morrison Chambers, 32 Nassau Street, Dublin D02 YH68, Ireland, https://eu-contact.penguin.ie.

For my children,
for the mothers who deserve wholeness,
for the children they are raising

Contents

Author's Note ... vii

1 Mmm, Raisins ... 1
2 Sorry, But No ... 14
3 Baby Parades ... 22
4 Mothering ... 36
5 Mattering ... 46
6 Perspective ... 56
7 Groundhog Day ... 61
8 Nailing It ... 69
9 Oceans ... 79
10 Changes ... 86
11 Quilts ... 94
12 Shoeboxes ... 100
13 Dumpsters ... 109
14 Selfless ... 116

15 Daddy Is Fun 126
16 Granola Bars 136
17 No Wonder 147
18 Icebergs 163
19 Sunshine 172
20 Rainbows 180
21 Dishes 185
22 The Contract 196
23 Gardening 207
24 Safety 224
25 Human 237
26 Rubik's Cube 250
27 Summers 262

Acknowledgments 270
Notes 274

Author's Note

This book wasn't supposed to be a memoir.

When I first sat down at my computer two years ago, I intended to write a book that combined research, *some* elements of my story, and the stories of mothers around the world. These would act as an illustration of what I've learned about motherhood and the life-altering impacts of practicing radical honesty. Truthfully, sharing the breadth of my life experiences simply felt too vulnerable (read: terrifying) and simultaneously not relatable enough to make the impact I wanted to make.

But in time, I felt my story was begging to be told. So, with a lump in my throat and the encouragement of my people, I have. I know now that we don't need to share universal experiences for you to find yourself in these pages or gain something from them. In fact, I think the uniqueness and sameness of my story are what make it compelling. Now this book is what it was always meant to be: my *honest motherhood, my* story, *my* truth.

Here's the problem: The truth is subjective.

Honest Motherhood is literally about honesty. But there are endless possible ways to tell every story, mine included: perspectives from other parties, details that we miss, forgetfulness, misremembering, or any number of "but what abouts" that fill our lives, relationships, and social media feeds. I'm no stranger to this phenomenon, which is maybe why I thought telling *my* truth felt impossible. I simply cannot capture the fullness of my experiences or that of those who have impacted my own story. (Nor do you have the time to read an encyclopedia.)

Still, the stories you are about to read are mine, from my perspective, pulled from my imperfect memory, told with my voice, with my biases, and with my own goal in mind: to help other mothers find their way to themselves.

I've remained loyal to the truth as I know it in every instance I can. I've also altered names, locations, and other details to protect the real people in my story—and occasionally, to get to the point quicker. I'm not a trained writer. I am a regular, small-town Canadian mom with a story to tell, a fiery passion for the wholeness of mothers, and a knack for disarming people with questionably dark humor. I hope that as you engage with my words (and also the world), you remember that the "villains" in every story have their own stories and that the "heroes" have their flaws, too.

Content warning: While this book is woven with stories that I hope will make you laugh, relate, and feel empowered, it also dives into heavier themes like depression, anxiety, complex childhood trauma, abuse, and other darknesses that may be triggering or difficult to read. If it gets to be too much, take a break, skip some pages, or talk to a therapist. If you are struggling with any of the above, please seek proper professional help.

Lastly, a spoiler alert—especially for the moms currently trudging through the trenches of life. There is a happy, nuanced ending to look forward to. (Not that our stories are ever finished.)

Take care of yourself. I'll see you on the other side.

Libby

1

Mmm, Raisins

I don't have time for this crap.

I sat in my car, looking down at the bottle of orange syrupy liquid in my hand that the lab tech had casually instructed me to drink. I took a sip. Nasty. But alas, I am a good girl, so I drank it. A few hours later, I was back at the lab, eyes closed and my arm outstretched while the tech pierced my vein and drew my blood to see how well my body was tolerating the sugar bomb.

A positive test result would mean I'd won the gestational diabetes lottery and that my body wasn't processing sugar properly. This diagnosis would come with a strict new diet to avoid health complications for both me and the baby. And sure, I wanted a healthy baby. But also? Sugar is one of my personal seven wonders of the world. The idea of giving up Twizzlers and Two-Bite Brownies for the duration of my pregnancy? Unrealistic. Sadistic, even.

Since getting pregnant, I'd become a blood-test frequent flyer. The amount of visits to the doctor, midwife, and lab made monitoring my health feel like a part-time job. I already had two of those.

By day, I worked a high-stress job on my feet as an educational assistant, supporting students with special needs in schools across my rural county. By night, I was a server at a fast-paced fancy restaurant. Between the two jobs, I crushed my step goal every day. By nearly all measures, I was a healthy twenty-five-year-old pregnant woman. Still, they had to check the boxes, I guess.

When I arrived at my midwife's office a few days later to get my results, I was greeted by a fill-in. Let's call her . . . Agatha. Think the Trunchbull from *Matilda,* whiskers and all. She called my name, and I waddled into her office.

"I've got your results here," she said with a thick Austrian accent, pursing her lips. "Are you drinking coffee?"

"Just decaf tea," I said, proud of myself for being a rule follower.

"Sugar?" she asked, with her head cocked to the side, as if she already didn't believe what I was going to say.

"No, just milk," I said, shifting in my seat, my legs throbbing after my long day at work.

"Good. Your result is negative. BUT! You *could* still develop diabetes at any time and *that* would be very bad for your baby! You *must* be careful. No junk food, no candy, no sweets, and no sugar in your coffee!" she asserted triumphantly.

Ludicrous! I felt my eyebrows lift and tried to pull them back down, desperate to hide what I was really thinking.

"If you really need a treat, have a handful of raisins," she added.

I held back my laughter like my life depended on it. "I can't have any sugar whatsoever?" I asked, in utter disbelief.

"Yes, no candy or treats. Eat whole foods and only those that are naturally sweet," she said. Did she live on planet Earth?

I gave a polite nod while my mind drifted to my hunger pains and the doughnut I planned to eat on the way to my second shift after this appointment. I'll try to cut a realistic amount of sugary things from my diet, but *hard pass on the raisins, Agatha.* I've got enough to think about.

She carried on with the rest of the appointment, weighing me, listening to my stomach, and listing off more rules. "Drink lots of water! Take your vitamins. Don't be stressed; the baby can feel it. No processed meat. Don't gain too much weight but make sure you are eating enough. Take care of yourself," she said.

INSIDE LIBBY: I'm tryingggggg, lady.
OUTSIDE LIBBY: Got it.

When she asked how I was feeling, I remembered the problems I was having with my legs.

"My legs have been bothering me a lot lately, getting more swollen as the day goes on, throbbing and even some of my veins are bulging out," I said, hoping for a quick solution.

"Stand up and let me see," she asserted.

I pulled up the skirt of my dress to show her and that's how the Trunchbull met Big Blue and his brother, Bulgy Blue—my enormous throbbing veins.

"Oh. Those are varicose veins. You'll have to stay off your feet as much as possible. Certainly, no standing for long periods," she said with stern certainty.

Did she think I was some kind of viscountess straight out of Victorian England? Like, I could while away hours in bed while my ladies-in-waiting fetched me cheddar scones and freshly churned butter? This is real life. I have bills to pay. I have a baby to prepare for. Such realities involve being a person who stands upright—a lot.

"That's not possible in my line of work. Are there other options?" I asked.

She looked at me, shaking her head, seemingly disappointed by my very being.

"Well . . ." she tutted. "If you really can't, you must wear thigh-high compression stockings whenever you are standing. You'll have to buy a pair as soon as possible," she said. As I got up to leave, she called out, "And don't forget to put your feet up!"

The next day I bought a pair of old-lady compression stockings just like she told me to. I used the money from tips I'd been saving to buy a maternity bra for my growing breasticles. Priorities, I guess. I wrestled the miniature uncomfortable elastic-y tubes of torture onto the pasty-white swollen legs of my five-foot-eight body that was once so slender, youthful, and freckled that my family called me Pippi Longstocking.

Now, when I looked in the mirror, that is not who stared back. Instead? A grandma—walker, dentures, and all. Like Pippi Longstocking gone rogue. I exaggerate. Still, I wasn't a fan. *Ugh.*

It was a good thing I bought the tights, because several weeks later, I needed to wear them on a long-haul flight—an activity infamous for turning swollen legs into full-blown conundrums.

We visited the UK most years. The south of England is where my husband, Greg, was born and raised. That big green island is also where I lived when we'd gotten married four years earlier, one rainy day just shy of my twenty-first birthday. But after living in Southampton for two years, we decided to move and settle in Canada. Now, with the help of Greg's mom, we simply visited England most years.

Despite the glory of rolling hills, cobblestone streets, historical landmarks, and five-star cheese, England was simply not a place we could afford to build a life. The decision to leave for Canada was easy. At the time, even with full-time jobs, we lived in a one-bedroom flat in the sketchy part of town and shared a car that was always on the verge of dying. Our kitchen was so small that we had to step into the hallway just to open the oven door. Making friends with English girls turned out to be harder than anticipated. I was lonely. Also, our downstairs neighbor sold drugs.

Any spare time we had wasn't spent gallivanting around castles or sipping pints in cozy pubs—it was spent surviving. So, we settled in southern Ontario, where life was affordable. Canada, my home country, also offered wide open spaces, strangers who acknowledged your existence, and houses without washing machines located in the kitchen (no offense, England). That and, of course, Tim Hortons, Canada's iconic doughnut shop with wonderfully average coffee. You don't know what you've got until it's gone.

Visiting England instead of residing there seemed like a better long-term decision. Besides, the trips back to the UK were always something we looked forward to. As we waited for our plane to jet off from Toronto that day, I smiled to myself. This visit was particularly exciting. I was seven months' pregnant with the first grandbaby in the family.

On the seven-hour flight, I tried to wear my compression stockings, but they were even more uncomfortable than usual. The hot, sticky beasts rolled down my legs. I wanted to yell in the flight attendant's face. I didn't. Instead, I went to the bathroom and peeled them off in relief—like a normal person. I enjoyed the rest of the flight, stocking- and shoe-less.

I stretched often. I walked the aisles every hour or so to keep my blood moving. The blood was making its way down to my lower extremities all right. It just didn't come back up. When the plane finally landed, Bulgy Blue and his veiny brother morphed into immense throbbing vessels of terror. My feet grew to two times their normal size. Before deplaning, I squashed my juicy feet into my little black flats and waddled my way through the airport, fearing I had made a grave mistake.

Greg's mom, Christine, picked us up at the airport and drove us to her quintessential English cottage, dreamy thatched roof and all. She made me a perfect cup of tea and I excused myself to take a bath in her big British tub. I am, and always have been, a bath girl. The bigger, the burnier, the better. If it doesn't scald my skin and make me sweat, what is even the point?

I poured myself the most lavish, scalding hot, bubbly bath possible, turned on the jets, and soaked. I opened the old wood-framed window, listened to the birdsong coming from her English garden, and breathed in the fresh air. I willed my tree-trunk calves to stop throbbing, waited for my veins to dissipate, and hoped my feet would return to their normal size. They did not.

After forty-five long minutes, I gave up and plopped myself on the couch beside Greg. Fear spread over me. Was I developing deep vein thrombosis, one of those diseases I'd learned about leafing through the pamphlets at the midwives' office? Was there a giant blood clot floating around my body that could travel to my lungs and give me a pulmonary embolism—and kill me?!

Nobody knew but Google. I searched "help swollen sore legs pregnant."

I read the list of things I already knew I should be doing. Then, I read something I hadn't seen before: sitting in hot water for long periods of time causes your veins to swell. Take showers or keep your bath water lukewarm. *WHAT? Whoops.* I showed Greg, while I anxiously considered the possibility of my own perishing. Hearing me complain, Christine chimed in: "When I was pregnant, I used to lie on my bed and put my legs up on the wall to help with the swelling. Have you tried that?" I had not. *Where had my mother-in-law been all this time?!* I thought. Oh yes, England.

My legs were flopped over Greg's lap. He lifted one up at a ninety-degree angle, high above his head. Within several seconds, the fluid eased up and I felt relief. My raised cankle was shrinking, along with it—my fear of death. We compared my draining leg with the other one. Greg laughed, either in amazement or at my stupidity for not knowing I could do this—I wasn't sure. Then it dawned on me. The Trunchbull. She *did* tell me to put my feet up. I guess she'd meant it literally, not figuratively.

PUT YOUR FEET UP.

It's a saying I'd heard countless times in my life when someone was being told to relax or take a break. Call me a dumbo, but I'd never once considered the necessity of literal elevation.

I am still paying for the brain lapse that caused me to wait until the eleventh hour to put my feet up. My legs never really went back to normal after that. As I write these words ten years later—nearly to the day—I am sitting in my living room with my legs propped up on a pillow, staring at the disgusting blue, purple, and yellow bruise that spans the length of my inner thigh where Big Blue and his brother resided up until last week, when I had them lasered out. Yes, it hurt.

Did I feel like a complete idiot for not understanding the need to *literally* raise my feet above my heart to help the fluid drain from them? Yes. Did I wish I could have taken it easy and not worked two physically demanding jobs that likely made the situation worse? Yes. Did I *want* to take care of myself, to put my feet up . . . even in a figurative way? Obviously. But it's not as simple as that.

I went to the appointments. I listened to the professionals. I read the books. I avoided hot dogs, caffeine, and alcohol. I stayed active and took my vitamins. It's not like I wasn't trying.

In the decade that's passed since I initially failed to care for my pregnancy legs, I've been misled or misinformed plenty of times. I've ignored, forgotten, or dropped the ball at plenty of self-care "shoulds." But when someone tells you to spend nine months eating raisins instead of a drop of sugar and, in the same breath, they tell you to put your feet up, how is one to decide which advice to heed? Which is literal and which to toss into the enormous and unrealistic pile of "shoulds"? When you've got limited resources and brain power, how is one to determine where said resources should go?

Pregnancy feels like you're walking around the world with a "give me advice" sign duct-taped to your forehead. *Free rein on the lady making a person! Let's help her out! She must know what we think is best!*

When the baby arrives, the advice just goes on steroids while the world watches on with a gown and gavel. Can't do it all? That's a *you* problem. If you're overwhelmed, just take care of yourself better. Here's a list of a million things you'll need to do for that to happen:

Just wake up before the baby, take all your vitamins, make breakfast, plan dinner, research developmental milestones, check on your fucking crystals, do a cold plunge, learn about the toxins in your food, return your mother-in-law's phone call, and don't forget to stretch. It only takes five minutes. Bounce back, girl. Keep up your skincare routine but also keep up with your naturopath. Can't afford it? Try harder.

Feeling down? Work out more! Maintain your friendships! Good luck getting time off work or preparing your partner to parent alone for a couple of hours while you're out. You're so lucky he babysits! Don't forget to open your legs and put out once in a while. He's got needs, too!

Oh, you keep peeing your pants when you sneeze? Just give up on all your other healthcare appointments for the next few months so you can see a pelvic floor physiotherapist. You don't have time for both. Actually, scratch that, the baby has checkups and you can't be in two places at once.

Sleep eight hours because sleep deprivation can make you insane and no one wants a loony mother, but also get up to feed your baby instead of starving them to death or breaking their spirit forever. Don't be selfish—they are only little once. Validate their feelings but also have boundaries for goodness' sake—kids need guidance! Trust your gut, just not if it tells you to drive into oncoming traffic because you can't handle another second. Heal your trauma! Most importantly, don't stress yourself out—it leads to all kinds of health problems. You wouldn't want that. If all else fails, just sleep when the baby sleeps.

THERE IS NO WAY TO prepare for the unrelenting, unsolicited, and conflicting advice in motherhood. We've never had access to so much information about pregnancy, parenting, and well-being. All of this should make our lives better, no?

We're navigating societal pressures and juggling a workload beyond our capacity while the world tells us to drink our greens, meditate, and build some Atomic Habits. *Okay, James Clear, have you tried that with a miniature version of yourself screaming in your ear?* "Let them!" says Mel Robbins. Does that apply to my children shoving their fingers in electrical sockets, Mel, does it?!

Most people telling moms how to live their lives and how they should feel about it aren't also the one juggling flaming swords with a baby on their hip. We've got the coaches coaching coaches to coach coaches, the positive thinking mantra that will apparently make you immune to toddlers coughing into your mouth and the pyramid schemes that will apparently skyrocket you to fulfillment. Maybe the MLM will even make you the proud owner of a brand-new white Lexus. You can't open your phone these days without someone selling you a quick fix to your overwhelm. There are entire industries profiting off our burnout, brokenness, and vulnerability.

Obviously, sometimes the easily accessible information on social media is valuable. The expertise and bravery of the Dr. Shefalis and Glennon Doyles of the world change lives. Some of the internet's health and parenting advice *is* helpful, of course. Let's face it, I wouldn't be where I am, and you wouldn't be reading this book if it weren't for the self-help industry. But the velocity at which we receive these conflicting messages from unverified sources and people with questionable intentions gets more intense by the hour. All of it adds to the feeling that we can't keep up, no matter how hard we try.

Navigating the pressures of raising decent human beings while taking care of ourselves is like trying to solve a rigged Rubik's Cube with some of your fingers missing, all while the sun burns your bloodshot eyes. You focus on solving one problem, but the rest of it falls to crap. Navigating "self-care" is challenging enough without kids. Parenting well is hard enough without unmet needs. Add in sleep deprivation, the mental load, and limited resources—and it's no wonder getting to the dentist feels like a monumental feat. Like, yes, I know that I can't pour from an empty cup, but how am I supposed to fill it when I can't get to the tap because there's a feral kid on my ankle?

I once thought that if I learned enough, followed the rules, tried my best, and did all the things I "should" do, I'd make it. I'd solve my Rubik's Cube, check all the boxes, line up all the little colored squares, toss it over my shoulder, and walk off into the sunset victoriously. I was wrong. I didn't realize I'd have to make the choice between one important thing and seventeen others—all with less time and energy than I'd ever had. I didn't realize how complicated it was all going to be.

Simultaneously taking care of ourselves and raising our little people is nothing short of a monumental crapshoot. And yet, it's our responsibility. So what gives? Despite what that rich motivational Instagrammer with a white marble countertop has to say, enjoying motherhood isn't just a mindset. We *don't* all have the same twenty-four hours in a day or the same access to healthy food, hours of sleep, money in the bank, or emotionally stable parents.

The mom who wakes up at 5 a.m. to work out probably doesn't have a colicky baby, a checked-out partner, and a two-hour commute to a job that barely keeps the lights on. The doctor who implores you not to stress and suggests you make a list instead probably doesn't have three kids under five and severe undiagnosed ADHD. The random lady who tells you to take iron supplements likely isn't chronically constipated, staggering through life with hemorrhoids the size of golf balls and a bathroom door that doesn't lock.

Moms are exhausted. We're overwhelmed with the information overload and the unattainable solutions sold by self-help gurus, the fear-mongering parenting experts, and the pressure to ensure our offspring excel at everything regardless of the cost to our sanity. We're mothering in a wellness-obsessed era where finding mothers who are truly thriving is a rarity.

The American Surgeon General has named "increasing stress and declining mental health among parents as the latest critical health issue" and has urged the government for more support due to the massive negative implications for parents and their kids. Systemic change is long overdue. And yet, my Instagram DMs are filled with moms asking me if it will ever get easier and what is wrong with them for being so worn out.

I entered motherhood blaming myself for all the ways I struggled to balance being a good mom with being good to myself—taking it as some kind of sign from the universe that I sucked—then bashing myself in the head with the corner of my rage-inducing Rubik's Cube hoping to ignite change. But blaming myself just made me feel worse.

You know what else makes it harder? The fact that other moms weren't entirely honest about motherhood. Women told me how wonderfully fulfilling it was—like some kind of all-you-can-eat buffet of joy, purpose, and giggles. They were right about the love. In fact, love didn't feel like a sufficient word. The scrumptiousness of having little humans to watch grow? The fierce protective instinct? Sure. I'd have tackled a rabies-infected raccoon in broad daylight if it so much as looked at my baby the wrong way.

But that love didn't mask the shooting pains that ripped through me while the doctor sewed up my second-degree tear after I pushed my first baby out—as if there were no human on the other end of her needle and thread. My full heart didn't ease the sting of that first bathroom trip. My renewed hope didn't stop my nipples from bleeding or my self-esteem from plummeting, either.

The drug-like joy didn't dispel the depression that seeped into my bones nor did it fill the black void of loneliness. The miracle of life couldn't erase the gut-wrenching pain of my own trauma that was unearthed. The beauty of my babies couldn't chase the longing I had to feel like I was more than somebody's snack bitch. The joy of childhood delight couldn't strip me of the urge to slash my husband's tires when he got to leave the house and think his own uninterrupted thoughts each day.

Right there at the beginning, I felt the true paradox of motherhood that I would go on to experience throughout the years: the indescribable good that comes with the unfathomably hard. The "I can't take my eyes off you" mixed with "What the hell have I gotten myself into?"

So many mothers struggled to be open about all the hard things that accompanied the joy and goodness. They were honest about the good stuff. Why didn't they tell the truth about the rest?

Before I became a mom, transcendent motherly love sounded like a magical unicorn I was eager to ride. The ease other women displayed suggested that motherhood might be easy. So, when it was my turn, when my experience looked very different from theirs, I wondered what was wrong with *me*. I wondered why it was so hard for me to love every second and be solely fulfilled by motherhood like they were. I wondered why I couldn't ignore the frustration, exhaustion, and apathy I would come to feel. Admitting that I didn't love it all felt like admitting I didn't love any of it. Feeling alone made it harder to figure out what I actually needed.

So yes, maybe I should have worn my compression stockings more often, quit my two jobs, rested more, and eaten raisins instead of Twizzlers and brownies. Maybe I should have put my feet up high above my head every day and stayed out of fiery hot baths. Maybe I should have called my mother-in-law more often and heeded her advice. Perhaps, then, I might not be icing my inner thighs right now. Although, it's *also* possible that quitting my jobs could have made me sedentary, leading to gestational diabetes, depression, or some kind of freak accident. I'll never know.

If I had a time machine, I'd go back and tell chunky-legged pregnant Libby a few things, starting with this: It's normal to want to throw your Rubik's Cube into the ocean and shout *fuck it*. You're not an idiot, or a failure, a broken person, or a bad mom. You are doing the best you can with what you have and what you know right now. That is enough. Being a mom feels like a lot, because *it literally is*.

But I don't have a time machine. I can't go back, just like I couldn't press fast-forward during my darkest moments. The best I can do is share my story with you and hope that my relentless honesty will help you feel seen in whatever place you currently find yourself sitting, lying down, or standing in your own literal or metaphorical compression socks. Possibly, in watching me find myself, you'll find yourself, too. *No pressure.* If nothing else, pat yourself on the back for reading an actual book when you could be sucked into TikTok or 647 other tasks pulling at you.

I know the conundrum all too well. Right here at the start of my story you'll find me in just that predicament: Do what's best for me or do what I've always done—what everybody else wants? Being honest is hard.

2

Sorry, But No

The phone screamed at me from my bedside table. Glancing over, I saw that it was the ungodly hour of 6 a.m. Knowing it was probably work calling, I considered dropping my phone into the toilet and going back to bed. Instead, I answered it. "Hello?" An automated voice on the other end offered me a day's work at a school twenty minutes away.

This is how my work days started. The early morning calls could send me to any school, any time. As a substitute educational assistant, I'd be assigned to work with any number of kids between the ages of four and twenty-one, each of them navigating life with some form of disability. In my four years on the job, I had seen it all. One day might start with an adorable smile from a ginger-haired kindergartner with thick-rimmed glasses, Down syndrome, and an uncapped affection for new people. The next day, I could be handed full-body padding to protect me from a towering nonverbal high schooler known for putting teachers through walls.

Chaos was common. I didn't mind. I prided myself on my ability to handle whatever life threw at me. I thrived in problem-solving roles. I understood how my students' disabilities or lack of impulse control, communication skills, academic support, and structure at home could lead them to make their needs known in alternative and sometimes aggressive ways. Having a stranger who didn't understand your wants, needs, routines, or struggles *would* be infuriating. I cared about those kids—a lot. My dad was deaf, disabled, and didn't get the help he needed as a kid. It's one of the reasons I went into that line of work. I wanted to help.

Since becoming pregnant, this was becoming harder to do. Partially. I was tired. No. First trimester had shattered me. The exhaustion was so intense, I often had to pull over on the side of the road to nap on the way home from work. More than once, I fell asleep mid–dinner party at a friend's house. I also forgot simple words like "bacon" and "sunshine."

The exhaustion and brain fog, paired with the unpredictability and sometimes straight-up aggressive nature of my job, made me enjoy the challenge of my work less than I did before growing a child in my uterus.

But like most normal people, I needed to earn money to live. I desperately wanted a long-term job placement. And not just for the cash. It would eliminate the stress of walking into a new and possibly violent work environment each day. Consistency and stability were things I yearned for. My goal was to land a hard-to-come-by permanent position before anyone knew I was pregnant. Disclosing my state of being could get in the way of any objectivity when hiring, of course, even though we all know that's illegal.

So I accepted the work offer that morning, made myself presentable, and forced some breakfast into my face. I kissed Greg goodbye, and waved to him and Roger as I left for work. Roger is Greg's dad and one of my favorite humans.

Roger was retired, and since his and Christine's marriage dissolved after Greg and I moved to Canada, he visited us from across the pond often. Along with my father-in-law's relentlessly positive attitude, he brought a desire to make mulligatawny soup, quick wit, and an up-for-anything vibe wherever he went.

Greg loved his dad's company, and I loved having a stable and supportive father figure around. So, after plenty of visits over a few years, Roger immigrated to Canada and the three of us purchased a home together, complete with an in-law suite. He became part of the very fabric of our family unit and one I was grateful my unborn kid would have.

That morning, like many others, Roger's bright smiling face and promises of the perfect cup of proper English tea on my return from work helped me get out the door. Twenty minutes passed between parting ways with Greg and Roger and rolling into the school parking lot for my workday. When I arrived at the office, the secretary handed me one of the generic binders I'd become all too familiar with, the kind that *should* have important information about my placement for the day but instead contained outdated, redundant documents that offered almost nothing to help me figure out what I was walking into.

"That way," the secretary said, pointing down the hall to the classroom where I would be working. The unknown portion of my job was my least favorite. Sometimes, my pregnancy made me question whether it was safe to continue working in a sometimes-violent job—but there was no choice. How would we pay the bills?

Greg and I were one of those lucky couples who said, "Hey, why don't we stop trying *not* to have a baby? It could take a while, so we can just see what happens," and then found themselves staring at two thin blue lines a couple of weeks later. Pregnancy happens. Listen. I understand the significance and blessing of this swift pregnancy, believe me. We weren't really prepared though. Greg was bringing home little more than minimum wage from a job he didn't like, and my unpredictable hours meant we were basically living paycheck to paycheck.

Still, the life Greg and I enjoyed was light-years away from the financial reality I'd grown up with. We had a mortgage. We each drove a secondhand car and had enough room on a credit card to fix a car if the brakes went kaput. Compared with a childhood where filling the cupboards with groceries from food banks, collecting social assistance, and pawning off our electronics for cold hard cash was as normal as putting on pants each day, we were loaded. But I could never trust that any stability we found would last.

I'd worked hard to end the cycle of poverty and couldn't risk ever going back. Being the girl who made it out came with an invisible weight that could only be carried with hustle. One wrong move always felt like it could be my ticket back to poverty lane. That was not a journey I was willing to take.

I was determined to give my unborn kid the life I never had. Our fridge would be unquestionably full, opportunities would be anything but scarce, and my love would be unwaveringly known.

Sure, standing on my feet all day wasn't exactly good for me, but neither was not being able to afford prenatal vitamins or a safe car seat. The risk of getting throttled by a teenager wasn't ideal, but neither was being jobless and pregnant, unable to pay the bills. Maintaining a bank account in the black was a way to create the life of safety and security I wanted so deeply.

Another way? Saying yes. It helped that I was someone with high capacity—for stress, for family shenanigans, and for workplace expectations and beyond. As far back as I can remember, my ability to take what life handed to me had only served to benefit me. Assuming responsibilities that were not mine made me a proactive problem solver. I was reliable—a "pleasure to have in class."

Listen. I drank tea I hated for two years when I lived in England because I didn't want to upset the people offering it to me. (Somehow, I ended up loving it. But that is not the point.)

My ability to say yes even when my insides screamed *no* got me jobs, promotions, friends, approval, accolades, and just enough validation to keep me feeling like I was worthy of the benefits I earned. My desire to show everyone I'd made it and they could count on me was unquenchable. The route to my happiness? Other people's happiness. Any success I'd found in my life had been found through my ability to be good.

That day at work I was determined to do what I'd always done. So I swallowed my fear of the unknown and made my way to the classroom.

I asked the teacher if she could fill me in on my assignment.

"The student's name is Emily. Just don't stand too close behind her or she'll headbutt you. She broke the last EA's nose," the teacher said. As I'd soon find out, Emily was a six-year-old girl who was twice the size of other kids her age. She had been bounced around the foster care system for a lot of her short life and her behaviors were evidence of that.

Emily came skipping into the classroom and the teacher gestured to her as if to say, "She's yours." Once Emily emptied her backpack, she sat at her desk avoiding eye contact with me. If you know anything about kids, especially kids with extra needs, you know that coping with change is their least favorite thing. Ditto, kid.

"Hi, Emily. I'm Mrs. Ward, I'll be helping you today. Would you like to build blocks or start the day with a snack?" I said, as I approached her. Choices. Kids love choices. She scowled at me and headed for the blocks. She picked up a block and threw it high in the air, smiling, then looked at me to see how I would respond as it landed on the floor beside her.

"Don't throw the blocks, Emily. Someone could get hurt," I said. She did it again as if I hadn't spoken a word. The teacher and other students carried on like it was just another day. My body filled with tension, multitudes more than I was used to feeling when dealing with the aggressive behavior of the students I supported. Was the small growing fetus inside me making me afraid of a violent six-year-old with a menacing smile and bucket full of wooden blocks? Was my pride being replaced by fragility? If so, I didn't like it.

Still, I kept calm on the outside and tried to distract Emily. Failure ensued. By the time Emily had thrown every block across the room, she was holding the attention of the entire class and I was holding on to my patience by a thread.

After recess, I was sitting on the carpet with Emily when she swung her elbow back and clocked me in the face. I tried not to react, but I couldn't stop a groan of pain coming out of my mouth. My cheekbone grew hot. *Thank goodness she didn't hit my stomach,* I thought. I reminded her to keep her hands to herself. In return, I felt the back of her head propel itself into my nose. I clutched my face and grimaced. Finally, the teacher noticed and buzzed the office to request support.

The principal's solution was not really a solution at all: spend the rest of the day in the hallways, library, and resource room—anywhere but the classroom. For the other children's safety, of course. I spent the remainder of the day supervising and attempting to regulate Emily, alone. She ripped art off the walls, threw books at me, ran, and hid. I counted the minutes until the end-of-day bell rang, weighing the risks of calling for the principal and admitting I couldn't finish the day's work. I thought, how could I keep working in positions like this when I was constantly in fear of my baby getting hurt? How could I protect my child while also protecting my reputation and job, especially as I was constantly the fill-in?

When Emily's school bus finally pulled away, I held back tears.

My body filled with relief, desperate to get home to that hot cup of tea. *Note to self: Do not accept any more calls to this school.* I was nearly out the door when the principal called me in to his office.

"I heard you had a pretty good day. You'll come back the rest of the week?" he said, with hopeful eyes.

INSIDE LIBBY: Over my dead body.
OUTSIDE LIBBY: Unfortunately, it was not a very good day and I don't think I'll be able to.

I'd never said no to returning to a school placement before. I'd *dreamed* of being asked for more than a day's work with a student. This was my chance to have the consistency and predictability I'd longed for. But I knew I shouldn't—I couldn't put my pregnancy at risk.

I felt myself shrink, desperate for this potential employer to wish me well and stifle my guilt.

"Are you sure?" he pressed.

I was a capable, hard worker who always said yes to my boss, to my husband, to my mom, to my friends, and to church volunteering. I liked being the girl who said yes, who was liked, and who was approved of.

But for the first time, I started to really consider the risks I was taking by choosing other people over myself because it meant choosing them over my baby, too. This was a new level of tension between other people's needs and my own that I'd never felt before.

"I'm sure. Actually . . . I should tell you I'm pregnant. I was hit a lot today and I don't believe it is safe to return. I need to keep myself and my baby safe," I said, hoping he would tell me he completely understood and that my well-being was the most important thing.

"Really?" he scoffed. "You *do* know this is part of the job. You might be making the situation out to be bigger than it is."

"I can show you the chart I used today. I was hit thirty-five times," I said, internally recoiling as I heard the words come out of my mouth. Offering this fact felt so unnecessarily dramatic, but it was true.

"We don't have anyone else," he continued, both of us knowing full well that it wasn't my problem or something my $16-per-hour pay grade made me responsible for. Not that it stopped me from feeling responsible.

"I'm sorry, but no," I said, physically incapable of not apologizing.

He shook his head in disappointment and got back to work. I left the school and made my way through the parking lot as quickly as I could.

I slumped in the front seat—equal parts infuriated with the principal, riddled with guilt, annoyed at myself for apologizing, and still certain I'd done the right thing. I'd always felt like I was expected to carry on no matter what the cost. But now the cost was too great. I'd never had a good enough reason to say no before. Now I did. The irony screamed at me like a siren I'd only just heard after my earplugs were ripped out.

After spending a lifetime hustling for approval, being honest about what I needed didn't feel brave—it felt unnatural. No, scratch that. Disappointing other people made me want to peel my skin off.

3

Baby Parades

I was standing at the back of our small country church waiting for my tea to steep. Heather arrived with a smile plastered across her face and waved—seemingly unaware that the one-year-old on her hip had a fistful of her hair. *Maybe she has an iron scalp,* I thought. Heather was also, somehow, carrying a tray full of shortbread and put it down on the café table. The condensation inside the plastic-wrap cover indicated the cookies were freshly baked this morning.

"Morning, Libby. Help yourself!" she said.

I picked up a piece of shortbread and it was, in fact, still warm. *Impressive.* Pregnant, albeit childless, I hardly had enough energy to do my makeup, never mind go to church with freshly baked shortbread and three perfectly dressed children and a smile.

I slid into the pew beside Leah, my best friend, who was also pregnant. "I got here early to grab our spot!" she whispered. Of course she had. Reliable, thoughtful, predictably prepared. Leah was the opposite of me, the ying to my spontaneous and scattered yang. She was introverted; I was extroverted. She was stoic. My face showed every thought and feeling that crossed my mind. Life choices, for my friend, were thought through logic and composure.

We'd met in youth group as teenagers. Leah was pretty, popular, and kind—the holy trinity of intimidation for a sixteen-year-old girl with the self-esteem of a socially awkward bridge troll. So, I kept my distance. But after I got back from England and got better at pretending I had my life together, we became fast friends.

We lived in the same town, attended the same church, and now we were both on the brink of motherhood. The timing? Freakishly good. And while her pregnancy was three months behind mine, she was always three steps ahead. Leah was just starting to show and she carried it with the same quiet confidence she carried everything else in life.

My friend was put together. Me? I was a sometimes put-together person. I could play the part when needed, but it was just that—a part. On Sundays, I put in my best effort.

We weren't the only women with growing fetuses. In our church, babies and children abounded. Our congregation was just a hundred or so, and the kids outnumbered the adults by a long stretch. Three or four kids, minimum, was the norm. "Be fruitful and multiply," it seemed, was taken literally. I'm sure it helped that many families were farmers.

"There must be something in the water," the pastor would joke, as if the water was what made our little corner of the world so fertile. Laughter would erupt. Proud smiles were shared. Our collective ability to fill those pews was something to be celebrated. The church BBQs were fun, too. I couldn't wait to join Club Motherhood—not that anyone called it that. The baby parades helped.

And what, you might ask, is a baby parade? Picture this: The congregation arrives like it's a routine Sunday. People take their seats. The service begins. Then a shining family floats through the back door bearing a newborn bundle of joy like it's Mother Mary carrying Jesus himself. I exaggerate. Still. The pastor announces the triumphant arrival. Everyone swoons. An electric joy ripples through the rows, as one of the parents carries the baby up and down the aisles for all to see. Voilà. Baby parade.

We were all eagerly hoping this unofficial tradition—a celebratory welcome for newborns—would happen that day. One of the moms, Ashley, was overdue and the people were eager to hear the news.

The people at my church were *my* people. I'd loved them ever since the youth group kids and their moms scooped me up and set me on solid ground amid the turbulence of my home life a decade earlier. They'd tamed my Eminem-lyric-spitting mouth and helped me stop writing the murder-suicide poems I kept stashed between my mattress and box spring.

This is not an offhand tongue-in-cheek description of my youth. I wrote those poems. Teenage life at home was enough to make me want out. So when my older brother, Harry, started asking me to stop saying "fuck" so much and invited me to his youth group, I thought I'd give it a try. The first time I walked through the community center doors, I was surprised by how many kids there were. Cute ones. Nice ones. Fun ones. Teenagers who looked me in the eye like I was a human worth talking to. Was this heaven?

The church people accepted me like family, inviting me into game nights, potlucks, bonfires, and prayer circles. People asked how I was doing and how they could help. *What is this sorcery?* I latched like a hungry newborn baby to its own milkless hand, became heavily involved in the church, and resolved to say "fuck" less. I burnt my "secular" CDs in the church bonfire and even vowed to abstain from kissing boys—not that I had the opportunity.

I became a hardcore Bible girly. It wasn't just the prayers, warm hugs, and soup Sundays that I liked. Church became the first place in the whole world where I felt like I belonged, like I was loved for no reason other than existing. It was the stability I needed. In a way, they saved me.

Now, ten years later, married and pregnant, I found myself in those same church pews, yearning for the community's acceptance, reveling in it, and committed to being good like I was expected. My church community offered guidance, celebrated my wins, challenged my failures, grieved my losses, and provided me with the guardrails I'd always needed. Also, there was the shortbread. Our little country church might have been in the middle of nowhere but being there, with them, made me feel like I was somewhere.

The women around me seemed to have life mostly figured out. Stability and self-assurance were innate to their way of life. The church moms seemed to harness a mysterious maternal power that I was hankering to replicate—one that spewed positivity and patience like a water hose. They made motherhood simultaneously look like the ultimate calling and a walk in the park.

Ashley and her family must have snuck in during the worship service because as soon as it came time for announcements, I saw a big *there's-a-new-baby-in-the-house* smile spread across the pastor's face. He invited Ashley and her husband to bring up the baby to the front so everyone could admire them.

As Ashley made her way around the church with her squishy newborn held close to her chest, I could practically smell her pride. We all oohed and aahed like we'd never seen a baby before in our lives. The baby was perfect. *How was this woman walking?!* I wondered. I didn't quite understand how she was so at ease after what I can only imagine happened. But what did I know?

After the service I found Ashley. "So, how are you doing?" I asked.

"I'm good. Everything went so well. I am just so in love," she said.

A few other moms joined the conversation. After adoring the new baby and congratulating Ashley, they turned to me.

"You could be next! Are you excited?!" one of them asked.

"Yeah, but I am terrified. I don't think I'll be a good mom. I'm not like you guys," I said.

They cocked their heads sideways in unison, genuinely puzzled. "Libby, you will be amazing. Don't worry about it," one of them said, scooping up her blond two-year-old who appeared from behind her skirt. "This is what we were made for. Motherhood will come naturally. Believe me." As a mom, she was so chill, so calm, so . . . certain.

"You'll just love that baby so much. The moment it gets put on your chest, nothing else will matter anymore," Heather, the warm shortbread mom, chimed in.

"Being a mom is the most fulfilling thing you will ever do, you'll see. I can't wait for you to experience it!" another said with finality.

I *did* love kids—the ridiculous things they said, the way they loved so unconditionally, the joy and hope they brought. I wanted kids for my own reasons like this, too. But these moms—they were so giddy around babies. I couldn't help but catch a little secondhand anticipation of joy and excitement. And it wasn't just newborns—for years, I'd listened to them and watched them love, sacrifice, and serve their big families without complaint. With even tones and seemingly boundless energy, they appeared to delight in their roles as moms unceasingly.

The motherhood positivity water hose wasn't just at church, either. Moms everywhere told me how motherhood would change my life for the better. Forty-five seconds into a Facebook scroll showed me just how happy women were with their little homemade humans who filled places in their hearts they didn't know needed filling. Cheesy Christmas photos. First steps. Morning snuggles. Fresh wonder about the world's mundane things. Without doubt, it seemed, children made life better.

Still, fear tugged at me. What if I couldn't become the kind of mother everyone seemed born to be? Was there magic pixie dust that would rain down from the skies that would deliver this maternal instinct to me? Would I learn how to function on no sleep or have all the knowledge I was looking for delivered by stork? Despite my fears, I couldn't wait for my own baby parade. Club Motherhood did seem magical.

THE FIRST FEAR I HAD to face was the one that involved a human exiting my body.

"What are you afraid of?" Tammy asked.

Leah, our husbands, and I were sitting together in Tammy's living room during our shared prenatal class. Tammy was the doula we'd both chosen to support us through our pregnancies and birth because she'd done so for hundreds of other women in our community. She was warm, wise, and straight shooting—just what Leah and I needed to help us navigate our mutual fear of birthing a human being. The plan, of course, was for Tammy to make the fear go away.

"I'm afraid I am going to poop on the table," I said.

"I'm afraid of not knowing what to do," Leah said.

"I'm afraid of how much it will hurt," I said.

"I'm afraid I am going to die," Leah said.

"I'm afraid I won't have what it takes," I said.

"I'm afraid the pain will be unbearable," Leah said.

"I'm afraid of being ugly," I said.

I laughed a little, because hearing that last one come out of my mouth sounded ridiculous. I didn't consider myself to be a vain person, but I'd be lying if I said I wasn't afraid of becoming a gross, sweaty, triple-chin, red-face, crazy-looking woman while pushing a baby out.

Tammy looked at us endearingly and took a breath before responding.

"You might poop on the table. That's just what happens," she said, addressing the first of our long list of fears. But that just scratched the surface of my fear. Part of the problem was that I knew, deep down, that there was a birthing hierarchy.

Take the baby parades, for example. It wasn't uncommon for the pastor to tell us how long it had been since the baby was born. Ashley's baby was born only forty-eight hours before *their* parade. The fact that she was up and walking around at church already was impressive—though not as impressive as when Jessica waltzed into her fifth baby parade just twenty-four hours after her latest birth. Jessica, the apparent birthing goddess, unofficially reigned supreme over the "bounce back with a smile" castle—not that anybody said that out loud.

Then, there was the birth itself. The gold standard? No drugs. "Natural" births, as they were called, were the crown jewel of the birthing world. Most of the church moms gave birth this way—often at home with midwives or doulas and their pride intact. No epidurals. Many of them in pools.

Did their poop just float around? Did it touch them? Did it smell? Could their husbands ever unsee it? I didn't want to know.

Tammy reassured us the research showed that uncomplicated pregnancies are just as safe at home with midwives as they are with doctors. I thought back to my conversations with all the crunchy home-birthing moms I knew and loved. "It was beautiful! Powerful! Amazing!" they'd exclaim, watery-eyed with euphoria.

Good for you! I'd think when they told their birth stories. *Seriously, impressive.* I wanted to do it like them. Except I didn't.

I wanted to want to.

One mom once shared regretfully that while she'd planned to birth at home, she'd ended up having to push the baby out in a hospital. Another mom reassured her. "That's okay, all that matters is that you are both healthy," she said sincerely, but also as if the new mom had just told everyone she accidently dropped the baby on its head but it survived.

Nothing about the birthing hierarchy was explicit. But I could feel the pressure. These micro-interactions made one thing clear: Birthing your baby in a hospital with a doctor after getting a needle in your back was a subpar option. Nobody *said* that doctors, drugs, or other interventions during labor made your birth less magical, but it was clear who everyone was most impressed by. And who doesn't like impressing people?

Unfortunately, the thought of birthing at home in a pool of my own bodily fluids and the remnants of my pride elicited intrusive thoughts about joining a nunnery or nosediving into a lava pit. No offense, my water-birthing buddies.

Tammy told us it was natural to be afraid. "One of the most important things is to ensure you are in a safe environment with safe people. Feeling safe will allow your body to relax so that the delivery goes more smoothly," she said.

Makes sense, I thought. This information made me even more grateful to be supported by a midwife. Otherwise, I would be in the care of whichever doctor was on call the day my baby decided to come earth-side. The options in the healthcare system where I lived were less than ideal. A midwife was what I wanted. The only catch with using a midwife in our local hospital was that if you did decide to get an epidural at the last minute, the rules stated your care would have to be transferred to a doctor. I did not want that.

Doctors could allow whoever they wanted in the room. I wanted my birth to be small, private, and emotionally safe—but also medically safe. That's why choosing to give birth in a squeaky-clean hospital, with a midwife, and creating the birth plan of the century—to ensure I wouldn't need the doomsday drugs—was a win-win.

I laid out the positions I wanted to try, the movement I wanted to fit in, the Coldplay songs I'd have playing, and the exact outfit I'd wear. The basics of the rest of the plan went like this: to allow labor to start "naturally"; to labor in the comfort of my own home with Greg, Tammy, and the midwife; and to practice all the techniques Tammy taught me until the contractions became too much.

Then, I'd go to the hospital at the opportune moment to ensure I'd be there for as little time as possible. I'd labor a little more until it'd be time to push. When it was time to have the baby, I'd summon all the goddess-woman energy that the crunchy moms talked about and ease that baby out with my small, safe group of cheerleaders by my side. No drugs necessary. Boom. Become a mom. Get a baby parade. Applause.

Women had been doing it for centuries, after all. If the women in *Call the Midwife* could do it in 1950s England, and my church friends could do it without drugs at home, I could do it in the safety of a hospital. This was a happy medium that I wouldn't have to ashamedly whisper about in hushed tones in the back of the church.

"Why are you afraid of it being ugly?" Tammy asked near the end of our session.

I pondered. Obviously, giving birth to a healthy baby was far more important than what I looked like doing it. I didn't *want* to care, but when I was honest, I did. I cared what people thought, what it meant about me, and my ability to control those things.

"I'm not sure," I said.

"Consider this, what if it *is* ugly? So what?" Tammy asked, letting her words linger in the air. "What if you let it be?"

Poignant, but hard pass, Tammy. I just need to follow the plan.

MONTHS LATER, DURING ONE OF my regular 2 a.m. pee breaks, my water broke and I felt a small gush. Then, a trickle. *Is this labor?* There were no contractions so I tried to go back to sleep. I couldn't.

At 4 a.m., Greg and I walked around the block while the contractions continued. We went home, tried to distract ourselves, and then went for a walk again. We ate breakfast and drank tea with Roger while I bounced on my yoga ball. By 8 a.m. the contractions were strong enough to stop me in my tracks. Officially, labor was happening.

By 11, I was ready for more support, so Tammy and the midwife came. "Let's check your cervix," the midwife said. I lay back, opened up, and the midwife put her hand inside me. Her hand. It felt like she was shoving an enormous rusty crowbar up there. And the sensation in my nether region? Sharp. Excruciating. I yelped.

"I'm so sorry," she said. "You are one to two centimeters dilated. I'll be extra careful next time, and we'll try not to check too much."

While I was grateful for her reassurance and care, I started to pant, remembering how petrified I was of anything else passing through that area again.

It had been nine hours since my water broke. At the twelve-hour mark, three more hours of laboring later, the midwife checked me again. Pain rippled through me, again. Three centimeters. Now I was really antsy for things to move along. By 4 p.m., I was spent. The relentlessly growing pain in my body coupled with my terror and lack of progress began to drain me of energy and hope.

I was dilated four centimeters by then. The plan was to wait longer but I couldn't. So we left home and headed to the hospital. Between the worsening contractions, the position in the car, and the reality setting in that a human being was really going to exit my body, I entered a full-blown panic. I became rigid and tight, my breath quickened, and fear made itself at home in my body. Relaxation was not in the cards.

Upon arrival, the triage nurse informed me that my registration was lost. "Name? Health card? Address? Reason for coming?" she rattled off. Entering into an administrative time warp was not in the plan. Every time a contraction came, I had to stop talking and the intake nurse would exhale in irritation, like I'd just butted in front of her in line at Disney World.

Once I was admitted, the momentary relief I felt was quickly followed by a contraction, which was immediately followed by an internal spiral.

It's been nearly fifteen hours, and I am not even halfway there. I can't do this. It hurts too much. I am too tired. I don't want to move. It's just going to get worse. I do want to move because it could get better. It's never going to get better. The church ladies were wrong. I should have come here earlier. What if I die? What if the baby dies? I bet they all think I am crazy. I look crazy, I know it. This was not the plan.

Tammy encouraged me to try a new position. I tried. No help. Every time I attempted to move, a new contraction came and my body stiffened with fear of making it worse. Then, the fear made me freeze more. The pain-fear cycle was incessant. At 6 p.m., the midwife checked me again. Five centimeters. Tears soaked my face.

Nothing was working. Knowing that I loved taking baths at home to relax, knowing that some women swear by the help of water during labor, I tried moving to the shower area. Greg poured water over my back and, immediately, the intensity of the pain increased. Less than a minute later, the contents of my stomach erupted all over the shower. Covered in vomit and embarrassment, I re-entered hyperventilation station. Was the moisture all over me vomit, water, tears, blood, sweat, or some other substance of my insides? *This can't be normal.*

I inched back to the hospital bed, perched on the edge, gritted my teeth, and waited. For two more hours I stayed frozen in fear with Greg by my side. The midwife checked me at 9 p.m. Six centimeters. *Nothing is worth this,* I thought.

"I can't do this anymore," I cried. "I can't do it."

"You can do it, and you are doing it," Tammy said.

"I wanted to do it without meds so badly. I don't want to let anyone down. I don't want to fail. I don't know what to do," I pleaded.

"There is nothing wrong with asking for an epidural. There never was. You have worked so hard. You are not weak and it is not the weaker option. We are so proud of you and will support whatever choice you make. Nobody is going to be disappointed. Do what you need to do," she assured me.

So I did. After about eighteen hours of labor I finally asked for the drug of glory: an epidural. I accepted that my care would be transferred to a doctor I'd never met and let go of the plan. I had no fight left in me anyway.

Not long after, the doctor came in, introduced herself in a hurry, and told the nurse to lay me back. "I'm going to check your cervix," she said. I wanted to tell her that I was afraid and to take it easy, but she didn't give me a chance. She shoved her hand inside and I cried while she made notes to the nurse. "I'm going to call the anesthesiologist," she muttered to herself. Later, the nurse informed me I was seven centimeters dilated.

The anesthesiologist was on call because it was a small hospital in the middle of nowhere. He finally arrived an hour later, swearing under his breath.

"I don't like being called in at ten o'clock at night!" he barked at the other doctor. "Especially when they are this far along and clearly losing it. I should have been here hours ago!"

Then the doctor yelled back, "Well, it's not my fault. I only just got the call that she was being transferred to my care. Don't get mad at me!"

I looked at them both, waiting to be acknowledged. Instead, they didn't. They just yelled back and forth, blaming each other while I braced for my contractions and tried to silence my groans of pain. Dr. Drugs came over, looked at me like I was some rabid animal that just defecated on his doorstep, and started prepping his drugs.

Reluctantly, he introduced himself, told me I should have asked for the epidural sooner, and reminded me to hold still. The needle went in. A few minutes later, the drugs were coursing through my veins and Dr. Drugs was gone. The relief was palpable, like the world's best noise-canceling headphones but for my uterus. Not long after, I fell asleep.

A few hours later, I woke up and it was time to push. The doctor decided it would be a good time to invite what felt like half the hospital's nursing staff in the room for "training purposes." One after another they filed in and stood in a horseshoe shape around the bed, watching, arms folded. The doctor and delivery nurse prepared their contraptions and Greg held my hand while I waited—spread-eagle.

I closed my eyes and took a deep breath. Another contraction came.

"Relax your jaw," I heard Tammy say.

Tammy held one leg, Greg held the other, and I let out my breath as I pushed. Several contractions and pushes later, I took one big breath, relaxed my jaw, and pushed with all my might. A few pushes later and nearly twenty-four hours after my water broke, I felt the rest of my baby enter the world. I exhaled. Then, I heard my baby cry.

"It's a girl!" I heard Greg say. They placed all seven pounds, six ounces of her on my bare chest. I gasped at the sight of my dark-eyed, full-head-of-hair, goo-covered squish ball of a baby. She was here. She was mine. She was perfect. We named her Eleanor. I basked in the oxytocin coursing through my veins and the glory of her existence. Bliss.

CHILDBIRTH MIGHT BE NATURE'S WAY of letting us know from the very beginning of motherhood that we don't get to call all the shots.

As it turned out, giving birth *was* ugly. In fact, it was disgusting. Riddled with fear, I'd clung hard to my perfect plans, hoping they could save me. They couldn't. I lost control of my digestive system, my birth plan, and the number of people watching a human exit my body. That wasn't all—despite my master plan, a great number of my fears came to full fruition. My grip on control created a counter-intuitive feedback loop from hell that made everything worse. And yet, I realized something: When any semblance of control sailed off into the sunset, hand-in-hand with my dignity, I finally surrendered. I succumbed to the pain. I let go. I survived the unknown.

I considered Tammy's words. *What if it is ugly? So what? What if you let it be?*

As I lay there, feeling the warmth of my little miracle on my chest, peace washed over me. Now, I felt like I was home. Not like I was at home. But like I was *her* home. *Together* was home. I *had* let it be. Accepting the mess showed me I could handle what I thought I couldn't. And now, I got to be a mom.

4

Mothering

I got my baby parade three days later. No records for the speediest return to church after ripping my undercarriage to shreds, but at least everyone smiled and clapped like I'd just solved world hunger. *I'll take it,* I decided. I'd never been prouder of myself.

That night, Eleanor—whom I decided to call Ellie for short—was in her bassinet beside my bed when I heard her making gurgle sounds. I sprang into action. And by action, I mean that I rolled over, picked her up, sat up in bed, and made a laborious attempt to latch her to my newly cracked nipple. The room was pitch dark, and Greg was fast asleep. Wincing in silent pain, I begged her to get a grip. Finally, she latched, and I had a letdown. Is exhausted euphoria a thing? If it is, that is what I felt. There is nothing quite like the drug of new motherhood.

Frankly, I couldn't tell the difference between the "I am awake, I am hungry, and give me the boobie" sounds versus the "I'm a new human who makes weird noises constantly, so you better get used to it" sounds yet. All noises were equally terrifying. I worried that if I let one squirm or cry or grunt go unchecked, I might let them all go.

Maybe I'd fall into a deep sleep and fail the task of motherhood in week one, making headlines across the globe: NEW MOM STARVES BABY TO DEATH BECAUSE SHE'S A SELFISH TWIT WHO JUST WANTED TO SLEEP. I couldn't risk it. So, I often stayed awake in the few hours she slept because I didn't want to miss the cue. Hypervigilance was the cure-all for uncertainty. Lessons are hard to learn.

I'd been pleasantly surprised by how the adrenaline rush of new motherhood carried me those first seventy-two hours. I thought I'd escaped the emotional turmoil Tammy had warned me of, but as I looked down at Ellie's little face while she nursed, something began to shift.

She was the most precious thing I'd ever laid eyes on—beautiful, vulnerable, perfect, and pure. How can a small squishy alien potato emanate such exceptionalism without the ability to even lift her head? *I get to raise a person!* The thought felt weird because she didn't seem like a person at all. My baby felt like an extension of me, someone I'd always known and loved. Looking at her was like peering into my own face. Only, I couldn't see the imperfections I saw so easily in myself. I gazed down at her little face in disbelief. A tidal wave of love for her washed over me.

I was so happy. But as a lump took shape in my throat, I wondered: Why was I also sad? Was I simply overcome with the miracle of her? New mom stuff? No. I rolled the word over in my head—*mom.* The gravity of the word felt like it was shifting in real time, now that I *was* one. *Why did the word feel so different now?*

I TRIED TO RECALL MY earliest memories of my mom. There was only a handful of fragmented pictures in my mind from before I was eight, filled in by the stories I'd been told. My older brother, Harry, was born first, and I entered the world less than a year later. Our parents fell in love almost as quickly as they fell out of it, though. I was a toddler when Mom left Dad, and I have zero memories of my parents together. Harry and I lived predominantly with Mom and the questionable boyfriends who entered and exited our lives. Harry and I took the bus to visit Dad on weekends.

Mom struggled to hold down a job and maintain friendships. Finances, transportation, and drama often kept us from seeing extended family or building community in the various places we lived. Our little family moved often. My earliest flicker of a memory was of one of our many moves. I was around five or six when the blue-and-white taxi dropped off Harry, Mom, and me at a large building with gates around it. Mom was leaving Frank, her abusive boyfriend.

The staff at the women's shelter were friendly, calm, and quiet. They showed us to our beds with freshly washed sheets. An older lady made me a peanut-butter-and-jelly sandwich and even cut the crust off. The sandwich made me feel special. Harry and I watched *The Land Before Time* on repeat, a welcome change from *The Young and the Restless*.

At some point, we moved to a government-subsidized townhouse on the outskirts of the city. The townhouse complex was arranged in a square, with all the houses pointing in toward one another. This made it easy for Harry and me to empty all the neighbors' mailboxes of Tide laundry samples or whatever other freebies were handed out by the postal worker that week. Unfortunately, the complex was miles away from the closest convenience store, where Harry and I walked to pick up essentials for Mom: cigarettes, Pepsi, milk, bread, and scratchers. I was seven-ish when Harry and I began our treks, buying goods on store credit and carrying them home in paper bags with proud smiles.

"Stick together," Mom would say. And we would walk shoulder to shoulder, the whole two miles to the store, laughing at ourselves.

That, or we punched each other and argued about who should carry the bags home. Sibling stuff.

Less than a year later, our little family moved again. Mom was talented at rebranding each relocation as a "fresh start."

"You'll get new bedrooms! We'll have a new kitchen, new neighbors, new school, and friends, too! Anything can happen!" she'd say, with hope in her voice and sparkle in her eyes. I loved how she could make anything feel like an exciting adventure.

It felt like, at any moment, our lives could transform for the better. So while change was common, Mom had an ability to make it hopeful. Her hope was contagious. On a good night, the three of us would crawl into Mom's bed and snuggle with the window cracked to let the cool air in and the cigarette smoke out. We'd surround ourselves with Kool-Aid, ketchup chips, and penny candy from the corner store. And we would talk all night about what we would do as a family if we won a million dollars in the lottery.

We could buy a house! A car! Go on a vacation! We could get all-new clothes from the fancy mall stores and go to restaurants! We could get new towels at Zellers or go for a steak dinner! We could leave the city! No more holding our breath every time we used a debit card. No more putting items back on the shelves when the card was declined. No more moving, food banks, and sketchy neighbors. These nights were my favorite.

With each move, we were filled with renewed hope that the change of scenery would bring the financial security, peace, and happiness Mom sought. With each payday rotation or new relationship, we'd reach the top of the roller coaster of hope, too. But eventually, Mom's rose-colored glasses would turn gray. We'd run into drama or out of money, and the roller coaster of hope took a nosedive into darkness. Mom would shut the world out and avoid leaving her bedroom again. Harry and I would fend for ourselves. Everything changed and nothing changed.

It was around the age of nine that I began to consciously pick up on the ways I could make life easier for Mom. My skills came in handy, particularly as there was always some kind of trouble—evictions, creditors, drama, broken appliances, and broken promises. I was seen as responsible and that it was a good thing. Harry was good at crying on cue, which helped us get out of financial pickles with landlords, creditors, and the school office asking for the fundraising money we'd "lost." I was good at telling Mom what she needed to hear, cooking dinner, and staying home from school when she needed me.

Harry and I also helped by learning the art of stretching pennies. We'd pull the cushions off our fraying couch to see if we could round up someone's lost pocket change. We'd clip coupons and damage cans at the grocery store so we could demand discounts and sold our furniture in the classified ads of newspapers.

No matter how hard we'd try, we'd end up broke again. One night, like many others, Mom made an effort to dig us out of financial trouble at the local bingo spot. When she came home, I could tell it hadn't gone well.

"Why are these lights still on?! What a waste of electricity! You're throwing away money we don't have!" she yelled. "This is why we keep getting the power shut off! This is why there is nothing to eat! This is why we can't do nice things." I bit my tongue.

"And look at this mess!" she yelled, pointing at the dishes left from the mac and cheese we'd cooked ourselves for dinner. I quickly got to cleaning, knowing the plates and bowls had been piling up for weeks, growing things on them I didn't want to touch. I rushed around doing whatever I could to calm the storm. I wanted to make her feel better. That's what made me feel better.

The next day, I concocted a little entrepreneurial plan to bring in some quick cash. That would do the trick.

"We're going to play hooky and we're having a yard sale!" I announced to Harry and Mom. It was a Tuesday in October and Harry knew the drill. Mom called the school to let them know we were sick, and we got to work.

The small brick bungalow we rented in the downtown core had a little front yard just big enough for a few blankets to cover in toys and a few pieces of furniture from the living room.

I stood on the top step of the front porch wagging my freckled finger in Harry's direction, yelling commands at him to set up. Customers would be here soon. Harry was older and clearly stronger than I was—which naturally made him our manual laborer.

The big stuff went out first: the coffee table, end tables, kitchen chairs, lamps, and even dinnerware. Who needs four dinner plates anyway? Who needs a dining room table or a microwave? Not us. We needed cash.

We paced the yard waiting for customers. Funnily enough, not many garage sale buyers were out strolling the inner-city side streets on a Tuesday morning. But around noon, kids from school began walking by, heading home for lunch. That's when Brittany showed up.

Brittany was our six-year-old neighbor with scraggly hair and shoes twice as big as her feet. She sauntered over, picked up one of my favorite stuffies, and told us she was buying it. "Fifty bucks," I demanded. "Deal!" she said.

Brittany ran home and came back two minutes later with a wad of small bills in her hand. Score. She bought the stuffy and we took the handful of happiness. We packed in the yard sale for the day and ran inside to tell Mom about our success. "We made fifty whole dollars!" Harry yelled. "A record!" I chimed in. Harry and I high-fived, and Mom's eyes lit up.

"Great job, honey!" she said, smiling.

I *was* a good girl.

Later that day, Brittany's mom realized her money was missing.

She stormed over to our front porch to demand we give it back. "You little shits!" she yelled at Harry and me. "Don't you fucking yell at my kids!" Mom yelled back. Harry and I stayed in the house and watched the moms with our noses pressed to the window. Mom came inside and told us she gave the woman her money back. "Oh well!" She shrugged.

Mom was chill like that sometimes. You just never knew. Apparently, Brittany had taken her mom's whole weekend's worth of tips. Brittany's mom was a stripper and not a very happy one that day.

I MAY NOT HAVE REMEMBERED much of my childhood, but I remembered this: I was Mom's best friend. I could sleep with her when I was scared. I could stay up late, help bring in money, and calm her worries. I could cook, clean, and fend off creditors like it was nobody's business. I got to be in on secrets and be out of school if I wanted. I knew Mom loved us and we loved her. I knew what she wanted and needed without even being asked and I enjoyed the glory of my maturity superpower.

When I decided to become a mom, I knew I didn't want to repeat my own childhood, but I honestly didn't think of my childhood that much. Now, looking at Ellie, my young memories seemed to hurt like they hadn't before. Memories I'd joked about just weeks ago. How could I be sad now? Why did it hurt . . . now?

I felt my jaw clench as I nursed Ellie and continued my spiral. I felt tense, like I often did when Mom was around. And Mom was around, a lot. Mostly, it was my choice. Mom didn't work or drive. The town she lived in was a half hour away and didn't offer public transportation. Getting around was difficult for her. She was lonely. Since returning from rainy old England five years ago, I'd made a concerted effort to support her. We spoke on the phone most days. I went out of my way to check in on her, to run errands with her, or offer rides to appointments. When it began to feel like too much, I kept saying yes anyway. She was my mom, after all.

I'd forgiven my mom for any pain she'd caused in my childhood. I wasn't angry. Her life had been hard. But now, I couldn't help but mull over the continuous problems I was navigating in our relationship.

My mind traveled back to six weeks before I had Ellie. Mom asked if she could join me for the day while I ran last-minute errands for Harry's wedding. To my delight, my brother was marrying my good friend Amanda. I'd been thrilled to hear the news and was honored to be asked to stand with them as their maid of honor. I loved planning events and making things special for people. But in a classic Libby move, I'd overanticipated my emotional and physical capacity. Working two jobs, growing a baby, and helping with wedding preparations were taking their toll. I knew I needed time alone—but I brought Mom anyway.

I pulled into the parking lot of her apartment building. She opened the car door, got in, looked me up and down, and said, "You're glowing! How are you?"

"Hey Mom," I said, pausing as I backed up the car, considering how much of my current struggles to share and focusing on the road.

"I'll tell ya," she said. "I'm having a day. My neighbor's dog won't stop barking and the landlord won't do anything about it. My friend Kat won't return my phone calls and I'm almost out of money for the month." Mom seemed unaware that I hadn't yet answered the question she'd just asked me. I bit my tongue and tried to hide my disappointment. "You know, I'm getting tired of living here. There's always something—"

"Do you want a coffee?" I asked, interrupting her as we pulled into a drive-through.

"Well, I don't get paid until next week, so no," she said. I knew this was her way of saying yes, just like I knew by the way she flared her nose at a family gathering that she felt left out and I needed to bring her back into the conversation. Just like when she texted "What are you up to today?" I knew this was my cue to offer her a ride somewhere. Just like I could read her body language when she cracked a joke and I hadn't responded the "right" way, I needed to force a laugh. I knew when Mom needed acknowledgment, space, attention, or words. I knew my mom inside and out. Still after all this time, anticipating her needs was my superpower. She didn't have to ask. I knew.

So, I ordered her a coffee.

"Thanks," she said, smiling, before continuing her story.

I wanted to tell her that my body ached in places I didn't even know existed, that I was excited to meet my baby, that I was worried about being on my feet all day at the wedding, that motherhood was feeling scarier by the minute. But my attempts to interject were met with a loop back to her struggles.

I was used to our dynamic, the one that had her leaning and me supporting. It was silly to hope for something different. On the way home from running errands, Mom leaned in for some advice.

"I'm stressed about the wedding and who I'm going to see there. What do you think I should do?"

"Well, Mom. We can only control what we do and say. We can't control other people."

She nodded at the advice and a proud smile crept to the corner of her mouth.

"You are so wise, Libby, so responsible and mature. What would I do without you?" she said, before getting out of the car.

Now, sitting up in bed with Ellie in my arms, something began to shift. *She doesn't know better,* I'd always told myself. But had she ever known better than to lay her burdens on my shoulders? Was there a time when I didn't feel that's where they belonged?

From my sparse early memories all the way to our most recent text thread, I began to see it. I'd been mature because I'd had no choice. I had longed to feel safe enough to make mistakes, to be guided with the wisdom I was assumed to have. But I couldn't.

For the first time, I thought consciously about the fact that I, too, was someone's daughter. I, too, longed to be dependent, to be mothered. Did my mom *ever* feel the way I felt now? So full of love and an overwhelming desire to protect, guide, and nurture her child? I knew she loved me—but I couldn't stifle the wondering. I felt my chest heave.

As I sat quietly holding Ellie in the dark of our room in our safe, happy home, I was struck by my reality. Real, wet, unstoppable tears rolled down my face and onto Ellie's little head. I cried for what I didn't have, what I longed for, and what I feared I couldn't give Ellie. I cried because I loved her so much and because I didn't want her body to tense like mine did when her mother walked in the room one day. I cried because I didn't have the first clue how to be what I didn't have.

I pulled her in close, took in one of those big newborn-baby-head sniffs, and exhaled with a fierce resolve I'd never felt before. I would be her mother, and she would be my daughter. Not the other way around. I would do whatever it took to be the mom she needed, to make sure she knew she was enough, safe, protected, and unconditionally loved. I didn't realize how much I needed my mom to feel like a mom, until I became one. And until that moment, it hadn't hurt that much.

5

Mattering

Somebody needs to call child protective services, I thought to myself. Two weeks had passed since Ellie entered the world, and for the first time, she was completely inconsolable. I'd fed, burped, and rocked her. The wailing continued. It wasn't until I laid her down on her back to change her diaper that I noticed what the problem was. Her whole body scrunched tight like it usually did, but her right arm rested limply behind her, unable to curl in. Of all the things I heard that could go wrong in those first weeks postpartum, not once did anyone mention the possibility of one of my baby's limbs not working.

It's broken, I thought. I broke her arm while I was maneuvering her into that stupid tiny onesie. I'm a monster, an awful mother who needs to be locked up. But then, as I lifted her arm to her chest, I could see her tiny body soften. Finally, she took a breath. The tears subsided. Relief. I realized that taking the weight off helped. So, I safety-pinned the sleeve of her shirt to the fabric on her chest. With a pit in my stomach that expanded by the moment, Greg and I strapped her tiny body into her car seat, I hopped in the back, and we drove to see the pediatrician.

Once the doctor assessed her, he told me that the crying was normal, that she was just fussy, and that he'd send us for an X-ray to ease my mind. Translation: You're a crazy lady but I'll check her anyway. I considered flipping his desk. I didn't.

I laid Ellie down on the adult-size X-ray table and did the only thing I could think to do. I sang, "Raindrops on roses and whiskers on kittens. Bright copper kettles and warm woolen mittens . . ." and continued singing as I smiled down at her, hoping to convince us both everything was going to be okay.

"You'll have to take the safety pin out and lay her arm back. Make sure to hold her still so we can get the set of images without having to do it again," the lab tech gently explained. I positioned her as delicately as I could but as soon as I laid her arm back, she wailed. She looked up at me through tears as if to say, "How could you?!" and I felt my heart break. With her fingers tight around my index finger and my hand on her chest, I attempted to breathe calm over us. I continued to hum "My Favorite Things" through teary eyes until the ordeal was over.

Afterward, I picked her up and held her as close as I could, feeling relief wash over me when her wails subsided. With the safety pin back in place, we strapped her back into the car seat and headed home, full of dread.

The phone buzzed and I answered from the back seat. "The X-ray was clear. We couldn't see anything to be concerned about. Just go home. If it's still an issue in a few days, you can come back," the doctor said casually. *What? That's it?* The pit in my stomach began to feel like a boulder while I simultaneously tried to convince myself he was right. *I'm a new mom. What do I know?* I thought.

But like any sane person with a fully functioning brain, I

couldn't shake the feeling that newborns should be able to use their limbs. By the time evening came, the spiral I'd dove down headfirst took me to dark places that could not be ignored. I nursed Ellie to sleep, brushed my teeth, got into bed, and tried to relax. I couldn't.

"Something's not right. We are taking her to the children's hospital," I said to Greg.

An hour later, we were in the triage area of the ER explaining the situation to the nurse. She unbuttoned Ellie's little pajamas, listened to her heart, checked her temperature, and placed little stickers on her tiny body to monitor her vitals. Greg rubbed my back as I held my baby.

Eventually, we were moved to a room in the ER. The nurse informed us Ellie would need to have an IV inserted. I looked at her miniature forearm. I looked at Greg. My stomach turned.

I held her as she screamed in pain and her eyes locked on mine like I'd betrayed her. If I could have combusted, I would have.

Finally, we were left alone and I could feed her. Luckily, after battling through the first couple weeks of exclusive breastfeeding, we were finally making strides and I knew it's what she needed in this moment. Only, I hadn't breastfed in public yet. I didn't really have a choice.

As I prepared myself to nurse her, I realized the mechanics wouldn't work. The IV and monitoring cords wouldn't stretch long enough for me to pick her up and hold her to my chest. I didn't have bottles. A pump. Formula. A clue what to do. Where was *this* in the handbook?

With the pale green curtains half drawn across the entrance to our room, I prayed it was enough to hide what happened next. I stood up, bent my exhausted body in a 90-degree angle, lifted up my shirt, and leaned over the side rail of her hospital bed. I stretched and shifted my swollen boob out to nurse her. Success. Latch. I fed my baby—like a cow—but I fed her.

With my boob out and what was left of my pride circling the drain, I felt a slice of goddess woman pride, followed by relief that she was calm. Ellie fell into the sleep she so badly needed. I carefully unlatched, filled with worry that one wrong move would wake her. She stayed asleep. Score! Apprehensively, I sat down in the chair beside her hospital bed. My entire being ached for reprieve.

But moments later, a new group of doctors and residents came into the room to ask me the same questions I'd already been asked and to prod Ellie the same way the others had. She woke. They left. I nursed her to sleep again. Minutes later, another nurse arrived.

"Time to go for your MRI," the nurse said, adjusting Ellie's IV and dissolving what little slice of calm had been created. Ellie became distraught again. The nurse rolled the bed down the corridor as I stumbled uselessly beside them, stroking Ellie's head. *How is this nightmare our reality?* I thought. As I lifted her miniature body onto the MRI table and watched it ease her into the enormous machine, I held my breath. Once she was out of sight, the cocktail of despair and worry that I'd been trying to keep at bay engulfed me. I wept.

Several hours later, the doctors informed us that while the MRI hadn't shown anything, we wouldn't be going home anytime soon. That's when I knew I had to send Greg home. The clock read 3 a.m.

My husband had always wanted to be a police officer. He'd trained hard and was nearing the end of the grueling application process. The job would provide our family the stable income we needed. His final interview was the next day and if he missed it, he would have to start the lengthy application process all over again. So, I told him to go. He offered to cancel, stay, and support me. But we both knew how big this opportunity was. He needed to rest and make it to that interview. Reluctantly he agreed. "I'll call my dad. He'll come," he said. He kissed us goodbye and as I watched him walk out, I realized just how alone I was.

A few minutes later, a young doctor came in, looked at Ellie's chart, and said, "I don't have good news." My stomach fell. "Because Ellie has a fever, we need to do a test for meningitis. The procedure is painful. But if meningitis is left untreated, it could be fatal," he explained. *Fatal. Death. My child. What?* The room began to spin. They needed to do a lumbar puncture, where a large needle is inserted into the spinal canal to collect fluid. He explained the need to "move fast" and "sign these papers" in case "the worst" happened "because there are always risks."

The doctor told me that if I said yes, I would have to leave the room because it was "a painful and traumatic thing for mothers to watch, and doctors need utmost concentration for the procedure." These words felt like the oxygen left the room.

"It's up to you whether to do this. You're the mom, you know best," the doctor said. But I didn't know anything. I was just a stupid twenty-six-year-old girl who'd had a baby a few weeks ago. I hadn't slept in three days, I was still bleeding from giving birth, my stomach was growling, my brain was misfiring, and yet, I was the one tasked with making a life-or-death decision. Allow the lumbar puncture to happen and hopefully save her life, or deny the puncture and hope for the best? I decided to sign the papers and let them do the test.

Luckily, not long after, Roger showed up, concerned yet calm. I needed him. We left Ellie with the doctors to do the procedure. I shuffled beside Roger, pacing the corridors, trying to disconnect from the reality that they were inserting needles into my baby. I swatted away the images in my mind of how scared she must be. In her two weeks of life, I hadn't left her side. Doing so in her most difficult moment was unbearable.

We returned to the hospital room a half hour later. "We tried three separate times, and we were unsuccessful in getting enough fluid to test. I am sorry but we don't have any answers," the doctor said.

So all the pain they caused her was for nothing? I thought. I sank. Still, I was grateful there hadn't been complications during the puncture and that I had my baby in my arms again.

The hospital staff didn't know what was wrong but decided to keep administering IV antibiotic treatment until they had answers and she got better. Ellie was admitted to the children's hospital and was moved to an expansive ward with dozens of rooms encircling the nurses' station. It was buzzing with hospital staff, parents, and kids of all ages and sicknesses. I was not buzzing.

THE HOSPITAL STAFF WERE KIND enough to let me, the mother of an exclusively breastfed newborn, stay with my baby. Unfortunately, since I was not the hospital patient, I had no access to care, food, water, and definitely not a bed. *What two-week postpartum mom needs those extravagances anyway?*

We shared a room with three other patients and their moms, each posted in the four corners of the large room. Our corners were separated only by a curtain. Beside Ellie's bed was a plastic chair that reclined a little, for my sleeping pleasure. In that green chair was where I tossed and turned for several days and nights, waiting for answers, for hope, and for my baby's crying to break my heart a little less every time a new IV was inserted into her arm or another test was administered.

At night, I was on alert at all hours, constantly wondering if the crying baby I heard was mine or one of countless other children around us. The more sleep-deprived I became, the harder it was to keep my balance in the middle of the night when I had to lean over her hospital bed like a moo-cow to feed her. Greg visited most days, but there was nowhere for him to sit, never mind sleep. Friends and family popped by, with a Subway sandwich here and an encouraging book there—welcome support, but not at all what I envisioned for our postpartum experience.

TEN DAYS INTO OUR HOSPITAL stay, my left boob started to throb. Heat radiated from my chest and the boob weighed heavier than usual in my hand. Puzzled and in pain, I noticed it was red with infection. Within a few days, it was excruciating. According to Google, I had developed a blocked milk duct and a severe case of mastitis. I asked the nurse if I could see the lactation consultant treating the mom in the bed beside us.

"I'm sorry but that isn't possible. You don't qualify for care because you are not the patient and you didn't give birth at this hospital," the nurse said.

"What? But my baby needs me. I am literally her source of food."

"There is nothing we can do. You can ask your family doctor for a referral," she suggested apathetically. But my family doctor was almost an hour away, and if I left, I couldn't take Ellie with me. We still had no pump, no bottles, no formula, and no need—really—to try formula. Ellie was an exclusively breastfed sick newborn who nursed on demand. Leaving my sick baby at a hospital to go get a referral? *Hard pass*. Do they *really* not see the irony in denying me care? Regardless, I had to figure it out myself.

Google told me to try massaging my boob in the shower. All I had access to was a public one. *Great*. I grabbed my toiletries, my towel, and the thimble of dignity I had left and headed for the showers. Greg was with the baby. Still, I couldn't help but wonder if every cry I heard in the hallway was hers. I shuffled down the busy corridor.

I looked at the faces that passed me as I walked, but no one met my gaze. I caught my own reflection in a window and grimaced. Same clothes as the previous two days. Cracked nipples. Swollen, leaking boobs. Itchy, irritated undercarriage. Dark under-eye bags. Greasy bun and hormonal acne. I felt like a ghost floating through an alternate universe.

Just six weeks before, I'd been glowing. At Harry and Amanda's wedding I'd stood as the maid of honor at thirty-six weeks' pregnant. It was the couple's day, of course, but as a giant first-time preggo lady in a bright blue dress, I drew attention. My body hurt in places that I didn't even know existed, and my organs had reorganized themselves in a way that hindered my ability to clear my intestines—but I was making a human and I looked the part. I felt beautiful, so full of life.

After the service, on my way out of the church, my uncle had offered me his hand on the stairs like I was some kind of china teacup on the cusp of shattering. Waiting in line for the bathroom, strangers had asked me about the gender of the baby, my nursery decor, my physical health, and my mental health. Everyone wanted to know how they could make my life easier and what my postpartum plans were. What was I needing to prepare? Had I been eating enough? Resting? Did I know the signs of postpartum depression?

On the dance floor, I'd watched people watch me, delighted by the sight of a pregnant lady dancing. At dinner, the catering staff served me before the other bridesmaids. I gushed. I smiled to myself all day, flicking my hair over my proverbial shoulder. Being pregnant made me feel like I was something to behold, something to care for, something to be treasured.

I suppose I saw the literal and proverbial baby parades as evidence that motherhood might feel as glorious as it looked. Or that the attention I received while pregnant could foreshadow motherhood itself. Mothers did important work, after all. Maybe all that care reflected how society values those who create and sustain life.

Now, as I stood under the scalding-hot public hospital shower, looking down at a squishy body I didn't recognize anymore, I began to fear I'd been wrong. That blissful feeling seemed like a distant memory. It wasn't just the changes in how my new postpartum body had looked. It was a sneaking suspicion that now everything had changed. Maybe motherhood would not be what I thought it would.

I began to massage the red-hot lump in my boob. Slowly. Deliberately. I circled over the skin and around the lump that felt so tender it might burst. I clenched my teeth. I whispered "FUCKKKKKK." With every press, the pain shifted, jolted like lightning, pulsed, and radiated out of me. I watched the wasted milk stream down my body and into the drain. I watched my tears cascade down, too. Eventually, I'd expressed enough milk to give me a little reprieve from this one physical ache.

What it didn't relieve was the other pain I felt—my aching back, the pinched nerves, my cracked nipples, my wounded undercarriage, and the relentless headache that throbbed like a beating drum.

The emotional pain was far worse. The roller coaster of bad news. The dizzying hormones of new motherhood. The uncertainty and worry about my baby that was baked into each moment of the day. The longing for a "normal" postpartum experience. The breathtaking fear.

These last weeks held some of the most physically and emotionally difficult moments I'd ever experienced. Learning how to be a mother while having fewer of my own needs met than ever before seemed like the right time to be cared for and supported. To be seen. I'd really thought all that care I'd had only weeks ago would continue into motherhood itself. But where was it?

Without a doubt, Ellie mattered most—to me and everyone else involved. It showed from the check-ins from loved ones who began to inquire more about her than about me. In the doctors', nurses', and strangers' concerns. It showed in the policies of the hospital that offered me nothing more than a plastic recliner while tending to my newborn 24/7, and in the refusal of lactation care. I mean, the main reason *I* cared about the throbbing dysfunctional boob was *also* for the sole purpose of feeding and nurturing my baby.

I wanted nothing more than for Ellie to recover and thrive. I *needed* my child to be okay like I needed air to breathe. Good moms put their babies first, sacrificing everything, from their iron stores to their bra budget and from their autonomy to the last slice of cake. It's what I wanted to do, what I needed to do, and what I planned to keep doing.

My body was a vessel, a powerful force capable of creating and sustaining life. I was honored to do it. I knew my purpose. But what happens if the vessel breaks down? As Ellie's mother and source of life, I mattered more than anything in the world to her. Simultaneously, in the eyes of those around me in that hospital, I felt like I'd stopped mattering. And yet, I couldn't ignore the quiet wondering as I sobbed in the hospital shower: *What about me?*

The tension between the indescribable love I felt for Ellie and my own desire to be seen and cared for filled me with shame. Like secondhand smoke in the back seat of a car—windows sealed with no escape—it clung to my skin, hair, clothes. I breathed it in with every inhale. The shame was inescapable.

Without a doubt, my daughter deserved to be healthy, happy, whole, seen, safe, and loved. Not because she was a sick kid in a hospital, or because she was my baby, or I was her mom, or because she was helpless, or she had earned it. Her worthiness and value had nothing to do with what she could do or how she could make others feel. She mattered simply because she was a person. No questions asked. When had that stopped being true for me?

6

Perspective

A few days later, Ellie had another MRI and they found a pea-size *something* in her shoulder bone. As I sat in the plastic recliner, the doctor came back with an update.

"Unfortunately, the tests are showing that she has osteomyelitis," he said. Osteomyelitis is a rare condition that affects one in five thousand babies. The bones get infected and can cause irreversible damage. Without treatment, Ellie could lose the ability to use her arm, or worse. My stomach sank. The doctor reassured us that while it was an uncommon infection, it was treatable and we could plan to go home, but only after Ellie got a port put beside her heart to make the administration of antibiotics at home easier. That meant surgery.

"She'll have to go under an anesthetic for the procedure, which means she will need to fast for six hours first," the doctor explained.

"But she feeds on demand and often every two hours. Nursing is the only way to soothe her," I said. But unless we wanted to stay in this hellhole hospital for another six weeks, the procedure was our only choice.

I would have to let Ellie suffer, to go without food and her main source of comfort. It was like asking me to betray my most primal instinct. And more, to feel like the cause of, and be the witness of, my own child's most distressing moments. I knew my heart couldn't bear it and also that we didn't have much of a choice.

The day of her surgery, I held her close and let her nurse for as long as she wanted. We finished at 4 a.m. I hoped to God that her surgery would be on time and that her suffering would be minimal.

At 6 a.m., she began to scream. I picked her up and paced around the room, singing, hushing, trying not to let her root for my milk caused me to entirely unravel.

"Unfortunately, there was another patient who required emergency surgery. Your daughter's surgery time will have to be pushed back," the nurse explained. *This can't be happening,* I thought.

By 10 a.m., Ellie was crying so hard she couldn't catch her breath. Red-faced. Frightened. Angry. Confused. She made her hunger known. I paced, holding her close, reassuring her, saying, "I'm sorry, I'm so sorry. Mommy loves you. It's going to be okay."

By noon, the time she was supposed to be put under for surgery, I began to sink into darkness. It had been hours of drifting up and down the corridors, cradling her delicate body, unable to put her down, unable to deprive her of a moment's comfort. I felt my back screaming at me. But I couldn't take a break.

I was drawn to feed my baby like a fish to water. Everything about each passing second felt unnatural. Criminal. Her pain was my pain and I couldn't look away.

The nurses told us that her surgery would be moved to 1 p.m. But when our appointed time came, they pushed it again. "She will be okay," they tried to reassure me. Their words felt empty. Surgery was pushed to 3 p.m., then 4, then 6. I knew that if I fed her now, the hours of suffering would be for naught. The surgery would be canceled. We would have to start all over again another day.

By the time the doctors wheeled Ellie away from us at 7 p.m. for surgery, she had been distressed for nearly thirteen hours. Greg and I waited for what felt like a lifetime at the hospital café, aching for good news. Eventually it came. The surgery was a success. We could go home to finish her six weeks of antibiotic treatment and start our new life. My baby was going to be okay.

THAT'S ALL ANY MOM WANTS: a healthy, happy baby. Well, that and to keep her personhood. Achieving the latter turned out to be harder than anticipated given the circumstances, but I didn't mind. If the church moms were right about one thing, it was that I'd have sold an organ on the black market or lain down in traffic if it meant my baby would be safe.

Who cares if I'm a little lonely? My baby has functioning limbs. Who cares if my belly button has stretch marks coming out of it so large they look like sun rays? My baby is alive. Who cares if the house is in disarray? I made a person and she's going to grow up, pick daisies, and if I am lucky, borrow my clothes one day. Those two weeks in the hospital had flattened me. But I decided to move on and soak in my mini-me, in all her squishy, milk-drunk glory—without a cloud of uncertainty circling over my head. Aside from a new person in the house, I had something that I hadn't had before: perspective.

Greg had taken two months of paternity leave. After losing out on togetherness in the first month due to our hellish hospital stay, he worked overtime to be dad of the year for the remainder of his time at home. We enjoyed finding our groove and became a strong team—dividing the work of diapers, tummy time, and burping.

I took showers without worrying about my baby perishing in the other room. I nursed Ellie in the comfort of my own home while Greg mowed the lawn or folded laundry. We took turns wearing Ellie in the wrap she loved and strolled around our little one-stoplight town. We didn't take turns breastfeeding the baby, for obvious reasons.

Our month of finding our feet was also helped by having a third and wonderful adult around: Roger. The three of us shared the load of dinner, dishes, and, of course, steeping tea. The sheer amount of Tetley consumed in our home was unfathomable to everyone but us. Roger played with Ellie while I took a breather and provided company on long drives to help Ellie get in a midday nap. When leaving the house, we tag-teamed things like pushing the stroller and holding Ellie during church services.

Roger would say stuff like, "Libby, you're doing a good job. Go easy on yourself" or "Aren't you expecting too much of yourself?" when I would push my postpartum body harder than I should have. These were welcome encouragements. The positive, supportive presence of Greg and Roger, the health of our baby, and my relative sanity were all I'd ever wanted. Life was perfect.

NOT. NATURALLY, OUR BLISSFUL MONTH back at home could not last. That interview that Greg had left the hospital for, back when we were first being admitted? Well, he nailed it. The police force offered him the job opportunity he couldn't refuse.

Greg was across the bedroom jamming clothes into his big black duffle bag while I sat on the edge of our bed, mildly numb. Do I scream or cry? Just keep calm and carry on? I weighed my options. The prospect offered us more financial security than I'd experienced in all my days on planet Earth.

Food on the table? Healthcare benefits? Money for extracurriculars? Maybe even a fancy Starbucks coffee once a month? Sign me up, buttercup. It wasn't the job that bothered me. It was the condition that came with it. Accepting the offer meant losing Greg to police training, Monday to Friday, for three entire months. Weekends would be our only chance to reunite. What new mom wants to make that sacrifice? Not me.

Tackling motherhood alone five days a week? Not in my plans. And worse, Roger was due to fly home to England for an extended visit. AT. THE. SAME. TIME.

"It's not ideal. But it won't be forever. We'll be back for good before you know it. I'll come home every weekend," Greg said, when I lamented about their departure. He wrapped his arms around me.

I held him tight, trying to ignore the images of Greg sleeping peacefully for eight unbroken hours without anything sucking on his nipple. I pictured him in training sessions, frolicking around the track with other alpha types, blissfully unaware of the world's screaming babies and their ragged mothers at home. I could just see him waltzing into the campus cafeteria set to 2000s rom-com music, filling his tray with meals he didn't have to cook. I batted away the desire to throat-punch him out of jealousy.

"I'll miss you," I said as I swallowed the lump in my throat.

7

Groundhog Day

Once the men departed, so too did any reason for me to give a crap. The sturdy routines we'd created together began to crumble. Before long, Ellie and I gave up on the bassinet and decided to co-sleep. And why bother wearing an over-the-shoulder boulder holder around the house? The girls were free at last. With the men gone, I could do whatever I wanted, whenever I wanted.

With my newfound perspective and overachieving nature, I was determined to fill our days. I nursed by night and strapped my baby to my chest while I kept house by day. I cooked, cleaned, organized, and crafted, all with Ellie attached to me. I soaked her in. That part wasn't so bad after all. But the charm of living in our little cocoon rapidly faded when I realized my life was turning into a remake of *Groundhog Day*. The minutes felt like hours, and the hours felt like days. Life was a four-hour cycle on repeat. The sounds in our empty house scared me. The vastness of each room swallowed me. The light flickering, fans whooshing, and beeping appliances taunted me. Suddenly, twenty-four hours felt like a week to fill.

I missed having my brain occupied with topics outside of

diapers and lanolin. I missed Greg and Roger, their cheery British greetings and piping hot tea. After so many days with my wordless baby, I began to see that "use it or lose it" also applies to your brain cells and word bank. I needed adults and two-way conversation. Despite never being alone, I began to feel lonely.

The peace I felt in the tender, sweet, loving moments began to devolve into restlessness. After a lifetime of hustle, the stillness made me spin—like a windup doll kicked to the curb and running in circles but going nowhere.

The church moms seemed wholly fulfilled by their children and the four walls of their homes. When I wasn't, I couldn't help but wonder what was wrong with me.

WITH TIME ON MY SIDE and nobody at home to spend it with, Mom's company was a welcome remedy. I made the thirty-minute trip to see her often. She also craved visits with her grandbaby. I'd take her to fetch groceries, chauffeur her to her doctor's appointments, or help her hang pictures.

When I had errands to run, she'd happily sit in the car with sleeping Ellie and let me shop without juggling a baby or a car seat. The small slices of freedom were glorious. Finally—conversation. Goals. Purpose! Our days together often saved me from monotony and, subsequently, my desire to pull my brain out of my eye socket with a fork. I'm a woman who requires intellectual stimulation. My baby was cute. But her ability to hold up her end of a conversation was subpar.

Not Mom. The woman, bless her soul, could talk. She could jump from one topic to the next, with a fervor and without input, in a way I have yet to see matched in another human. If stimulation was all I needed, Mom was the perfect antidote. With her, life was never boring.

"You'll never believe what happened yesterday!" Mom said as she flopped down across from me on her burgundy couch. "Libby, I came home and there were all kinds of fire trucks at the building. I'm like, which idiot set a fire? Turns out it was me! Ha! I'd put the pot on to boil and forgot about it when I went out. But there was no fire luckily. Thank GOD. My neighbors would've been pissed!"

I raised my eyebrows and tried to pull them back down, to laugh along with her. "Fire trucks! Uh oh," I said.

"It's not a big deal, Libby. It's fine. Nothing got damaged," Mom said, rolling her eyes as she sensed my thoughts from the other side of the couch—the couch with a singed hole in it, a parting gift from a cigarette she had dropped and forgotten about ages ago.

It's really not that bad, I tried to convince myself. Burns happen. Accidents happen.

One time, she offered to help carry Ellie's car seat down the hallway to her apartment. "My balance is getting better. Promise," she said. I felt uncertain but didn't want to hurt her feelings. She was Grandma, after all. So, I obliged. I walked close behind while she struggled to keep the car seat level and herself upright. She tripped but caught herself on the wall.

"Thanks for trying, Mom, but I will carry her from here," I said, gesturing to let her know I'd like the car seat back. She exhaled sharply and slumped in annoyance. I felt guilty. I knew it was an accident. But I also knew that protecting my baby was now my number one job, even if it hurt people's feelings. Even if those people are connected to me by blood.

Before I had a baby, Mom's moments of absentmindedness were simply silly quirks. Now, with a baby in tow, those once innocent moments were no longer events I could brush off or giggle at. I *had* to care. To make it even more complex, Mom's reactions to her own potentially harmful mistakes left me wondering: Did she?

Despite returning for visit after visit, I declined all of Mom's offers to babysit. My heart was plagued by equal parts guilt and frustration over her audacity for asking. I wondered if things would get better or if I'd always have to have my guard up. Was I just lonely and self-serving or was I helping Mom like I thought I was? Would our relationship ever become what I'd always hoped it would be: healthy, reciprocal, normal-ish? Could I fix us?

The visceral sense of responsibility I had was interwoven with my being. She was my mom. You only get one, after all. And we loved each other. Even after everything we'd been through, this remained true. We were just . . . complicated.

MY DAYS OF SOLO PARENTING were also helped by a few friends who checked in: my cousin Jacquie who worked around the corner, my old coworker who made the long drive to have coffee with me, dinnertime visits with Harry and Amanda, and church friends on Sundays.

But the real camaraderie didn't come until Ellie was three months old and I had been on my own for a month. Listen, the joy of some things in life simply cannot be measured. Like the first time I saw the viral "salad fingers" YouTube video in 2004 and rewatched it four hundred times, laughing so hard I stopped breathing. Or, like when the British boy I met at summer camp turned out to have a big fat crush on me and invited me to visit him in fairy-tale England.

Or like when you hold your pee for so long you think you might die but then you get to a bathroom and it feels like angels from heaven are singing around you. That's what it felt like when my best friend finally had her baby. With three months of motherhood under my belt, I was ready, locked, and loaded to be there for Leah when she needed me. I needed her, too.

Together, we determined that new motherhood was best done side by side. We went for walks and texted about our milk supply and sleepless babies at 3 a.m. We joined a weekly baby-and-me salsa dance class. We swapped recipes and digestive tract updates—and not just for the babies. When Ellie got her first distressing cold, Leah shared her mom's advice. I shared tips for peeing less when you sneeze. I texted her pictures of my postpartum hair to see if I looked as much like Gollum as I thought I did and she texted me about the color of her baby's poop. We eased each other's loneliness, fear, and worries that we were screwing up our children.

HER: Am I overthinking the weight of his baby sleep sac?
ME: Yes.
ME: Can you die of monotony?
HER: LOL. No.
HER: I haven't slept. I don't think I can make it through the night.
ME: Yes, you will.
ME: I miss when my time was mine.
HER: Me too.

Day after day, we wove our little threads of uncertain new motherhood into a rope of strength and solidarity. Finally, I had someone to be honest about motherhood with.

My friendship with Leah mainly consisted of simultaneous cover-free breastfeeding sessions in her living room and taking turns coaching each other out of our mental breakdowns. As much as she reassured me that I was doing a great job, I couldn't help but remind her of the reasons she was incorrect. That—and ogle at her clean countertops. As I ate the freshly baked peanut-butter-and-jam cookies she made, I gazed upon her dust-free baseboards and glistening light fixtures. I dissected the order of her perfectly folded, organized matching towels in the linen closet. I admired her ability to keep up with it all with such ease.

"Sorry for the mess," she said one day as I made my way into the living room. She was moving the tummy-time mat that had previously been on the middle of the perfectly clean living-room rug to the corner where it lived when it was not in use. Then she walked back into the kitchen, opened her spotless fridge, and started wiping it out. I did not do such things. Cleaning my fridge was a once-in-a-blue-moon thing, not a tea-date thing.

But maybe it should be? When was the last time I cleaned my fridge out? That's embarrassing, I thought, suddenly self-conscious. *Was it just a difference of standards or was I a gross person? Did it even matter? Was this fridge tactic something I missed from the blueprint?*

I wanted to be a put-together person. I just didn't know how. I mean, my house was clean. I prepared a hardcore diaper bag, organized the nursery, and tried to keep clutter to a minimum. I swept the floors and wiped the counters daily. I rarely went to bed with dishes in the sink, and I threw in a load of laundry most days. Sure, clothes hung over the designated clothing chair in the bedroom, maybe on the floor, too. Sure, I couldn't remember the last time I'd wiped down my light fixtures or cleaned out my oven. But I was a clean person. Certainly, our home was more well-kept than the houses I'd lived in growing up. I made sure of that.

Still, I questioned myself. Leah held herself to high standards with ease. After playdates, toys were sanitized. Inside her kitchen drawers? Not a crumb. Her coffee tables? Spotless. I tried so hard not to look at her side of the proverbial fence—at her career, her parental support, her house, her family finances, and her ability to spin all the plates. But I struggled. I probably had things she didn't, but who keeps track of those things? It's easier to compare the other way.

Did her ability to stay put-together have anything to do with what she had that I didn't? Or—did I just suck? Maybe she just loved cleanliness. Who was I to get in the way? Maybe I needed to stop overanalyzing everyone.

Besides, none of that really mattered. My friendship with Leah altered my entire experience of motherhood for the better. She was a life raft. When she told me she wanted to scream into the abyss, I said, "Me too, girl. Me too." When I admitted I was jealous of my husband's useless nipples, she didn't judge me. We were each other's safe place. You don't have to be the same as someone to be safe *for* someone. With each other, we knew we weren't alone. That's what mattered.

THE NEXT WEEK, LEAH CAME to my house between the babies' nap times. I clicked on the kettle to make tea for us when she offered to grab the milk. "No, that's okay! I got it," I said, remembering I hadn't cleaned out the fridge. "You don't want to see the state of that thing."

"Lib, I don't care what your fridge looks like. Promise," Leah reassured me. But what if she did care? What if she found me out for the grown-up imposter that I was?

"Leah, your floors are so clean I could eat off them," I teased.

"I know," she said, and took a deep, sad breath. "Honestly, Lib, I wouldn't envy me. I'm a wreck. Everything in my life feels completely out of control. I clean so much because it's the only thing that quiets the anxiety. I wish I could relax but I can't. I'm always filled with dread over stupid things that other people don't even think about."

Wait, what? Here I was desperately trying to live up to her standards, feeling self-conscious, and all the while, she was strung out anxiety-cleaning? And the worry? She must be exhausted.

"I'm so sorry, Leah. That's hard," I said. I meant it.

"Thanks. It is. I can't drive anywhere with the baby; he cries so much. It's way too stressful to leave the house. So, I don't," she said. "I just stay home and clean."

I couldn't imagine. I *needed* to leave my house, like it was the air in my lungs. Long drives were what helped Ellie sleep. And the only reason I rage cleaned when company came was because I thought that's what I was supposed to do. I swept, mopped, sanitized, and stacked towels into neat piles because other people did—not to calm anxiety.

Leah's admission perplexed me. I'd always assumed motherhood came easier to her. How could someone look so put together while quietly unraveling just beneath the surface?

There was so much about Leah that I wanted to model myself after. But anxiety sounded rough. Or maybe it was par for the course? Maybe anxiety-fueled perfectionist cleaning was normal. What even *was* normal?

8

Nailing It

I'm not normal.

This belief was as natural to me as salt is to the sea. I wanted to fit in. And Leah wasn't the only person I modeled myself after to achieve such goals. For years I'd held up my little monocle, inspecting the ways other women who seemed to have their shit together lived their lives, washed their walls, and rolled their pie crusts. Both consciously and subconsciously.

I observed how Linda—the church mom who took teenage-me in for a few months when our home life was falling apart—baked her cookies. I studied how my aunt tucked in the sheets on the bed, how my mother-in-law wrote her Christmas cards, and how my church friends hung their matching family photos.

How did the mothers I admired do life? What is the magic sauce to keeping all the plates spinning? What plates should I even use? What is the measure of a good mother?

If I studied them close enough, for long enough, I could learn their ways. Maybe by proxy, I could figure out how to be a grown-up. Lord willing, I might become "normal."

Without a blueprint or healthy measuring stick for success, I found it difficult to determine the most essential expectations I should strive to meet. Should I be the clean queen? The Pinterest mom? The matching-clothes mom? The read-my-infant-classic-books-only mom? The bake-together and free-hugs-for-everyone mom? The crunchy mom? The fun mom? I didn't know which of the things I lacked in childhood made me least normal. How was I to choose? I didn't want to screw it up.

So, what did I do? I stretched my snow-plow arms as wide as they could go, collecting knowledge, routines, priorities, interests, immaculate habits, unrealistic expectations, and values that did not belong to me. Then, in the most "normal" act of all, I tried to execute on all of them.

With a tank filled with the fuel of hope, guilt, and grit, I went hard. I took my cue from friends, family, the women at church, society at large, and the fabricated places in my mind. I baked, crafted, taught my baby sign language, read books, sang songs, cooked, and rage cleaned like my life depended on it when company was coming. I wore other mom's perfectionisms like a badge of honor and my hard work paid off.

Ellie and I found our little two-person groove. And I just kept going—impressed by my ability to innovate and achieve—exhausted, but proud. In the three months Greg was away at Police College, I wasn't just *playing* house, I ran a house. Maybe I didn't *want* to do it mostly on my own, but I could, and I did.

ELLIE WAS SIX MONTHS OLD by the time I had Greg and Roger back home. My desire and ability to appear "normal" and function on less-than-ideal sleep had grown exponentially. Greg slipped back into daddy-of-the-year mode. He learned Ellie's daily routine and took an active role in it. When he wasn't working, he would lie awake with her in the night, sing her lullabies, and pace the house with her until she fell asleep again. He followed my lead in teaching her simple sign language, played her the guitar, changed her diapers, and blew raspberries on her tummy like dad-hood was the most natural thing.

Having Greg's and Roger's help again reinforced my once flailing arms to keep the plates of motherhood spinning and we found our family's new normal. With a full house, a full heart, and the confidence of a toddler running full speed toward the top of an escalator, I continued to strive.

On Saturdays, I prepared the weekly schedule and batch-cooked pureed solids for the week. On Sundays, Ellie and I wore matching outfits to church. We joined our library's baby reading group. I scheduled nap time, tummy time, and dinner time as if the Queen herself were coming over. I started volunteering again. I started a Bible study. I deep cleaned. I tracked milestones. I supported Mom. I visited Dad. I joined a book club. I figured out how to nurse with Ellie in the baby carrier and did housework while my boobs worked overtime. My pride soared. I loved being a mom. And considering all things, I was doing it pretty well. Possibly, I was nailing it.

MOST REWARDING OF ALL, I was giving my baby the life I'd never had. On a particular visit with my dad, I felt this truth deeply.

"Hah Lih-bee, izz ni tuh eeee yoo," my dad boomed, greeting me and giving me a hug in the hallway outside his apartment while patting me on the back. I mostly understood my dad. I'd had enough practice—unlike strangers, who often struggled to piece together my dad's speech. As a twin, he was born prematurely in 1951. From birth, he was deaf and had a learning disability. But for reasons unbeknownst to me, he didn't get the help he needed until adulthood. I never met my paternal grandparents. Dad was a capable person. He could take a car apart, put it back together, lay roofs, and beat just about anyone at a game of chess—but he never learned to speak clearly, sign fluently, or read or write properly.

After Mom left Dad, Harry and I still visited Dad on weekends. That lasted only until my eleventh birthday. Once my mom, brother, and I moved out of the city where he lived, I wasn't allowed to see my dad. Seven years later, when I turned eighteen, I picked up a phone book, found his name, and called him. The next week, we met at a bayfront park where he used to take us fishing when we were kids. We had a long awkward hug and he told me he'd tried everything he could to locate us all those years. His inability to read or write made it impossible for him to find out where we'd gone.

Less than a year after our reunion, I moved to England and got married. When we moved back to Canada, I got a job, went to community college to become an educational assistant, and we bought a house and started a family. I visited my dad a few times a year, but he wasn't a regular part of our lives. I felt guilty about this. It was just . . . complicated.

He lived an hour away, and like Mom, he didn't drive. Therefore, I bore the responsibility of maintaining our relationship. And let's be real, I was young and had other things on my mind. Even before I became a mom, time with Dad often left me feeling drained.

Communication was hard work.

His lack of literacy meant letters, emails, and texting were out of the question. Talking on the phone was so difficult that we only did so to make plans to meet in person. It took time and energy. Dad's being deaf (even with hearing aids) often made what should have been five-minute conversations take thirty minutes. There was so much to say and so many barriers to saying it. Since having a baby, finding time together was even more difficult to manage, but I determined to try harder. He was a grandpa now.

Dad held the door as I walked inside his apartment, then he pulled out a chair for me around his little kitchen table, beaming.

"How is the baby?" he bellowed, happily gesturing to Ellie.

"The baby is good. She's pretty happy most of the time," I said, signing "good" and "time," some of the signs I knew without thinking too hard.

"Greg has a new job," I told him.

"A new dog?!" he asked, surprised, signing the word "dog."

"No, Dad, a job," I said. The way Dad misheard me was often endearing. Other times, it was sad. No matter how hard I tried, I knew there was only so much we could talk about, only so much he could know of me and I could know of him.

I pulled out my phone to google how to sign "police officer." Sometimes, it took several minutes to clear things up. With Dad, we used what's called "total communication." Essentially, it's where you use every possible tool to communicate—a simultaneous mixture of speaking, lip reading, sign language, pictures, body language, contextual cues, and anything else that could convey a message.

He asked more about the baby, how I was doing, what Harry was up to, how Roger was liking Canada, and if there was anything I needed. Then, it happened.

"Let me tell you about my life," he began. He told me this life story on most visits, so I was not surprised. I bounced Ellie on my knee as I leaned in to listen. Dad's story went something like this, except much, much less clear.

"I was born deaf, you know? Me and Bill [his twin] were the size of your hand. Just this big," he said, gesturing. "Mom and Dad didn't know what was wrong with me. They sent me to a special school for slow kids. Kids called me stupid. Dad was mad all the time. Did lots of drinking beer, lots of beer. I couldn't hear anything. Nothin'. I was frustrated. Really mad. I got in trouble a lot. I didn't understand what was going on. One day when I was a teenager, maybe thirteen or fourteen, I got really angry. I did something bad. They sent me to the hospital for crazy people. They weren't very nice. I was there for a long time. A long time, Libby. Not a good place.

"One day a man came to help and found out I was deaf. That's when I got hearing aids for the first time. They sent me to the school for the deaf so I could learn to read and write. I was older then. Nineteen or so. It was hard to learn to read and to learn sign language. I didn't understand the sign language all the other kids used, but I tried and learned some. I didn't learn very good. But I learned how to fix cars and build things. I liked that. I didn't fit in with the hard-of-hearing kids or the deaf ones.

"I had to leave that school when I was twenty-one. Then Mom died. It was cancer. You know. C-A-N-C-E-R," he said, signing the letters one by one. I looked at the pictures on the wall behind him. There was one of Harry and me, one of him and his four siblings, and a portrait of his parents. I'd met his sisters when I was younger but didn't hear from them much after that. As I sat there with Ellie, I discovered I didn't know my family on his side and only now realized how strange that was.

"It was not good after that. I had a hard life. A hard, hard life," he said. "I am not stupid. You know?" And the way he said it told me it was something he'd been trying to convey to the world all his life.

"I'm sorry to hear that, Dad. You didn't deserve that. It must have been hard," I said.

I'd always viewed our separation through the lens of my childhood eyes. But now, as a parent myself, I was struck by the magnitude of *his* loss. What would it have felt like to lose your kids and not see them for seven years? Listening to the story I'd heard countless times, I felt a new sadness I hadn't felt before.

"Well, that's just what happens. It's not your problem. I'm the father. You are the daughter," he said. Dad always wanted to make sure I knew two things: First, he wasn't my responsibility. Second, there were reasons he was the way he was.

Before Harry and I moved away from the city, we went to Dad's house on weekends. Usually, we took the bus. He stocked our favorite snacks: orange pop, Mr. Noodles, and strawberry wafer cookies. There was always something planned. He took us to the park, the bowling alley, the public pool, and car shows. Before we watched a movie, he would get out his giant hardcover *Sesame Street* ASL book to teach us to sign.

If we wanted hot dogs, we signed. If we wanted the bathroom, we signed. In the pool, between being thrown in the water, we signed. I saw the way people looked at my dad, like he was stupid when he wasn't. I saw the extra work he had to put into every moment of his existence. I saw the things we didn't do with Dad that other kids did with theirs. But sign language? It felt like a special code only we knew, one of the only things we had that other kids didn't.

During our years apart, I missed his company. I missed our card games. I missed his unconditional love and the feeling of being protected by him. I missed my dad. Now I wondered, what would it have been like to have a dad who taught me how to ride a bike, encouraged me to try harder at sports, or read me bedtime stories? What was it like to have a dad tell you that you are beautiful or to talk about college applications with? And now, what would it be like for me to have a dad now who was more able? One who could fix my air-conditioner or text me when the roads were covered in ice to tell me to drive safe? What would it be like to talk to your dad about what was really going in your life?

When our visit was over, he walked me and Ellie to my car. As we drove off, he stood in the parking lot, one hand on his hip, the other waving a big happy farewell. I knew this time spent together meant the world to him.

Seeing him reminded me what I'd missed out on and was still longing for. I realized I had more questions than answers and more longings than I'd previously been able to acknowledge. The guilt-laced grief that crept up my throat wasn't something I felt anyone could ever understand, much less that I could say out loud.

I looked in the rearview mirror and gazed at my own little girl with the bittersweet understanding of things as they were. I couldn't go back and give little me what she needed. I couldn't give Dad what he needed, either. But I could give it to her. Knowing Ellie would experience the joy of having a loving, present father like Greg filled the crevices of my heart and was the full-circle perspective I needed. But I couldn't help but wonder: Would it always hurt a little?

ROGER DIDN'T REPLACE MY DAD, but in many ways he filled gaps as a father figure and enriched our lives in ways I didn't know I needed. It was impossible not to love this man—and not just because he made a sick cup of tea or vegetable curry. His easygoing nature and unassuming, witty British charm just drew people in. Roger had this magical ability to make you feel seen, no matter who you were. He took every opportunity to help people, to listen, and to encourage.

Before long, he began receiving invitations to our friends' Halloween parties, Christmas soirees, bonfire nights, family fishing trips, weekends away, and Sunday lunches. I would tell our friends that he really was fine to stay home when our family unit was invited places. They didn't have to invite him just because he lived with us. But always, people would laugh and remind me how much they wanted him there.

Roger made friends everywhere he went: the post office, the church, the corner store, and on park benches. Eventually I noticed the women of his generation were particularly intrigued. I began to wonder why he wasn't dating. He was single, after all. And after all the good he did for other people, he, too, deserved goodness in return.

Roger often joined in on my daily activities with Ellie. One day, we were out scouring the local thrift shops for decorations for Ellie's first birthday party when we stopped for lunch at McDonald's. As usual, Roger did his best to pretend a table of older women weren't swooning in his direction, again. So, I shot my shot.

"Have you considered dating? There are apps you can join," I asked.

"No, not really." He laughed bashfully. But a few weeks later, after several cups of tea and promises of taking it slow and maybe trying it as a joke, he agreed to try a dating app. I set up a profile for him, and we began to scroll. What could it hurt?

I USED THE EXTRA CAPACITY from having Greg and Roger around to plan the first birthday party of my baby's dreams. And by "my baby's dreams," I mean my dreams. I love a good party. I wasn't necessarily trying to impress anyone. I simply enjoyed having a creative outlet, seeing an event come together, and rising to the challenge of "bougie on a budget." There was much to celebrate!

I spent my evenings scouring the corners of Pinterest for ideas. One of those ideas was a sugar-free cake. Cake smashes were all the rage but I was committed to the no-sugar journey. So, I sourced a recipe that was 70 percent bananas. *Fancy.* I also made four dozen perfect cupcakes with real sugar for the *not* one-year-olds because I am not a psychopath.

The day of the party arrived. Together, Roger, Greg, and I transformed our backyard into a British garden party—minus the rain. I borrowed tents from friends to make shade, strung a pretty homemade bunting banner on them, and dressed the table in all its fanciness. I baked and bought English party treats. There were cucumber sandwiches, squares, and scones. I even went to the effort of buying clotted cream from the only international specialty shop in the county. After decorating, I placed the treats on their respective teal and pink vintage standing trays, the dainty ones I'd sourced from thrift shops to complete the look.

I timed the end of Ellie's perfectly scheduled nap with the perfect party start time and brought her out in her perfect pink party dress. When it came time for the cake smash, Ellie did what any one-year-old would do with a gigantic pink cake made primarily out of bananas. She took one bite, spit it out, and looked around as if to say, "Why did you give me this trash?" I didn't blame her. At least we got a good picture.

While I sat with her opening her presents, I looked at the circle of friends and family around us, smiling wide, bearing witness to such a special moment. We'd made it.

For a year, I'd wondered if we would. I'd second-guessed everything. I'd inspected every mystery rash like her life depended on it. I'd hovered over the top of her crib—like a deranged twitching maternal zombie—watching her chest rise and fall to be sure she was breathing. I'd spent my days neurotically micromanaging everything, from the angle of her headbands to the timing of her naps. Now, I felt relieved. No—I felt proud. My baby had everything she needed. Most of all, our love.

I'll admit the tea party for a one-year-old was hardcore. Maybe I hadn't planned the party for the adoring looks or to impress people. But I'd be lying if I said it didn't feel good. Was I normal yet?

9

Oceans

A few weeks later, we went on our first family road trip. I wanted to use the last of my one-year maternity leave as best I could. I adored being a mom and I also couldn't wait to go back to work and engage my brain in other ways. The great thing about having a humane amount of parental leave is that it gives you essential time with your baby until you cannot wait to rejoin the workforce. Go Canada.

Ellie loved the car, which made a road trip possible. We loaded her up and headed east for an epic 1,200 mile journey toward Canada's rugged Atlantic coast. Not that we measured the trip in miles. Canadians are known to measure distances in time. We broke up our twenty-hour voyage by visiting some of the country's most charming, historic East Coast cities.

We stopped for poutine in cobblestoned Québec City before rolling through lobster-crazy New Brunswick, the province that borders Maine. We watched the chilly water ripple next to us as we drove across the Confederation Bridge and made our way to Charlottetown, a tiny city tucked away on picturesque Prince Edward Island, home of Anne of Green Gables.

We toddled around our nation's iconic lighthouse at Peggy's Cove, took a whale-watching trip that yielded no whales but still delighted our senses. We popped into Halifax, where, on a park bench with her dad, Ellie enjoyed her first taste of sugar: vanilla ice cream. At last, we landed at our final destination, my favorite place of all, Cape Breton Island. Sparsely populated, Cape Breton is famous for its jaw-dropping good looks and magnificent hiking. Think Scotland's ancient landmarks and weathered coast but with a Canadian accent, and if you are lucky, moose.

"You sure you want to do this?" Greg asked, as we pulled up to the Skyline Trail with our hiking boots, backpack, and well-worn baby carrier. It was a ten-kilometer (six-mile) walk each way with no possibility of pushing a stroller. "I can handle it," I assured him.

I strapped Ellie to my chest, and we began the walk through the pine forest trail. Ellie, inches from my face, took every opportunity to look around, cooing at the birds and shrieking in delight. Thirty minutes into the walk, we came upon a group of people who were whispering and pointing. As I looked in the direction they gestured to, I saw two enormous moose—the first I'd ever laid eyes on.

I pointed and whispered to Ellie, "Look at the moose!" Her eyes scanned the woods. Then her face lit up. I said it again. "Moose! Look!" She whispered back to me, "Mmm, mmm," and waved at them. My heart lurched with joy.

We continued walking for what felt like forever until we emerged from the heavily forested area to a clearing that explained why the place was called the Skyline Trail. The dirt path ended. A long wooden plank trail began, with hundreds of shallow stairs leading to the beach. It curved back and forth ever so slightly to the left, toward the cliffs and an endless view of the sea. The vast blue sky stretched for miles and was speckled by *Simpsons*-like clouds. The sun was hot and the ocean breeze fresh. It felt like we were staring at the edge of the earth itself.

Ellie began to squirm. She wanted down. I handed her to Greg and watched from behind while he led her, holding both hands for stability, down the wooden stairs toward the ocean.

I meandered behind and took pictures, wanting to capture the magic of the moment. She was so lucky to have him.

When we reached the bottom wooden plank platform, I sat down and welcomed the relief to my back. I opened our picnic lunch with the rocky cliffs in view and birds swirling overhead. Then, I watched Ellie watching the world: content, happy, loved. I'd seen beautiful parts of the world before. It sure was more work to travel with a baby. But experiencing the wonder of the Earth's beauty with the person we made was somehow better.

I got to see the ocean, yes. But more so, I got to see *her* see the ocean. I got to see *her* see the moose. I got to see *her* see me. And nobody looked at me like she did.

Sitting there, with the ocean as our backdrop, I was unbothered by the slowness of it all. I didn't care about my exhaustion, my throbbing back, or the lack of signal on my phone. I didn't care that my identity shift in motherhood was still hanging in the balance or think about the other nagging frustrations of motherhood.

The difficulties that came with being a mother felt inconsequential because I knew that moments like this could never exist without the hard parts. Little regular moments, too. Like watching her roll over on the living room floor, smile at Granddad Roger in the living room, or giggle at my made-up songs. Like first steps, first sneezes, and first crawls.

It wasn't just about a trip to the ocean. It was about getting a front-row seat to the wonder in my child's eyes. Being present for every inch of growth and learning. How ludicrous that I could be the source of that joy. How lucky I was to have someone to love so much and be loved in return.

It's easy to take the privilege of motherhood for granted when you are living and breathing it every day, when the moments feel like hours and the days feel like years. When the crying won't cease and the lists are never done—it's easy to forget what an honor it is to create and nurture a whole person to adulthood.

Motherhood woke me up and helped me see the world with new eyes and helped me appreciate the magnificence of life itself. Did I miss my freedom and former life? Sure. Being a mom *was* hard in ways that are difficult to describe. But as it turned out, the goodness of motherhood was impossible to describe. It was every feeling at once, and I knew then just how lucky I was to experience it.

IN A SURPRISE TO ABSOLUTELY nobody, our epic experience on the beaches of Cape Breton combined with my maternal epiphanies led to my desire to make more babies. Lucky Greg. A few months later, shortly after I returned to work, we decided to stop trying *not* to have babies, again. A few weeks after that, we were reminded just how fertile I was. Helloooo, thin blue line.

Approximately nine months later, I woke up in the middle of the night in so much pain I thought I was dying. I woke up Greg to inform him. The ache in my midsection was so intense and so unlike my labor pains the previous time I'd given birth that the thought didn't occur to me that my pregnancy might just be coming to an end.

"You're not dying," he groaned, half asleep still.

"Okay, well, I am going to get in the bath and then—AHHHHHHHHH," I said, interrupting myself with a yelp. When he didn't instinctively know exactly what I needed, I wanted to drop-kick him. Instead, I dialed Theresa. Doula Tammy had moved away in the last year, so I'd brought on a new doula, Theresa. My abdominal pain skyrocketed while I waited for her to pick up. So, I threw my phone at Greg and groaned while I waited.

Roger had planned to be at the house to watch Ellie when I went into labor, but since he'd met someone new on that dating website I'd signed him up for, he was away that night. Greg called and asked him to make the one-hour drive home so that I could go to the hospital if needed—which was also an hour away but in the opposite direction.

When Theresa arrived, she pulled Greg aside. In a hushed but very serious tone she said, "This baby is coming soon and based on the sounds Libby is making, her body is pushing. We need to get her to the hospital as soon as possible." Greg called Roger back and told him to drive faster.

I waddled out to the car, plopped myself in the back seat, and tried to breathe through the intensifying contractions. I was focused. Oddly quiet. "Try and hold it in, try not to push," I heard Theresa say. By the time Roger's headlights made their appearance at the end of our road, I'd been waiting "patiently" in the back seat of the car for what felt like the longest thirty minutes of my life, willing my cervix to close. Greg hit the gas, we drove to the hospital, and this time, I planned to ask for an epidural right away. I didn't need to be a hero. I was going to pop this baby out easier than the last one.

Theresa asked me if I wanted a wheelchair. I declined because I'm an independent woman. *I can walk just fine by myself, thank you.* The hospital was a ghost town in the middle of the night, but we tried to follow the signs to labor and delivery. I waddled into the elevator, held onto the railing inside, and let out what felt like the largest, most-in-chargest bearing-down moo there has ever been on planet Earth. The poor little old man beside me looked at the wall of the elevator and pretended this was normal.

My midwife appeared. She measured my cervix, and I could hear her voice quicken as she told me I was ready. Maybe this labor would be different? Maybe there would be none of this twenty-four-hour labor business? Weirdly, I wasn't panicked.

Less than two hours had passed since I woke up in pain, so I reminded myself to be patient.

"Will the anesthesiologist be coming soon to give me the epidural?" I asked. She smiled at me in an *oh, bless your sweet heart* kind of way and said, "There isn't going to be time."

That can't be true, I thought. *I can't do this.* I could hardly do it last time, *with* drugs! There was another contraction. I breathed deep, gritted my teeth, and focused. Then there was another. *I have to do this.*

Ten minutes later my midwife looked at me, pointed between my legs, where I felt all the pressure I was trying to pretend wasn't there, and said, "You know you could have this baby now, right? It's right there."

Oh.

So with the next contraction I stopped holding it in. I blocked out the noise. I ignored my six chins. I listened to my body. I felt the pressure. When the next contraction began, I leaned in. I mooed. I yelled. I squeezed Greg's hand like mincing his finger meat was an Olympic event. There it was: the epidural-free ring of fire. AND I WAS DOING IT.

First came his head. Then I gave a final push and out my baby popped like a banana from its peel—all nine pounds five ounces of him. He was a wet, chubby, goo-covered ball of glory. We named him Oscar. He was perfect and I was proud.

THE TRUTH? PUSHING OUT THAT behemoth of a baby without any pain medication made me feel like the most primal and powerful woman on earth. Ellie's birth had taken equal but different strength. In the end, there was no hierarchy. Birthing babies is just badass.

The strength it takes to go home and sustain that baby's life—without sleep, without control, without enough support or information—is like what I imagine the settlers of rugged Cape Breton Island needed when they first landed on the coast after bearing storm after storm. Constantly on the lookout for danger, for the next wild animal they'd never seen before. Woefully unprepared. Unable to turn back. Broken and lost. Forced to keep pushing through regardless. Amazed by the island's breathtaking beauty, its ferocity, and, eventually, by their own ability to weather its storms and call it home.

Moms. When it feels like we can't go on another day, another hour, another minute . . . we do. When we're scared, when it hurts, when the future is unknown—we show up anyway. Giving birth, like raising our children, doesn't hurt for no reason.

Motherhood hurts because it matters. And it gives back, too. Of all its gifts, one of the greatest is the chance to discover our own strength. I didn't know how strong I was until I was forced to find out. Spoiler alert: I was forced to find out even more.

10

Changes

Whatever secret sauce I'd had before Oscar entered the picture seemed to evaporate when he arrived. Motherhood with two small humans was not twice as hard as raising a single child. The challenge grew tenfold.

Getting out the door was like trying to evacuate a circus tent during a tornado. Nap schedules? A chapter of ancient history. Putting the kids to bed felt like World War III. Newborn Oscar didn't sleep for more than two hours at a time, and two-year-old Ellie entered into some kind of sleep regression from the seventh layer of fresh hell. Any semblance of control seemed to up and leave in an instant, including that of my pelvic floor. Also, I had a baby who reacted to feeding like I was pouring toxic waste down his throat.

Nursing Ellie into drunk baby heaven past the one-year mark made me feel like I was the source of all things good: bonding, nurturing, growth. I didn't realize how much it made me feel like a capable mom until I had the opposite experience. From day one, I'd attempted to exclusively breastfeed Oscar, assuming I could recreate the experience. Wrong!

I tried every angle, every posture, every tip and trick in the book. Nothing worked. He wouldn't latch, and when he did, he'd come off screaming like I was spraying him with a fire hose of lava. The lactation consultant I was referred to cut Oscar's apparent tongue-tie, which changed absolutely nothing except for how I felt about myself as a mom. I worried he wasn't getting the nutrition he needed. Scratch that—I became completely consumed with suffocating anxiety that my baby was not going to be okay and it was all my fault.

After a few weeks, I tried to pump exclusively instead. Listen. I don't know what your boobs are like or what technology existed if and when you ever attempted to pump milk out of them. But let me paint you a picture of my experience.

There's a buzzing machine plugged into the wall making a low mechanical *hummp . . . hummp . . . hummp . . .* and slowly extracting what few drops of liquid gold and any dignity I have left. There are two lines coming out of the machine that connect to bottles that have squishy suction cups on them. Suction does not actually happen. Not to my boobs. So, I hold both pumps on manually, adding a borderline-aggressive amount of pressure in hopes of squeezing any drops out. The constant suction makes my nipples feel like they are being slowly sanded off.

The baby was usually screaming. The toddler was usually asking questions. Pumping and parenting turned out to be like cooking in a kitchen that's on fire. The pump parts and bottles? Always waiting for me to sanitize them, staring at me from the messy kitchen as if to say "You're behind again. You suck."

The monotony of washing partially consumed bottles got old fast. I spent half my life apologetically pumping and the other half praying that what I produced was enough to make my struggle worth the effort. It wasn't. Oscar refused my liquid gold. When he ingested it, the milk came right back up.

After six weeks, I gave up on the pump, too. The future was formula, or a one-way ticket to the lobotomy clinic. I thought the powder would free my time, ease my mind, and satisfy his appetite. Wrong. I was constantly hyperaware that my energy, tone, or posture could make or break the moment.

Would he finally give in and accept what I was offering, or pull away again like he often did? My mind would race, trying to remember what angle had worked before or what temperature the room was or what he'd been wearing—exactly—the last time he gave in and let himself eat.

Oscar's larger-than-average weight began to drop. Drinking milk seemed to cause him pain. *I* seemed to cause him pain.

He was never truly satisfied. That meant he never slept, which meant I never slept. When we were awake, he cried. Well, sometimes he didn't. Colic or not, I felt my sanity slipping away like sand through an hourglass.

Something was wrong. The doctors I brought him to assured me there wasn't. Everyone told me not to worry. But worrying was my job. Plus, they weren't at home witnessing the treachery of our feeding sessions every hour on the hour. What did they know?

Would he grow? Was I depriving him? Would his distress have some kind of long-term impact? Did he know he was loved? It didn't seem like it. My heart ached for him.

Whenever it was time to try and feed him, my nerves magnified infinitely. Could he sense my apprehension? The internet gurus told me he could, that maybe my stress was part of the problem. Naturally, this helped me to stress less. *Not.*

All I know is that over the course of the first few months, as a mother of two, any pride or confidence I'd had in my ability to mother all but vanished.

TRUE OR FALSE: DECIDING TO uproot your entire life and move house in the early weeks of newborn life is a perfectly sane idea. False? Correct.

Here's the thing. When I said yes to moving our family, I was two-weeks postpartum and hadn't considered just how different babies could be. *He'll be three months old by the time we move. It'll be easier then,* I told myself.

Another thing I misjudged was the steep decline in support that generally happens after a sibling arrives. When Ellie was born, our church swooped in like they did for all new moms in the congregation and arranged a meal train. I didn't have to cook for a week. There were frozen casseroles, fresh chicken Caesar wraps, or cheesy rigatoni waiting on our doorstep each day. I had the support of Roger and Greg, so the VIP food service wasn't entirely necessary, but it was extremely welcome. Knowing people were thinking of me bolstered my confidence.

In those early days with Ellie, Tammy checked in to make sure breastfeeding was going as planned. When it wasn't, she arranged for a latch guru to come over and help. Friends sent texts every few days just to ask, "How is it today?"—no pressure to respond, just a reminder I wasn't alone. When Ellie was admitted to the hospital, friends and family showed up with snacks and company. The support wasn't perfect, but I felt held.

With the entrance of a second baby, my web of support wasn't quite the same. There was a meal train, but it lasted only a couple days rather than a week. When feeding became an issue, I navigated it alone. Roger was busy being newly in love. Greg was supportive, but that manifested in being on Ellie duty. I appreciated his help, but it also left me alone with a baby I couldn't figure out and nothing to stifle the inner voice that was tearing me to shreds.

The calls and texts came in at a fraction of the rate they had the first time. People around me must have assumed I knew what I was doing. But now, with a mountain of moving boxes to pack and two miniature humans who needed me 24/7, I needed *more* support than I did the first time.

I couldn't shake the feeling that everyone had moved on while I was sinking below the surface. Maybe I'd spent so much energy trying to show the world I was nailing it that they believed me.

THREE MONTHS AFTER OSCAR JOINED our family, moving day arrived. In the past we'd enlisted the help of friends and family, offering pizza and good vibes as payment. But Roger was out of the country, Leah was about to pop out another baby, Harry was having surgery, and well . . . we were grown-ups. So, we hired a moving company.

I packed the diaper bag, loaded up the car, and waved goodbye to Greg—who had agreed to finish things up with the movers. Ninety-six seconds later, Oscar began to scream. My body filled with tension. *It's only a thirty-minute drive,* I told myself. *Calm down, woman.*

Over the last three months, every single time I got in the car with my children, Oscar wailed as if I was sawing off his toes with a butter knife. Was it motion sickness, light sensitivity, gas, general crankiness, or starvation? Nobody knew. I'd tried everything. I put up mirrors and installed an inordinate number of sun blockers. I tried singing, talking, silliness, and silence. Nothing. Worked.

Ellie spent the drive to our new town plugging her ears and frowning, bless her soul. Despite my nervous system feeling like it was being electrocuted, I attempted to focus on the road. The vehicular torture chamber was just one of the long list of reasons we'd decided to move in the first place.

Living in a one-stoplight hamlet in the middle of nowhere had once made sense. Our church felt like the only community I knew. We wanted to be close by. The housing market was affordable there, and I'd thought rural living was a wholesome way to raise a family.

Instead, it was inconvenient and isolating. There was so much we hadn't considered or anticipated. Big things, like Greg getting his dream job an hour away, making his already long twelve-hour shifts turn into fourteen. That didn't even count overtime. His absence left me alone with two kids a lot and (due to the car torture chamber) having major anxiety about leaving the house, ever.

When we did venture out, everything was far away: Mom, Dad, Harry, playgroups, dance studios, and grocery stores. The church moms? Well, pre-baby Libby didn't think things like homeschooling, farming, or generational ties would get in the way of infiltrating the mom circles. But, while Sundays were smiley, it turned out a lot of people already had their people.

Leah and her family had also just moved out of our little town. With another baby on the horizon, her family's life was about to get significantly busier. Roger's choice to take my advice and find love was another factor we had failed to consider. He was marrying and settling down with his new wife an hour away. We no longer had a use for such a large house with an in-law suite, nor the desire to maintain it.

We wanted to move before the kids were enrolled in school. We wanted to give the kids more opportunities and hopefully to make life with littles somewhat more manageable. So moving closer to where Greg worked and closer to civilization was a no-brainer.

Still, I felt guilty about the decision to move. I worried how the changes would affect the kids. I didn't want to uproot them. After moving eighteen times before my eighteenth birthday, I swore I'd never do that to my children.

ONE OF THE MOST SIGNIFICANT of my countless childhood moves happened my eleventh year on earth. We were living in a small subsidized bungalow in the inner city—the same one where we'd raked in pocket money selling our housewares on the front lawn. We'd resided there for more than two whole years—a record—when Mom met a new man, Karl.

Our cat was for sale, along with several household items we'd advertised in the local paper to generate cash. Karl had seen the listing in the newspaper and come to pick up the cat. I suppose he and Mom hit it off because a few weeks later, I came home from school to find this poorly postured, disarmingly tall, gray-blond man I'd never met painting our kitchen.

"Your mother is outside," he said to me, straight-faced, as if I knew who he was and why he was in my house. His accent was strange. Thick. Deliberate. Hard. Quick. Clipped. Russian, I later found out. Shortly after that, we shared a meal around the table—a fairly uncommon event in our house. He told us we needed to work on our dinner table etiquette, whatever that was.

Karl was old—or least that's how I felt about a man ten years Mom's senior. He lived on a hobby farm an hour outside the city, and on that farm were cows, chickens, and goats! *How fun,* I thought.

On that farm also lived his four teenage children and his wife. Karl had lamented to Mom about how mean and abusive his wife was. Naturally, Mom wanted to help.

A few months into their courtship, Karl announced that he was going to change our lives. "You can go back to school, get a job, drive a car, and have a vonderful life with za kids out in za country!" he said to my mom. He wanted us to move to the rural town nearest to his hobby farm.

While we'd moved a lot, we had stayed within the same city all our lives. I didn't want to move again—especially so far from my dad, my friends, and everything I'd ever known. But a few months later I was saying goodbye to my fifth-grade pals and we were packing our lives into boxes again.

"It's for the better," Mom assured me as we unloaded the moving truck into our townhouse rental in a new town I'd never heard of. "We've got a car now!"

Mom said she wanted better for us. That's why we'd moved. That's why she got a full-time job at a group home. That's why she was going back to school to get a college diploma—to make a better life.

I assumed that's why she said, "He's only doing it because he loves you," when Karl scoffed and threw my carefully folded laundry across the floor of the laundromat when I hadn't folded it exactly how he liked it. "He might be your dad one day. He's only trying to teach you," Mom said. And he did. Before long he'd taught us how to set the table properly, how to fold clothes properly, and most importantly—how to stay invisible and out of the way.

We lived in that townhouse for eight months until Karl finally left his wife. Before sixth grade ended, we were packing up to move four hours north. Over the next two years as a "new family," we moved six more times, Karl's divorce went through, we moved onto his hobby farm, and Harry and I learned how to run the farm. By the time I was thirteen and entering eighth grade, Mom and Karl were married, and the few ties we had to family or old friends were cut for good.

HOME WAS NOT A CONCEPT I grew up with. Therefore, creating one for my kids that was stable, loving, and safe was priority number one. As we drove to the new house, I reminded myself that our move that day was different. This move was made with intention. We were relocating for our kids' benefit—and their experience of it was anything but an afterthought.

11

Quilts

The move meant some of our loved ones would live farther away from us, but others, specifically Mom, would be closer. My feelings about this swung like a pendulum. I felt hope, because close proximity would make supporting and visiting her easier. I felt trepidation, because saying no would become harder for me—and *that* was already a challenge.

Still, Mom tried. On moving day she offered her apartment as a place for me and the kids to kill time while we waited for keys to our new house. As I pulled into her driveway, she was eagerly waiting for us outside on her front steps.

"Hi, Grandma!" Ellie said as she ran toward her.

"Hi, sweetie!" Mom said, before wrapping Ellie in a hug. I tried to mask the stress on my face from the drive over and contort my mouth into a smile of gratitude. I was thankful to have somewhere to go while we waited.

Then my phone rang.

It was 10 a.m. "The lawyers said we can't get the keys to the new house yet," Greg told me. "They're still waiting for our bank to transfer the money to the sellers. I talked to the bank, and they said it was sent, but the sellers' lawyer said they don't have it."

"Did they give you any idea of how long it could take?"

"Not really, but it shouldn't be too long," Greg reassured me with the optimism I'd become accustomed to. I said goodbye and hung up, unsure.

There is still time. We can still make it into the new house for the kids' naps, I told myself. I fed and entertained the kids, drank the tea Mom made me, and listened to her stories. We continued to pass time like this for two hours until I called Greg at noon. There was still no news. I attempted to put the kids down for naps. Failure. I called Greg on the hour until 2 p.m. No news. I was desperate to get into our new house.

Pacing Mom's apartment, surrounded by the smell of the cigarettes she pretended not to smoke anymore and the reality that we may not get the keys before night fell, I pondered my options.

At 4:30, I called Greg again. "Still no luck," he said.

"I've been here all day. The kids are cranky. I am cranky. We need to get into that house. We have nowhere to stay tonight," I told him.

"You can just stay overnight here if you want," Mom offered.

"Thanks, Mom. I'll think about it. Hopefully that won't be necessary."

I finished my call with Greg and imagined trying to fit my family of four onto Mom's single bed and the chaos around it. Then, I imagined what it would be like to be able to say no to your parent without becoming riddled with fear of their reaction.

I got lost in my thoughts, wondering what having healthy, stable, supportive parents might feel like as I navigated motherhood. What did it feel like for my church friend Lindsay, whose mom came over every Tuesday and Thursday to watch her kids for no reason other than she wanted to and could? What would it be like to tackle life like Tamara, who called her mom every time she had a question about what to do next?

There was Leah's mom, who cooked dinner for her adult children and grandchildren every Sunday. Sundays were usually the saddest day of my week, especially when Greg was working all weekend and most of my friends were busy with their families. By the time the weekend ended, I was often spent and desperate for connection—for support, routines, and traditions I didn't have to create or maintain. I longed for Sunday dinners.

I longed for the village they say it takes to raise a child. But *what even is a village?* Physical proximity to your people? Intergenerational care? Genuine loving and reciprocal connections that don't suck the life from one party or another? Family? Friends? Both?

I imagined a village like a handmade quilt. Greg and I had been gifted a few of them when Ellie was born. Each one was colorful, soft, strong, unique, and very clearly stitched together over time with great care. There is something about that mixture of these qualities that makes a quilt particularly comforting. They take work, skill, resources.

Some moms seemed to dodge the hard work of quilting their villages from scratch. They raised kids around close friends and family who happened to share similar values. They took their place in the village and contributed to its maintenance rather than build it from scratch.

In past generations, moms in individual families didn't need to singlehandedly be the cook, cleaner, teacher, coordinator, playmate, holiday magic maker, and everything in between. They had other trusted adults and children interwoven into their lives who they did everyday life with.

I witnessed it in several of the church moms—women whose parents were their steady foundation, keepers of family secrets, and sharers of wisdom and recipes. The thick border and top stitching on their intergenerational village quilt. They relied on each other, bolstered each other. Watching how they lived was like stepping back in time and witnessing village life at its finest—except it wasn't a story in the past. It was right there in front of me, like a snow globe: magical but untouchable. Impenetrable.

Maybe that was a small part of the reason we decided to try a new church after the move. We could never really fit in. Sure, my church family had carried me through hard times and they were wonderful in many ways. When somebody needed help, we were there with prayers and muffins. When babies were born, we threw parades. We had board game nights, prayer nights, friendly Sunday mornings, and community events. These things had once made me feel like I belonged. But when the deeper layers of community life began to feel like something I watched from the outside, something didn't line up. It hurt.

Their way of life was simply not a reality for women like me in modern-day society. Whether it was because of finances, choice, chance, or the families we happened to be born into, fitting into their lives was out of reach. I mean, for most of us, twenty-first-century life in the West is basically the antithesis of village living.

Those of us who didn't inherit a quilt have to go fabric shopping and make our own. We have to slowly stitch together a trustworthy, empathetic network, one meaningful relationship at a time. We're never sure if we are even doing it right. Sometimes, our scraps of material are scattered around the globe or hidden under giant boulders in some kind of sick scavenger hunt. Our quilt gets shredded or quilts are handed to us covered in toxic waste.

Our generation often lives in silos, intentional or not. We don't always have the time, energy, and skill to stitch a quilt properly. Our hands are busy doing all the other tasks of motherhood, trying to make it through each day without breaking. Building and maintaining a village falls to the bottom of the list. If we're not handed one, it's hard. You've got to make do with what you've got.

Nobody had perfect parents, of course. Sometimes the helpful grandparents were also the judgmental and overbearing ones. Honestly, some moms I knew expected far *too* much from their parents. No one completely escaped misunderstandings, tricky dynamics, and challenging boundaries.

But that didn't stop me from wondering what it might feel like to mother with all our family members on the same continent, with able parents, cousins for my kids to play with, or from wondering how this day might feel without the knowledge that Roger was leaving.

My father-in-law had been a tremendous support to us. He didn't owe us anything. Roger deserved happiness in his new life. But as I sat on my mom's couch, pondering the prospect of staying at her apartment that night, I realized just how much I was going to miss him—his conversations, encouragement, and everyday immersion in our lives. His kinship had helped carry me the last couple years. And now, when motherhood was getting harder, he was moving away. I didn't blame him—I was the one who had encouraged him to see what was out there, after all. I just couldn't believe it was all happening at once.

AT 4:49, THE PHONE RANG with good news. The money had gone through, and we finally had our home. We thanked Mom and hightailed it to our new place. I took a detour at the golden arches, shoved a Big Mac down my throat in an effort to stave off hunger, and fed my babies. Walking in the front door, my body filled with relief. We were home.

It was nearing 6 p.m. when Greg and the movers began to pull bed frames and lamps and boxes galore from the truck. I watched the kids and attempted to unpack. But every time I tried to put

Oscar down in the bouncer he sometimes loved, he'd cry, and every time I tried to soothe him, Ellie came running with a burning question or five. Eventually, I gave up on the notion of unpacking anything but the essentials.

I settled the kids into bed in their new rooms and, eventually, crawled into my own. I looked down at my phone, hoping to see a text from someone—telling me what I needed to hear, informing me that they were coming to help, or asking if I'd survived. Instead, I saw an empty screen. And it hit me. Had we made a big mistake?

No, this is just the reality of modern-day life, I told myself. It's just one day. People are just busy tending to their own lives. Maybe, in this new town, we could find community with new people who were also walking the tightrope of twenty-first-century motherhood. Maybe Roger will still come around a lot. Maybe we'll get more time with Greg. Maybe I'll still see Leah. Maybe I will fix things with Mom. Maybe everything will be okay, I told myself.

But it was too late. Panic had set in. For someone who'd moved more times than she could count, the four years in our little hamlet had been the closest thing to permanence I'd ever known. Leaving felt like the right choice, but I'd miss the familiarity and warmth of the people who'd been a part of the fabric of our lives for so long. There were so many unknowns in our future. So many changing rhythms and routines, so much I already longed for but was too busy to really think about.

This was the end of an era and reality was hitting. Whatever patchwork village I'd created was coming loose at the seams. The soft, colorful fabric squares were littered at my feet. Would I find the right pieces again? If I did, how could I sew them while my hands were busier than they'd ever been?

When we'd decided to move, I'd told myself our move would be different from the many moves I'd endured as a kid. I believed it was for the best. But now, I wasn't so sure.

12

Shoeboxes

"I just cherish these moments, they go by so fast," Idiot Lady said.

> INSIDE LIBBY: Please fuck all the way off.
> OUTSIDE LIBBY: Yeah . . .

I nodded politely and used whatever energy I had left to stop my eyes from rolling into the back of my head.

The only thing *I* had been cherishing of late was the sound of silence after I buckled both kids into the car and snail-walked to my car door.

Idiot Lady is the name I gave the woman who imparted this wisdom one afternoon while I paced the pediatrician's waiting room with a screaming baby in my arms. Several weeks had passed since the move. And while Oscar's silly, charming personality had entered the chat, his appetite had not—nor had his interest in my comfort, or sleep, apparently.

My child was having problems that I was desperate to solve but couldn't, no matter how hard I tried. Lord knows I tried. I explained

Oscar's struggles and all the ways I'd attempted to help to the pediatrician. But he just parroted a version of what all the other professionals I'd reached out to for help had said: "Well, he's still growing. You must be doing something right. He will eat if he's hungry. I'm sure it's just fine."

If by "something" they meant practically force-feeding him through both of our tears to get the bare minimum in, and by "fine" they meant having panic attacks every time I had to feed him, I guess he was right.

"I'll see you again in a few months if you're still concerned," he said, which was code, again, for *you're crazy, please leave me alone.* A few months sounded like a decade. The verdict was in: No one would care as much about my baby's struggles as I would.

Sure, my baby's needs were high. But that didn't stop me from keeping my standards high, too. A good thing—because a few weeks after meeting Idiot Lady, Greg's mom, Christine, decided to visit from across the pond. She reminded me that she was not coming to be hosted.

I was grateful for the support. But also, could I hold it together? It's one thing to keep your metaphorical ducks in rows when you leave the house or when visitors come for a few hours. Despite the difficulties I faced, I was still a pro at that. But it's a whole other thing to have extended visitors, and ones with higher standards than yours—especially of the in-law variety.

My mother-in-law is the kind of woman who maintains the cleanliness of crevices of her home that you didn't even know existed. She's British, which means she hangs her clothes to dry and she irons everything. *Everything.* She cooks wholesome meals and eats hamburgers and pizza with a knife and fork, unapologetically. I'd never seen her go to bed with dishes in the sink. The woman wears dresses and high heels on airplanes, okay? We're talking transatlantic flights.

On Greg's mom's last visit, Ellie had given her the name Grandma Pearls, because she always wears a string of them. Real ones, of course. Grandma Pearls also happens to have a perfect pearly white smile and a furry white hat that she wears in the wintertime. Her house is white, her couches and rugs are fluffy white, and the insides of her well-used teacups are bleached white. She is an active person with high heels and higher standards. The only thing of mine that was whiter than hers was my skin, because she spends time on sunny holidays making sure she is always bronzed and looking her best. Grandma Pearls lived up to her name and then some.

Was she kind? Yes. Was I nervous to stand in her presence and wash my own dishes the wrong way in my own sink? Also, yes. When we got news of the visit, I got to work in our new house. On top of carrying on the rest of my monotonous and unending mom duties at an inhumane pace, I committed to the extras. We painted, organized, and hung the family pictures. I prepared the spare bedroom, shoved the unpacked boxes in the far corners of the basement, and stocked the cupboards with snacks I knew she would approve of.

Who wants their mother-in-law to think they live like a slob? Not I, my friend. Not I. Oscar was the kind of baby who would drag his way around the house on his elbows instead of crawling. He also spat up milk as he went and then heaved himself through it, manically giggling like it was the funniest thing that had ever happened. And after deep-cleaning the carpets of milky puke, I scrubbed the baseboards and walls like Martha Stewart was standing next to me with a stopwatch. I did everything—minus the ironing. That was where I drew the line of my pretend put-together-ness.

The outside of our new redbrick home helped me feel like one of the normals, too. It had an average-size front lawn with the greenest and most weedless grass I had ever called my own. A maple tree stood in the middle of the lawn, its branches full of yellow leaves that were just beginning to change color and drop. The neighborhood was quiet and well established. The winding streets were lined with big trees and older neighbors who waved at you every time they saw you. The houses weren't exactly new, particularly big, or luxurious. But none of them had garbage on the lawn or overgrown shrubs or beer bottles on the porch. Our street was the kind of place I once thought only existed in movies. Moving there felt like we had made it.

One of the reasons I loved the house was that it was open concept, so no matter where I was in the house, I could pretty much see or hear the kids. Hooray for safety! What I didn't consider was how *not excellent* it would be for buffering my night-shift working, daytime sleeping husband from the sounds of his noisy children. Also, hiding mess.

We stored everything we didn't want anyone to see deep down in the basement next to the massive stash of donations I was collecting for a charity event I was organizing. It was for The Shoebox Project, an organization created to give shoeboxes filled with gifts to women at risk of homelessness during the holidays. In every basement corner sat boxes of new items: makeup, winter hats, face masks, jewelry, pretty notepads. I had sourced them from local businesses who wanted to help.

Each local chapter was run by volunteers, and the previous year, when I still had only one baby, I'd tried to volunteer but was told no local chapter existed yet. So, like the overachieving lunatic that I am, I offered to head it up. And that was how my new basement and my brain got filled with so much stuff.

Because I spent much of my childhood going without, by the time I reached adulthood, my desire to help people who needed it was woven into my being. I couldn't *not* help. Christmas was always a time when the gap between me and my peers was most obvious. Harry and I had gotten gifts from toy drives in the city. But often, there was nothing for the moms—an oversight I only now recognized as an adult. My drive to help women like my mom, or women who could have easily been me, was strong.

When I said yes to coordinating the whole thing, I thought I might spend a few hours each week reaching out to people, sourcing donations, and coordinating pickups or drop-offs. In reality, it was more like a three-month crash course in running a startup with no experience, budget, or staff. Oh, and with a sleep-deprived postpartum brain. Have I mentioned my inability to predict time constraints?

I planned to take advantage of Grandma Pearls's help with the childcare and host a few Shoebox packing events for the volunteers. Did I also plan to receive her generosity and chill out? Let her cook and clean while I put my feet up? Absolutely not. The last thing I wanted was to be seen as incapable. That was probably why I insisted on making homemade meals like shepherd's pie and coconut curry while she played with the babies. That's probably why I put on a bra when I didn't want to or tidied up the living room at night when I knew full well it would be trashed the following morning anyway.

Greg was working his regular shifts, so Grandma Pearls and I spent the week together at home with the kids. A week into her visit, the night of the Shoebox packing party arrived. I worried how she would fare with both kids alone but I knew she loved spending time with them. I knew I could trust her. Also, her time would probably be more enjoyable without me looking over her shoulder, hyperventilating with a tense smile.

After writing what felt like a manual for life itself, with every possible instruction necessary for keeping children alive for *checks notes* *four* hours, I put on real pants. I straightened my hair, caked concealer under my eye bags, checked my clothing for bodily fluid stains, and kissed the kids goodbye.

I stacked the back of my SUV to the top, every crevice packed with the empty shoeboxes I had been collecting for the last month. Then, I prayed to the gods of gravity that everything would stay in place until I arrived at the venue, our church. As I waved goodbye to the kids and Grandma Pearls through the car window, I felt a moment of freedom. Hooray for time to think my own thoughts!

On the drive to the church, my mind ran over the litany of things that needed to happen when I arrived. Tables and chairs had to be set up, donations needed to be sorted into categories, food and drinks would need to be put out, volunteers would need to be coordinated, and instructions would have to be given. Once the donated items were categorized, volunteers would grab an empty shoebox, fill it with a variety of gifts, write an encouraging message in a holiday card, and then wrap the shoebox in holiday paper.

Each shoebox lid had to be wrapped separately from its base, so as not to seal the parcel shut. Every shoebox needed to be filled correctly and pass an inspection to make sure we followed protocol.

As I pulled up to the church, it occurred to me that I should have had some of the volunteers come early to set up. *Whoopsie.* I climbed out of my car and fumbled in and out of the front doors with arms full of boxes, swearing under my breath, scrambling around the ice patches on the stairs like a lone baby mountain goat.

When the volunteers showed up to help, the questions began: "Where do you want the snacks to go?" "Is there decaf coffee?" "I forgot the plates, should I go out and buy new ones?" "Where should the wrapping paper go?" "Are we allowed to donate nuts?" "Are these cookies gluten-free?" "Who's watching your kids?"

So much for a break from questions.

I texted my mother-in-law: *How is everything going?* I didn't want to sound insane, but I needed to know if my kids had been screaming their brains out for the forty-eight minutes since I'd left.

All good here, enjoy your evening, she replied. I couldn't tell if she was telling the truth or telling me what I needed to hear.

I looked around, floored by the sheer number of people waiting for me and the number of things to be coordinated. I took a deep "let's do this" breath. Forty women got to work. Some were loading up the wrapped shoeboxes with donations, while others wrote greeting cards. There were ladies passing out snacks, too—God bless the snack ladies. As I stood back and looked around, my heart soared. *So this is life outside of diapers and tantrums. So this is what it feels like to create something that stays intact.* It felt good to be with other adults, making a difference, even if I had to silence the growing sense that I was in over my head.

"You look great," one of the volunteers said as she smiled and looked me up and down. I glanced down at my ill-fitting pre-pregnancy clothes. I considered my caked makeup, a failed attempt to cover the hormonal stress-acne and glaring evidence that I hadn't slept a full night for six months straight. I had dyed my hair red and gotten bangs a week prior (a stark shift from my usual long blond hair) in hopes this would spruce up my appearance and, by proxy, my wilting self-esteem. Instead, my hair stole any sliver of confidence that I had left. Did getting bangs foreshadow a future mental breakdown? Is the Pope Catholic?

INSIDE LIBBY: Are you blind? I'm a train wreck!
OUTSIDE LIBBY: Aw, thanks!

As I finished wrapping another shoebox, the paper ripped straight across its bottom. I exhaled in frustration, pulled the paper tight, and tried to tape it together. The shiny, happy paper ripped in another place. Then another. Then another. I contemplated bashing my head against the table but ultimately decided not to scare the other women away.

Finally, I was able to wrap the box without anything ripping. I put a fancy bow on the side, slid a rubber elastic band around each end to make sure the lid stayed on top, and added the parcel to the stack of finished presents. *See, you can do this,* I told myself.

It wasn't so long ago that I'd felt proud of myself for nailing it. But that pride, along with most other positive emotions I felt, was evaporating by the day. My days felt like a nonstop hustle to do things that never stayed done. Often I found myself counting the minutes down to the moment Greg returned from work, woke up, or the kids went to sleep. I had expected the transition to two kids to be hard, just not someone-get-me-a-sedative hard. I missed the days when I wasn't plagued with guilt for not having the capacity to be what both children needed.

But The Shoebox Project could help! Grandma Pearls could help! Keeping everything in order could help! I told myself. Staying busy had always slowed the self-loathing, drain-swirling thoughts. Being productive gave me a sense of purpose again. Keeping up appearances and spinning plates are what I excelled at. By the end of the night, I began to realize how full my plate had become.

Once we made the final count of boxes, took a group photo, and cleaned up, it was nearing 11 p.m. and the volunteers had begun to trail off. A few loaded up the back of my SUV with as many boxes as they could fit and squeezed the trunk closed. I locked the church doors, set the alarm, and made my way to the car.

I arrived home shortly before midnight. Outside, the air was just above freezing, uncomfortable but no longer icy. I was rubbing my eyes, desperate for bed, when I popped the trunk from the driver's seat. As the trunk door lifted, I heard *thud, thud, thud, thud, crash, crash, crash.*

I jumped out of the car to inspect the damage, and saw ten of the carefully wrapped shoeboxes, previously stuffed to the brim with gifts, now upside down, the contents scattered across the driveway in an icy-cold puddle. The elastic bands holding the shoeboxes closed had snapped. I looked down at the scarves, mittens, and hats, now sopping wet. Hairspray and shampoo bottles rolled away from my feet and into the street. A glass candy jar smashed to smithereens. Broken candles, dented water bottles, and wet greeting cards stared back at me as if to say, *You'll never fix us*. Everything was a mess. *I* was a mess.

Standing under the streetlight, I sank down to the ground in surrender. I wanted to quit but I couldn't. From the outside, my life looked put together. I was *normal.* I organized themed pictures for our Christmas cards, volunteered at church, rage cleaned, and put myself last like I thought I was supposed to. I was good at keeping up, keeping everything in.

From afar, I always felt the eyes of the world watching me—my friends, my family, the neighbors, the church moms, the Facebook lurkers—waiting to see if I'd screw it all up. I worked hard to show them I was doing just fine, that I was different from where I'd come from. I wasn't the one in need anymore. I was the helper, not the helped. I'd wrapped my jam-packed life in pretty paper, a shiny facade, hoping to convince the world I was doing so much better than I was.

I wanted to be a good mom and be seen as one, too, but the effort it took to do the latter was actively breaking me. Crawling around on the cold pavement at midnight, I gathered up the gifts we'd carefully placed in the boxes just hours ago. They were ruined. Useless. And it didn't matter how pretty the wrapping paper was. If everything inside was broken, what was the point?

13

Dumpsters

I fantasized about putting Oscar in a dumpster. There, I said it. I didn't really. It's just, he'd been screaming for an hour straight, again. I was parenting alone, again. Ellie was asking me to play, again. I was staring into the abyss of my kitchen, swatting away the intrusive thoughts that might get me psychologically assessed, again. It had been a month since the shoebox incident, and pushing through was not working.

Obviously, I didn't wish my baby any kind of harm—and if you do find yourself wishing harm on your most treasured humans, seek professional help immediately. It goes without saying that I loved both my children with my heart and soul; I just couldn't control the solutions my brain came up with for my ongoing perilous predicament, the rocks and hard places I continually found myself between.

Instead of putting him into a dumpster, I picked him up, wrapped him in a blanket, rocked him, and walked outside into the crisp winter air, hoping it would jar us both out of mental oblivion. It worked—for thirty seconds. We went back inside. Ellie followed, carrying her bowl of crackers and eagerness to "help."

Eventually, it was nap time. Once both kids settled down, I dove into my bed in hopes of getting a break. A couple minutes later, Ellie decided that sleeping was stupid. She marched down the hall, hollering my name. I gave up on the fantasy of enjoying a moment of silence and carried her downstairs to play.

I kindly reminded her to use her whisper voice since Daddy was still sleeping after his night shift and baby Oscar needed to sleep. She nodded sweetly in agreement, tiptoed into the wood-floored living room, and then looked me dead in the eye before emptying out a basket of hard plastic toys that I had put away just hours earlier. *Bang, crash, bang!* Oscar woke up instantly and began to scream. My cortisol boarded a rocket and blasted into space.

Moments later, I was sitting on the floor playing with my babies. A usual scene. Through the bay window, you might have seen a calm, normal looking family enjoying time together. Ellie was stacking Duplo blocks. Oscar was watching her, smiling. They were happy for a few minutes. I was there, too, answering toddler questions, pretending to be delighted by things I once had been truly delighted about.

I looked like I was present there. But I wasn't. Not anymore. I was floating up above, dissociated, exhausted, apathetic, looking down at myself in disgust. I could see joy, but I could no longer feel it. I could see my kids' cuteness, but I could no longer appreciate it. I could see their wonder, but I wasn't a part of the experience like I used to be. I was dragging myself through life on autopilot. Detached.

Six months into being a mom of two, I was no longer enjoying myself. And more, I felt like a failure. I just kept pushing and hoping, desperate not to disappoint the people who had applauded me for making it through my first two years so well. I was waiting to cross some magical threshold of crisis to justify saying: I'm not okay. But with increasingly less willpower to wake up and do life again each day, I feared it would never come. So, in that quiet moment of darkness I simply texted Leah.

> ME: I can't do this anymore. I think I need help.
>
> HER: There is no shame in that, Libby. You've been struggling for a long time. Talk to your doctor. I'm here for whatever you need.

The doctor suggested I might be suffering from postpartum depression, which sounded stupid. I was six entire months postpartum on my *second* baby. People talked about postpartum depression like it was something that made you overwhelmingly sad and rendered you useless as a mom. I wasn't the picture of postpartum depression I'd read about, the lifeless mother lying on the couch, crying into a bag of bonbons, neglecting her home and children. That wasn't me.

I may have *felt* useless and emotionally stunted, but I carried on with all the monotonous tasks of my day, cooking dinner, singing songs, making appointments, reading Peppa Pig, and changing diapers. I kept the floors and my children's little armpits clean. I socialized them and engaged their little brains.

Plus—I wasn't sad. I was mad.

Still, I was apparently a part of the 30 percent of moms who struggle with postpartum mental health—and that's just the ones who report it. The stigma around mental health didn't help, of course. But also, the state of my mental health might have been more obvious to me if I'd been told that staying so busy you never stop to feel how hollow you are might just be a sign there is a problem. Possibly, if I knew that resentful hypervigilance, apathetic zombie-autopilot mode, and blinding rage were gigantic flashing arrows pointing to PPD—I might have understood my predicament sooner. Who knows.

Regardless, my doctor suggested therapy. I begrudgingly agreed. A few weeks later I was sitting on a cold metal chair in a cramped waiting room, preparing for the first therapy appointment of my life. As I fidgeted with my fingers, I rehearsed what I would say to make sure the therapist knew I wasn't *crazy* crazy. I needed her to know that I was normal and that I just needed a little help with loving motherhood again.

I was averse to professional help, partly due to pride but also because I'd spent the better part of my nearly thirty years on earth trying not to be like the kind of people who need therapy. My magical concoction of overfunctioning had gotten me this far, by golly. Going to see a professional felt like the equivalent of hot-glue-gunning a sign that said "problematic, needy, and best to avoid" across my forehead. I had worked too hard to avoid such labels. I was a *normal* person, and the therapist needed proof.

That's probably why I started by telling her about everything I *could* do: like running The Shoebox Project, caring for my parents, supporting my husband, and mothering my kids.

ME: Like, I am not okay, but I am. You know?

THERAPIST: Tell me more. Tell me about what you are feeling.

ME: That's the thing. I don't feel much at all. I do lots of things—but I don't feel them. I guess, that is, until all I can feel is pure rage . . . at everyone, for everything. I keep it inside, but I'm angry at other moms, the ones with easier lives or more support or the ability to gracefully handle whatever life throws at them. I'm mad at my mom and my dad for everything they aren't and everything they are. I'm mad at my childless friends for having autonomy and mad at my kids for needing me so much. I'm angry at Greg for still having a life outside parenthood. More than

> anything, I am mad at myself for feeling so angry at the world. What kind of mother does that? Moms are *supposed* to be patient. They are supposed to love being moms. But I don't anymore. I've been waiting day after day, week after week, to love motherhood again—and I just don't. I'm scared I will always feel like this. My kids don't deserve that. Sometimes I want a new life. But I don't really. Sometimes, I loathe more moments than I enjoy. What does that say about me?

I exhaled, certain I'd just proven how nuts I really was. I've never been good at putting the lid back on once it pops off.

"It says you are having a hard time. It says that you are carrying a lot," she said, relaxing back into her chair.

She let the silence sit in the room for what felt like a year while she wrote her notes and I fought every bodily urge to crack a joke or leave the room entirely.

INSIDE LIBBY: No shit, Sherlock.
OUTSIDE LIBBY: Am I a bad mom for feeling like this?

"No. Being angry or not loving everything about motherhood does not make you a bad mom. You're allowed to be mad. In fact, it makes sense. There is a lot about your circumstances that *isn't* fair. There is a lot that is not in your control. There is nothing wrong with you for not enjoying motherhood right now," the therapist said.

INSIDE LIBBY: Sounds fake. You are just saying that.
OUTSIDE LIBBY: I don't know. Sometimes I hate myself for feeling this way.
THERAPIST: Do you often feel bad about feeling negative emotions?

INSIDE LIBBY: Obviously. Who doesn't?!

OUTSIDE LIBBY: I thought everyone did.

THERAPIST: Not necessarily. You are allowed to have hard feelings. It's human. What you are experiencing sounds like shame. It just makes you feel worse about what you are already feeling and the cycle continues. You know, you are allowed to grieve that your experience doesn't look or feel like what you expected. That doesn't make you a bad mom.

INSIDE LIBBY: As if! Fantasizing about putting your baby in a dumpster or wanting to scream in people's faces isn't exactly an aspirational quality.

OUTSIDE LIBBY: I just want to stop being angry. How do I make it stop?

THERAPIST: You can feel better. But it's not that simple. What would happen if you let yourself be angry? Anger *can* be healthy, you know. It's often a sign of an unmet need. What would happen if you stopped stuffing it down and shaming yourself and just . . . felt it?

INSIDE LIBBY: I HAVE NO IDEA, LADY. When are we going to get to the part where you tell me how to fix it? WHAT AM I PAYING YOU FOR?!

OUTSIDE LIBBY: I'm not sure. I'm afraid I might not be able to make it stop.

I sank, enveloped in red-hot shame, wishing I could pull out some kind of coping mechanism like intellect or willpower to shut it up. But I couldn't. Not anymore.

THERAPIST: Just think about it.

Then, it was time to go home.

When I'd walked into that therapist's office, I'd wanted a quick fix. A little "bibbity, bobbity, back-to-not-feeling-like-a-basket-case" spell that would fix me without anyone ever knowing that I was broken. I'd have given my left tit to feel better and not loathe myself. But this? I wasn't so sure. I pulled out of the parking lot as the therapist's words rang in my ear. *What would happen if you let yourself be angry?*

I decided to try. I ignored the shame and ruminated on all the things I was pissed about. I pulled apart the emotional layers and let myself miss my old life, the part where I wasn't needed 24/7 and the part where staying busy worked. I grieved the loss of what *might* have been six happy months with Oscar and ached for a time when I felt more in control. I raged about how my marriage had changed, how other moms had support, how hard my childhood had been, and how ill-equipped I felt to be the mom my kids needed. I loathed all the menial, mind-numbing tasks that made every day feel like a marathon. I let myself feel angry about not being able to take care of myself anymore and how it made me feel like I was no longer a person.

A single hot tear spilled out and ran down my cheek. Then, another. I sobbed for the entirety of the forty-five-minute drive home down country roads. Eventually, I pulled over because I couldn't see through the tears. I wasn't just mad. I guess I *was* sad after all.

Allowing myself to feel the anger helped me uncover what was underneath it, and to my surprise, it did bring a slice of relief. I wasn't crazy. I wasn't a bad mom. I was depressed. Unfortunately, admitting the truth didn't fix anything immediately—but it was an important first step.

Starting therapy was like tugging on a loose thread in a ball of yarn—it unraveled so much more than I expected about the problems that existed long before I landed in that therapy office. Still, as I arrived home that day, unfixed, I had a new inkling of hope.

14

Selfless

"I hear you saying that you are exhausted. That you don't feel like yourself anymore. Have you considered prioritizing yourself? Doing things just for you?" my therapist asked. I shifted in my seat.

> INSIDE LIBBY: Have you considered trying to ride a unicycle with a backpack full of feral skunks?
>
> OUTSIDE LIBBY: Yeah, it's just hard.

Self-care: just another thing on my never-ending to-do list, just another thing to fail at. I desperately wanted time and space to be me. I just didn't know *how* to make it happen without sacrificing all that my kids needed. I didn't know how not to feel guilty.

Validating my difficult feelings was fine, but that didn't change the practicalities of my life. Before I was tits deep in diapers, tears, and unmet expectations, I never imagined the act of caring for myself would become so complicated.

But it was amazing how quickly sleeping five hours in a row began to feel like I'd just spent a month at a five-star resort in

Cabo—a sure sign my baseline standards for well-being had shifted. The logistics of taking time and space for myself felt like just another snag in my rigged Rubik's Cube that I didn't have the energy to solve.

I could barely coordinate taking a shower without someone needing me, never mind making time to go to the flipping audiologist to get my ears checked for the hearing aids I knew I needed and couldn't afford. It had become normal to do a number two with a baby on my lap. How was I supposed to find the time to go for coffee with friends?!

Eating a hot meal might mean sacrificing my kids eating their food at all. Going to sleep on schedule might mean giving up on having clean underwear laundered for the next day. Post-dinner solitude meant sacrificing stories and bedtime cuddles. There was no winning.

Pristine, childless, self-helpy types, people who had no idea what reality entailed, hurled self-care advice at me. How could they possibly know what it was like to be needed every second of every day? Their wise words felt as useless as a paper bag in a rainstorm. There were physical hurdles: time, money, and childcare. But there were mental obstacles, too.

Mostly, it was guilt. The guilt I felt about taking time and space for myself was incessant. It followed me around, haunting me, reminding me of all the bad things I was and all the good things I was not. Like some ghost of Christmas past except louder, more relentless, and believable. I couldn't relax when Greg cleaned, cooked, or functioned while I didn't.

No matter how tired I was, I felt bad leaving him alone at the house with the children he fathered, the ones I cared for most of the time. Despite his encouragement, I couldn't shake the feeling of not-enoughness that accompanied my desire for rest.

I felt guilty going to therapy, guilty that I didn't want to play, guilty for counting down the minutes to bedtime or skipping pages in our bedtime story or wishing the kids would stop crying. I felt guilty for wanting to sit down. Putting on the TV? Guilty. Feeding them snacks to keep them quiet? Guilty. Asking for help? You guessed it. Unless my femur was snapped, it simply felt like too much to ask. No matter how I balanced the scale, my kids' needs always seemed to outweigh mine, even the simple need to feel capable of thinking in full sentences.

Plus, everyone applauded the selfless moms. My church friend Lindsay, a mom of four, had told me that she didn't feel the need to be away from her kids. "They are my world! Why would I want to be with anyone else?" she said with a neon smile. When I asked another mom about what she did just for herself, she laughed and said, "I don't. But that's okay! Being a mom is the best. They are all I need."

When other moms seemed solely fulfilled by motherhood, my feelings of guilt only intensified. The guilt didn't register as a feeling but a fact. Moms everywhere either lacked the need for solitude or they felt guilty for not doing everything for and with their kids.

I'd have carved out my spleen to have a night alone. But if I did, what did that say about me? Was I selfish? Selfish, from the start, was the last thing I wanted to be. My kids came first. And while this choice was informed by the pressures of the world, I came to realize it was also deeply connected to the ways I hadn't felt like a priority when I was a child.

"DO IT AGAIN! THAT WAS HALF-ASSED," Karl said as I hammered shingles on the roof of the chicken barn we were building. I slammed the hammer down, accidentally hitting my finger. I yelled out in pain. I was thirteen. "Don't be a crybaby, Libby. You're fine," he barked.

Harry was in the cow barn, shoveling months' worth of cow dung into wheelbarrows as punishment for making an honest mistake while repairing the electric fence. He had just turned fourteen.

We'd been living on our multiacre hobby farm for nearly a year. The white-paneled farmhouse sat a couple hundred feet back from the road and had a long gravel driveway lined by enormous willow trees. Beside the house was a maple tree with a doghouse tied to its trunk by a long metal chain. It's where our dog, Russell, lived 365 days of the year, through rain, snow, and blistering southern Ontario heat. Despite our petitions, Karl wouldn't allow the dog in the house. It was his farm after all—and his rules.

Once we moved in, Mom drifted further from us and closer to him. Maybe their closeness was warm at first, but it quickly turned into a choke hold on her—and, subsequently, on my brother and me. Karl insisted we call him Dad, and, from there, his expectations of Harry and me steadily increased, along with the metaphorical eggshells that scattered our floors.

There were literal eggshells, too. Every day, there were eggs to collect from the barn. There was feed to pour out, coops to mend, and poop to shovel.

Karl was a hobby farmer but he pretended he was a real one, particularly when we frequented the local farm auction to buy animals. Sometimes chickens, other times rabbits, or, if we hit it lucky, black-nosed brown cows, too. Jersey cows.

The farm auction took place each Friday. Harry and I would sometimes take the day off school. We'd cross our fingers for a bargain, and, if we got one, we'd drive our baby Jerseys home in the back of our derelict Dodge Caravan. Eventually, we were the owners of about a dozen cows of various ages. Karl's master plan was to raise the cows for meat. The bull calves were adorable and a lot of work. In large part, that work was mine and Harry's. "Dad" had to work in the city, after all.

MOM FINISHED HIGH SCHOOL AND got a college diploma. Yay! Except that this meant she got a job in the city with a one-hour commute, too. So, Monday to Friday Mom and Karl were often gone from the farm long before Harry and I left for school and returned once dinner was almost on the table.

Mom loved the gardens on Karl's farm, and Karl loved having two able-bodied teenage farmhands to eradicate stubborn, overgrown weeds. On summer days, Harry and I tended to the wraparound flower garden next to the farmhouse. Then, we'd spend hours pulling the stubborn overgrowth from our large vegetable garden that sat beside our willow trees.

Mom and "Dad" would sit watching, coffee in one hand, cigarette in the other, to ensure we weren't slacking.

When my brother and I weren't busy with yard work, farmwork, household chores, or at school, we tended to the yard sale. And by "yard sale," I mean the tables of junk that lined our long driveway for six months of the year. We kept the tables covered with big blue tarps when we were busy elsewhere. Rather than selling our housewares, we sold the boxes of "antiques" found stashed in the attic or unused barns. No cute scraggly neighbors came with wads of cash. The kids on the bus that picked us up for school found it amusing, though, and they showed it by rubbing wads of sandwiches in my hair.

One day, Harry and I had been raking and bagging up freshly trimmed willow branches from our two-acre lawn for hours after dinner. My back ached. I needed to get to my homework. We thought we were done and asked Karl if we could go inside. He came out to inspect, determined that we'd done our work half-assed, emptied the bags of branches we'd collected to teach us a lesson, and demanded we do it again. Nothing was ever good enough for him.

On Monday nights, we had family meetings that involved listening to a long list of all the ways Karl believed we'd failed to be a good son and daughter that week. There was the single Cheerio my vacuuming didn't pick up. The animal stall Harry didn't shovel thoroughly enough. The lack of pleasantness in our greetings when our parents walked through the door. Afterward, I would find Harry in the closet, letting out the sobs he'd kept under wraps for the hour of lambasting. Then I'd find myself screaming silently into my pillow. This tradition picked away at the fabric of my self-worth—a slow conditioning that wore me down like the soft green grass around our dog's house until it became bare, hardened, and unrecognizable.

By the time I was fourteen, the hobby farm was like a full-time job on top of school. There were no extracurriculars. No sports teams. No large family gatherings. Just us, the farm, and my decaying self-perception. One morning, I woke up and went to the laundry room to prepare formula for the calves. It was 6 a.m. Groggily, I picked up several large white 5-liter bottles and their matching orange nipples. I scooped in the formula, filled each bottle with warm water, covered the hole in the nipple, and one by one shook the bottles as ferociously as my arms could handle.

Outside in the cool dark hours of the morning, I fed the calves. I held onto a bottle as tight as I could, but one calf kept pulling on the nipple, eventually pulling the bottle from my hands. I finished, went inside, washed the bottles, and got ready for school.

"Don't wear that shirt out of the house. You look like a slut," I heard Karl say, as I passed him in the kitchen. I was wearing a white tank top and wondered to myself what a slut was anyway. I changed into a blue T-shirt and jeans.

"Good girl," he said, slapping my butt before leaving for work.

After my long day at school, I made roasted chicken legs and mashed potatoes for dinner. Harry and I did the dishes, collected the chicken eggs, and raked the leaves before doing our homework. I went into the living room, where Mom and Karl were watching TV, each lying on their own couch.

"Can I go to bed now?" I asked, hoping there was nothing left for the day.

"Your dad had a long day. Why don't you just lie down and snuggle together for a while," Mom said. Disappointed, but relieved it wasn't more work, I tucked in front of Karl on the couch. I left my body and stared at the TV until I was excused to go to bed. It was our nighttime routine, after all.

I missed the days when it had been just Harry, Mom, and me, when she would tell the corner store owners to fuck off and tell the neighbors to shove it if they even looked at us wrong. I missed seeing the hope in her eyes. I missed life before *him*. I missed feeling like I mattered.

AS I LOOKED BACK AS a mother myself, my nighttime teenage couch-spooning with my stepfather made my skin crawl. But at the time, it was all I knew and it was far from the worst of my memories. Were there other experiences like this in the memories I cannot access? I might never know.

What I *could* access was marrow-deep resolve: to prioritize and protect my children no matter what the cost. Regardless of my mother's intention or understanding of what happened, I couldn't help but perceive her actions and inaction during that time as selfish. So, I did the only thing I could think to do—I ran in the opposite direction, overcompensating, until the cost became my ability to function.

I wanted to take care of myself, to put myself higher on the proverbial list, but I struggled to find the line between selflessness and selfishness. Once again, I found myself asking, What even *is* normal?

But with every poor night's sleep, every microwaved cup of coffee, and every failure-filled day, I began to see how my inability to close the door while tinkling without feeling selfish was, well . . . a problem. I didn't want to be a selfish mom, but I equally did not want to be a mom who couldn't stand it anymore.

I couldn't seem to push past the roadblocks to take care of myself unless I knew it was worth it, unless I knew I'd still be and feel like a good mom first. I didn't know how to choose me without it meaning I wasn't choosing them.

ONE DAY, WHEN I HAD reached the threshold of my sanity, I decided to take a baby step. I was desperate.

It was the dead of winter. After Greg got home from one of his twelve-hour shifts, I said, "I need to leave this house." Full stop. I handed him the baby, pointed to the toddler, put on my snow boots, said goodbye to the mess, the kids, and I went for a walk despite the guilt.

I don't remember what music was playing, but I'll tell you what I do remember: It wasn't the flippin' *Paw Patrol* theme song. I hated the cold but loved the silence. Feeling anything other than a little hand pulling at me was glorious. Not being needed was scrumdiddlyumptious.

The next day, when Greg got home from work, I went out walking again. I felt so refreshed after my small dose of freedom the previous day, that leaving this time was a little easier. Just ten minutes changed my mood for the rest of the evening. The day after, before I hit the pavement, I made a playlist full of music I loved before Ellie and Oscar arrived: Macklemore, Taylor Swift, and Eminem—of course. I began to look forward to having some time to not think about all the ways I was failing at motherhood and all the laundry that still needed to be folded. Then, I began walking farther.

Over time, despite still answering five thousand questions a day, I noticed myself becoming lighter (emotionally, obviously). My window of tolerance had started to widen. I fell asleep a little easier. The morning heaviness that lived in my chest lifted. Fantasies about smothering Greg's sleeping face with a pillow because he got to sleep when I didn't happened less often. The urge to wear real pants again returned. My energy reserves expanded. I could feel my kids' laughter in my bones instead of just seeing it on their faces. Shrill screaming children still made me feel like a lion was chasing me, but the lion was a tinge smaller.

Several months into this walking routine, I got the most ludicrous urge of my life—to jog. Listen, I was the kid who avoided all physical activity. Running for fun as an adult? No thanks. Who would intentionally exert themselves to the point of pain or breathlessness? Psychopaths, that's who. I do enough hard things.

But, for a reason I have yet to determine, I jogged—for precisely one minute. Then, I alternated one minute of jogging and one minute of walking. It hurt so much I wanted to punch the innocent old man I ran by, but I didn't. I kept running. The next time I went out, I did it again. A couple weeks later, I started running for a song after walking for a song, and then I started running longer stretches, even past the point of pain. After the pain passed and my red face turned freckly white again, I felt . . . good?

Eventually, I ran a full five kilometers and straight into what I can only describe as a strange cloud of energetic pride, happy exhaustion, and satisfying relief. I felt alive. For the first time ever, I began to enjoy moving my body—not just because it gave me a break from wiping bums and answering questions about why birds have feathers—but because I liked how it felt.

I'd started walking to deal with my emotional inferno, and to my surprise, it became the catalyst that helped me feel better in ways I couldn't have anticipated. That first walk created a domino effect of changes to my habits, energy, mood, and ability to get through each day. I began to see flashes of myself as someone other than an extension of my kids again.

Doing something *for* me helped me see that the rewards of my actions far outweighed the costs. Experiencing the benefits helped me to see how stupid the guilt I felt for taking care of myself was in the first place. I had wanted to figure out how to stop feeling guilty before I stepped away to care for myself. But as it turns out, I just needed to do it.

Choosing myself despite the guilt helped me to stop feeling guilty for other unnecessary things, too, like missing the kids' bedtime routine once in a while or changing my tampon without an audience. Solo grocery store trips eventually stopped feeling like self-care. Walking around the block, guilt-ridden, was a stepping stone. Sure, the practicalities of taking time for myself still remained, but the guilt? Well, it slowly subsided. Turns out, the guilt wasn't a fact after all.

I didn't want my kids to grow up the way I had, wondering if they mattered. So I'd absorbed society's obsession with selfless moms being the best moms. But plopping myself on the back burner wasn't the answer. In reality, it only served to make me a shell of myself.

The truth was that I was not my mother nor was I the church moms or my neighbors or the moms on Facebook. Selfless and selfish were not the only options. I could choose *me* without neglecting *them*. I could choose me while protecting them. In fact, choosing me was choosing them because it gave them a mom who wasn't shattered. Taking care of myself inched me toward feeling more human again. How could I feel guilty for that?

15

Daddy Is Fun

"Shhhhh, Daddy is sleeping," I whisper-yelled to the kids as they giggled manically one Saturday morning. I could feel my blood pressure rising as I reminded myself that it's normal for children to delight in the wonder of life. There were cardboard boxes strewn around the entirety of the house, and Ellie and Oscar were crawling in and out of them, playing hide-and-seek.

The kids promised to be quiet, but they were four and two years old, so promises meant diddly-squat. One minute later, cackles rippled through my eardrums at a higher decibel than before. They were having delicious fun. I was not.

Daddy was sleeping because Daddy had worked a twelve-hour night shift again. Mommy was not sleeping because the children couldn't watch themselves. Our thin walls and my delicate nervous system didn't stand a chance against small humans living their best lives.

It was June, the month both my children had decided to evacuate my uterus. With two birthdays to plan, a preschool graduation, and a dance recital, it was the busiest month of the year. I was back working as a part-time educational assistant and full-time as the Ward Family Life Coordinator. This unpaid domestic role was particularly grueling, given the wildly unpredictable nature of our lives.

Our beloved and hardworking Greg continued his full-time breadwinner shifts that felt more like double full-time for the rest of the family. That's because my broad-shouldered, dark-haired, crime-fighting husband's flip-flopping twelve-hour night and day shifts followed a pattern so complex it might as well have not been a pattern.

When you factored in the requisite alternating sleeping patterns, the kids and I rarely saw him, particularly on a string of night shifts. He wasn't just gone all night, missing dinner, bath, and bedtime, he was unavailable for a large part of the day before and after—catching up on essential sleep. The shift could start at 4, 6, or 7 p.m. and go until the same time the next morning. He'd come home as the sun rose, crawl into bed, and then attempt to sleep as long as his body or the children—or I—would let him. And I often let him because he needed it.

Police College made sure to warn new recruits of the perils connected to sleep deprivation. Losing sleep isn't just about feeling tired—it screws up your health, increasing the likelihood of depression, anxiety, heart attacks, strokes, obesity, and hypertension. Rest up at all costs, they said. Sleep loss wreaks havoc on your memory, mood, and attention span, they said. I didn't want a bleak future for Greg's health, so even when he told me not to worry about keeping Oscar and Ellie quiet, I still tried. When he *was* home overnight, if the kids woke for any reason, I took charge of caring for them, for the same reason. My dashing policeman needed to be in peak form.

Greg missed us when he was working or sleeping. Sweet, right? Except that once he shared that with me, I started making fewer plans. I stayed home when I had opportunities to go out with the kids so that he wouldn't miss those small windows of opportunity to see them. He didn't ask me to, but I did it anyway. I wanted to be considerate.

In the limited time he had with the kids, he was Mr. Fun Dad, putting on butterfly wings and flying around the living room, taking the kids to the park, reading endless Peppa Pig stories, and generally being five-star fun. Greg would be all the things I wish I had the time and energy to be. All the things I used to be.

When the kids began to fight over who owned which cardboard box, I snapped at them. "Shhhhhhhh. Daddy. IS. SLEEEPING!" I exhaled in lieu of the scream I wanted to let out.

"Mommy, why are you always grumpy in the morning?" Ellie asked.

She was right, I *was* grumpy. I couldn't remember the last time I'd slept a whole night or gotten to wake up when my body decided it was time. *Ssshhhhh, Daddy is sleeping* felt like it had become my middle name. Routine was the ghost of our childless past. The lack of reprieve meant that along with Greg's flip-flopping shifts, my moods tended to follow suit. My determination to make sure Greg got his shut-eye had turned me into a less-than-ideal version of myself.

OUTSIDE LIBBY: I don't know, Ellie. I'm just tired, I guess. I'm sorry I snapped.

I knelt down and hugged her. She looked up at me, innocently, sincerely.

"Why isn't Daddy grumpy in the morning?"

INSIDE LIBBY: I DON'T KNOW. WHY DON'T YOU GO WAKE HIM UP AND ASK HIM?!

I WAS PACKING BAGS FOR Ellie's dance recital while the kids ran circles around me and lobbied me for snacks. I was genuinely thrilled to be taking my baby girl to her first ballet recital.

Let's be honest. Recreational ballet for a three-year-old isn't exactly an Olympic sport. Certainly, her classes hadn't involved much more than rolling around on the ground and twirling with her pals once a week for the last eight months. But that didn't matter. She had fun. It filled my heart that she had something just for her. I'd always dreamed of taking dance classes when I was a kid. Now, she got to. Watching her shine filled holes in my heart that I didn't know existed.

We were on the verge of leaving, so I gently shook Greg awake after his night-shift sleep. He smiled at me with his rested eyes, and I did my best to hide the daggers in mine.

OUTSIDE LIBBY: We've got to get going or we'll be late for the recital.

INSIDE LIBBY: How nice it would be to wake up and be told where to be and when.

When he walked down the half flight of stairs into the living room, I was preparing the snack my children begged me for. The kids ran into his arms with the most exasperating delight. I called Ellie over and lovingly forced her to sit still so I could pull back her wispy blond hair into one of those tight dancer buns, the ones that make little girls hate their mothers. Meanwhile, Greg played Magna tiles with Oscar. As I huffed and puffed and loaded the well-packed bag into the car, Greg told Ellie how beautiful she looked. He was right.

Unlike many of the dads we knew, he didn't let being the

bacon-bringer-homer stop him from being involved at home. Greg cooked, cleaned, played with the kids, took them places, and engaged in home life. As the attentive, compassionate, and patient father he was, he was the furthest thing from Homer Simpson types.

In our rural churchy circles, we were the progressive ones. Since the moment we began cohabitating all those years ago, Greg had made his own lunch. He had tidied up his own dishes. I'd never once had to put the toilet seat down. He put his laundry in the basket more often than I did. My life partner was a self-sufficient, considerate human being.

When I first found out that I had friends who packed their husbands' suitcases, I had to scoop my jaw off the floor. When we got married, Greg and I earned the same income and split the bills down the middle. Greg began to outearn me around the same time I birthed our children and began to raise them, giving up dreams of a university degree, sufficient nutrient banks, and the elasticity of my nether regions. Mutually, we agreed our money was our money, that our children were our children, that the house was our house.

Greg was the type of dad to say "I love you" every day. And he was never, ever too good for some nail polish from his daughter. His ability to play pretend far outweighed my own. So, too, did his ability to look like he was enjoying it. God bless the man. Often, I witnessed him delighting in the time he had with the kids, full of patience, energy, and positivity. He wasn't faking it.

My husband *also* had no clue what it was like to live a day in my shoes. He hadn't experienced early parenthood like I had. Greg certainly didn't hold the mental cards for our family. Alone. Nearly every day. With no breaks. As involved as he was, our everyday realities were a canyon apart.

I was on duty morning, afternoon, and night. I coordinated childcare. I took time off work when someone got sick. The kids came to me first, even if they had to walk right past their dad and into another room to find me. When bums needed wiping, it was always "Mom!" not "Dad!" I knew how Ellie liked to be reassured and how she liked to play. I coordinated our calendar and tracked the milestones. I did the research. I booked and attended appointments, communicated with our loved ones, and maintained holiday traditions. I oversaw nearly all the logistics required to make our lives work. Or at least I tried. Golly, I tried.

By no fault of his own, Greg was the backup to my default. He was a helper in our home—the occasional staff, not the manager. I bore responsibility for everyday logistics and survival. My husband did what he could when he could. But it just wasn't the same as being in charge of multiple overlapping things every single day. And over time, with two kids now in the mix, the complexity of family life multiplied.

As the constant presence, delegator, communicator, and initiator, I started to wonder—When had virtually *all* of family life become my responsibility? As the default parent, I was always on call, day and night, handling the endless tasks no one noticed. I knew the food aversions, the sensory triggers, the needs and fears. I could see the meltdowns coming and was always, always anticipating them. The gap between what Greg and I did—and, more importantly, *thought* about—became a gigantic infuriating cavern for me.

Having a husband who engaged with his kids with ferocious tenderness and playful delight was a gift. After long stretches of parenting on my own, I was grateful when he clocked in. I knew he worked incredibly hard at his job. Policing was demanding and, by nature, riddled in conflict. I couldn't understand what it was like to be in his shoes. Yet I couldn't help but consider what it would be like to focus on one thing at a time, to have colleagues see and appreciate your hard work. To know when, for the most part, your shift would end. To have a boss tell you where to go or what to do next. To know what it would be like to be alone with your thoughts on the way to and from work or in the long, dark hours of the night, on lunch hours and coffee breaks.

I couldn't help but wonder how much better I might function or how much happier I'd feel if I had a clearly defined job description and some objective metrics for success. Or if I got some kind of sticker reward chart every time I chose to take a deep breath instead of scream in my kids' faces.

How much energy could I have if I got to sleep until my body woke up? How silly could I be if I wasn't also concerned about the toddler falling down the stairs, or whether we'd taken the ground beef out of the freezer for dinner, or if we'd packed a spare onesie for our trip to the zoo, or if we were running low on wipes, or if I still had time to order a Play-Doh set before Ellie's birthday party, or if Oscar's classmate needed a gluten-free cupcake instead of the standard ones I planned to buy? How present could I be if I got to engage my wilting brain outside of the house more often? I couldn't stop myself from recognizing the disparity in the hours of our days, the competing pressures and simultaneous responsibilities.

I wanted to let down my guard and love my kids in fun ways, too. I wanted to play without having to wonder what was for dinner or calculate when I had to start cooking. I constantly felt split in two, never quite fully present—like there was never enough of me to go around. If I cooked, I couldn't clean, and if I cleaned, I couldn't play, and if I played, we'd be dirty and hungry. I felt robbed of the opportunity to *be* with my kids because I was always doing things *for* them. If I wasn't doing work, I was mentally managing it. I'd always wanted to be a fun mom, but that desire had become more of a fantasy.

When I was honest with myself, I felt a little bit jealous of Greg.

I'd thought about asking him to take on more, but delegating a task, remembering to remind him, and ensuring it was done right took more work than doing the job myself. I longed for the ability to put my responsibilities into boxes like he could, to focus on doing one thing without thinking of the forty-five others tugging on my sleeve. It was another problem to solve in my Rubik's Cube of motherhood. But solving one issue made five more problems.

So when it came time to fully engage in Ellie's dance recital, I was determined that she be my only focus and responsibility. Greg might have naturally taken responsibility for looking after Oscar anyway, but I wanted to be sure.

"CAN YOU PLEASE TAKE CARE OF OSCAR? If there are any issues at the recital, I want to make sure you have him so I can be present for Ellie," I asked earnestly. Greg obliged, happily.

Backstage, I blotted bright red lipstick onto Ellie's little lips and begged her not to wipe it off with the back of her hand. I kissed her on the head and admired her twirling in front of the mirror in her purple-and-teal tutu, the silver-sequined lining bouncing as she went.

Once she was ready, I took my seat in the auditorium with Greg and Oscar. The lights lowered. Ellie followed in line with a dozen other three-year-olds. She pranced across the stage with no concept of rhythm or beat or poise, lipstick rubbed up the side of her face, hair already coming loose. It was the most average and spectacular recreational ballet performance the world had ever seen. *That's my girl,* I thought.

When the number finished and her group lined up to bow, she scanned the crowd for my face. As she caught my eye, her face lit up and a big, sparkling smile spread across her face. She was proud. So was I.

In that moment, she had my full attention. In that moment, I felt truly present. I wondered if she would remember our moment, the way our eyes locked or the flood of happiness that followed.

I wondered how many other times had she looked for my eyes at home when I was too busy to meet her gaze? How many times had I missed a moment for connection because I was lost in my thoughts? How many times, even that day, had she longed for my attention or sought my reassurance when I was distracted or tired? Too many. But my heart rejoiced knowing I was *really* there for her for her big moment on stage. I longed to feel more of that in our everyday lives.

On the way to the car after the recital, we stopped at a beautiful fountain to take pictures. I coached Ellie into various poses, snapped pictures, and cheered her on. I took photos of both the kids, of the kids with Greg, of Greg with just Ellie in her perfect little tutu.

I hoped Greg would offer to take some pictures that included me. Generally, pictures were something I had to ask for. But part of me felt like I shouldn't have to ask—especially on occasions like this. I waited. I wanted to be in the picture, too. But as he made his way to the car once we thought we were finished, it was clear he wasn't going to.

"Could you take some pictures of me and the kids?" I asked.

He fumbled for his phone, snapped a few, and carried on. As we pulled out from the parking lot, I exhaled in frustration. Why wouldn't he take a picture of me and Ellie without needing a prompt? *Don't the memories matter to him? Doesn't he care? Why do I always have to ask?*

On the drive, I thought about all the tasks that needed to be done the rest of that day, the rest of the weekend, the rest of the month. There were outfits to plan, appointments to make, gifts to buy, parties and ceremonies to plan for and attend, food and decorations to prepare. Was my husband thinking about any of this?

Did he lie awake at night wondering if our kids were developing properly, if we were running out of milk, if the kids had summer clothes that fit? Did he worry about if the kids felt loved and seen at daycare? Did he wonder if they would grow up with memories of both of us loving them?

I hated being annoyed that he didn't offer to take a picture. *It's just a picture,* I told myself. But it wasn't. The picture represented all the things he didn't have to think about or realize that I thought about; everything I carried that no one saw because it was always carried. If I didn't make the list, the list wouldn't get made. If I didn't ask for the picture, it wouldn't get taken.

The picture represented every second of invisible labor that pulled me away from the little people who mattered most to me, all the work that stole my ability to be present in those moments and remember them, too. With a pit in my stomach, I decided to say something.

"It would be nice if you offered to take pictures of me with the kids," I said.

He responded, "But I did take the picture. All you had to do was ask."

16

Granola Bars

There is something magical about seeing your kids' personalities come to life. The age of two was when that really started to happen for my younger child. One day, I was carrying a load of laundry up the stairs to put away, when, on the third step, I nearly ran into Oscar, who was face down, motionless, stiff as a board. His face was just inches from the step, with his little blond head of hair hovering there. His arms were straight by his side and his little trunk was flexed.

I called his name. He didn't move. A full panic came over me as I dropped the laundry basket and dropped to the ground to pick him up. I was a few inches away from him when he quickly sat up, screamed, "Baahhhhh!" and burst into a fit of laughter. My dearest son was alive and well. He was just planking, 2010s style. Remember that weird trend?

Planking was *the* bizarre internet craze of the early 2010s—where people would lie face down, rigid as a board, in the most random and inconvenient places possible. Sidewalks, park benches, grocery store aisles—nowhere was safe from the wave of human planks. It was pointless. It was hilarious. And for reasons I'll never fully understand, the world was briefly obsessed with it. Apparently, so was my toddler.

My child was not only planking but also pranking me—again. Knowing he was the source of my laughter made him laugh more, which made me laugh more, which made him laugh more. We sat there, teary-eyed with silliness—a usual scene. That day marked the beginning of a six-month planking era that left our entire family in hysterics.

Sometimes it was daily. Other times, weeks would pass between his planks. In the most random of places, he would lie down, silent, motionless, waiting to be caught. On the beach, on the dining room table, at the top of the slide at the park, under the coffee table, in the driveway, in the sandbox, anywhere. Every time, he wouldn't respond to us when we called. Every time, he would burst into laughter at his own tomfoolery.

Not a day went by when Oscar didn't delight us with his silliness and joy. Along with being smart, curious, sensitive, and sweet, he was the resident family clown. Slapstick was his specialty. This physical humor was handy considering he couldn't yet speak. Halfway through his second year, Oscar's ability to speak hadn't "resolved itself" like so many loving friends and family had suggested it might. Neither had my anxiety about it. Despite immense effort on our part, Oscar's vocabulary was limited to a small handful of singular syllable sounds. Not words. Sounds.

I pulled from the toolbox of skills I'd collected over the years as an educational assistant and daughter of a disabled and deaf man. I taught Oscar baby sign language like I had with Ellie. I repeated back to him what I thought he was trying to say. I would ask a lot of yes-or-no questions. Our daily schedule became even more hardcore than it was before, with pictures and symbols to help him understand. In the car on the way to daycare or when we sat down for dinner, I anticipated what he might be wondering and tried to fill in the blanks. I verbalized what he couldn't so that he felt included in family conversations and tried to give him some semblance of control.

Oscar helped himself by resorting to other methods of communicating, too. He used some of the sign language we taught him and also made up his own gestures and sounds. He pointed to pictures on posters, in books, and on signs outside. He created his own unique and unbelievably accurate facial expressions. Eventually, Oscar began to combine the various tactics to get an idea across.

One day we were running late when I was trying to get both kids out the door. He refused to wear his sandals. No matter how I tried to convince him to put them on his feet, he wouldn't budge. Instead, he pointed and yelled sounds I could not comprehend. My attempts to understand the holdup went nowhere. Eventually, he stuck up his finger as if to say, "I have an idea." His face brightened and he ran upstairs to his room. Upon return, Oscar held a book, flipped it open to the third page, pointed to the red shoes in the book, pointed to himself, and then pointed to his feet, and signed "please."

"Do you want to wear your red shoes? The ones I packed away last week?" I inquired. He nodded ferociously. Once the shoes were on, he smiled at me, hugged me, and we left the house. As we drove off, I couldn't help but be impressed that a toddler—who by nature of being a toddler had limited executive function and attention span—could communicate so creatively. That one small phrase had required so many steps to get out. But he did it, I supposed, because he had no other choice. While his efforts were often ingenious, they were also painful to watch—especially when we'd reach a dead end.

Like when he wanted to play with other kids or use their toys in the sandbox. He would attempt to ask, pointing and signing "please," but the other children would turn away and keep playing.

Or when he and Ellie had a conflict but he couldn't tell me his side of the story. Or when I took him to a playgroup and all the children shared about their weekend, but when it was his turn, he sat silently. Or when the kids in daycare would all sing nursery rhymes together or recite the alphabet, and he would watch from the sidelines. Or when he'd try to tell me a story or ask for something with the sign for "want," and I'd spend fifteen minutes attempting to understand, only for him to give up and go off and play silently.

I knew he had just as many thoughts, feelings, questions, and needs as the rest of the two-year-olds. He just couldn't express them, and his face would drop, shoulders would slump, and he'd walk away, realizing his mouth was defying him again. My heart broke.

Other times, his frustration would get the better of him and he would collapse on the floor, devastated, scream-sobbing, helpless and unseen. Like when Ellie took the toy he was playing with or when he lost his favorite stuffy and couldn't tell us where or when. Or when he was struggling to complete a task or build a tower and didn't want help but wanted something else that I couldn't pinpoint. Or when he would run to me in tears, signing "hurt," and I didn't know what or where or how serious the pain was. When the tears turned more dramatic, I couldn't tell if he was in grave danger or just unbelievably frustrated.

How are you supposed to know if the reason a toddler is torture-screaming is because you opened the banana peel a little too far, if he can't even tell you that? Every small task and request took more effort to understand. I always had to be one step ahead, predicting what he might want or need, or what might trigger him. And there were countless triggers: a simple look of disappointment from me, the wrong socks, the sun shining too brightly, an unexpected schedule change—you name it.

Of course, all toddlers have a lot of feelings about life. But having those feelings without being able to articulate them takes those feelings to a whole new level. Like his mother, Oscar wore his joy and heartache on his sleeve. And while I believe that feeling deeply is a superpower that should be harnessed in all humans—particularly in little boys—it felt like our house was a minefield of emotional grenades. The tiniest conflicts easily morphed into borderline apocalyptic meltdowns, and home life continued to be an all-consuming game of survival.

Eventually, after plenty of nagging phone calls, we got an appointment with a local speech and language pathologist (SLP) to help us understand what was happening. After one session she confirmed my suspicions.

"It is not a speech delay," she said. "Your son has a motor speech condition. He has the language; he just can't get the words from his brain out of his mouth. There is a chance it will resolve, but there is also the possibility he will live with a version of this condition for the rest of his life." This last line was like a knife to my gut.

"What do we do?" I asked.

"Early and frequent speech therapy intervention is the best treatment. He would benefit from multiple sessions a week. Unfortunately, the system is really backed up so I will only be able to see you once every other week, and only for a few months."

It was clear that if we wanted to provide Oscar with the help he needed, we needed a secondary SLP and to pay out of pocket. So, Greg sold the truck he'd just purchased to free up some cash and we got to work.

I began to schedule and reimagine our lives around what our son needed. I researched everything I needed to know to support him, joined Facebook groups and advocacy threads. I took him to the specialists, started a binder to track the appointments and progress, taught him more sign language, attended all his speech therapy sessions, implemented a PECS (picture exchange and communication system), and did the daily speech practice with him.

I communicated his needs to all other caregivers who had even less of an idea of what he was saying than I did. All the while, carrying all the regular day-to-day work of keeping our household running and the humans inside emotionally regulated.

The cycle of parenting, advocating, learning, and teaching consumed all my time and brain power. Progress was so slow it was nearly imperceptible. I didn't know if or what efforts made a difference or how I was making it worse.

Meanwhile, my dear, sweet, sensitive, caregiving, do-gooding, creative firstborn, like all little human beings, had needs that required my attention and patience. She could speak clearly, but this didn't stop her from doing things like drawing large-scale pictures of the Lion King on the wall in our freshly painted basement—using a Sharpie. She cut her own bangs. Her lack of urgency to get in and out the door tested me daily.

Ellie was eager to help, delighted to learn, and hungry for time with me and, also, snacks. Normal preschooler things. When I struggled to give her the time and attention she needed and deserved, I felt terrible. There was never enough of me to go around. Guilt shone in my eyes like a floodlight every night, keeping me awake and forever vigilant.

The pressure to keep all the plates spinning of our everyday lives would not relent. I was still an active volunteer in our new church community, I continued to support my parents, I kept my house clean, and I made sure my mother-in-law got a birthday card. I advocated. I translated. I cried. I got up the next day and did it all again.

Well into Oscar's second year, my capacity for dealing with my kids' shenanigans was evaporating quicker than a muddy puddle in the Sahara Desert. Nothing prepares you for how fast you can switch from *I would do anything to protect you and make you happy* to *please leave Mommy the fuck alone for five minutes.* (For the record: I never actually said that out loud.)

It's not like I wanted to blow my top over the sound of the word "mom." But now, unexpected or incessant sounds that hindered my ability to think filled me with seething rage. Getting slapped in the face or having my hair pulled made me want to scream. So did whining. So did being touched. When a kid was rolling around in the entryway and refusing to put on their coat, or when we were running late, or when the fan over the stove blared, or when milk spilled, my insides filled with fury. Being ignored? Triggered. Being woken up? Triggered. Kids playing loudly and gleefully? Triggered. Running late? Triggered. Overstimulated? Triggered. Being *awake?!* You guessed it.

I knew what it was like to live on edge, never knowing when a parent would blow. The term "gentle parenting" had never entered my orbit, but I'd determined long ago not to be the rage-fueled mom dominating through terror and power. Logically, I understood that my children were small humans learning how to be big humans. They didn't need punishment; they needed love, guidance, boundaries, rules, and structure. I wanted to be the kind of mom who raised decent human beings by *being* a decent human being.

I loved my children from the marrow of my aging millennial bones, but ignoring the knee-jerk reaction to scream in their faces when they were just being kids became harder than I'd ever anticipated. Parenting a constantly dysregulated child with high needs and little support became the single most dysregulating thing I have ever experienced in my life. I struggled to separate "they are having a hard time" from "they are giving me a hard time." Their dysregulation caused my dysregulation and mine set off theirs—a never-ending vicious cycle that I felt more incapable of handling by the day. And so, I lay awake each night and replayed all the ways I hadn't been the mom my kids deserved.

I TRIED TO TAKE CARE of myself. I did. But something always got in the way. I attempted to go for walks when Greg was home, but because of his schedule, maintaining any kind of routine was impossible. I continued therapy. I washed my face. I intended to go to bed on time—but nighttime was the only time I had to think my own thoughts all day, so I stayed up instead. I went to the doctor when I was sick, but they just told me to rest. *Yeah, okay, buddy.*

I knew I had severe high-frequency hearing loss, which made everyday hearing hard enough as it was. The listening fatigue drained my energy stores, and not being able to hear my small children's unclear voices each day only magnified that stress. I went to a hearing clinic to be assessed for hearing aids. The cost? Five thousand dollars out of pocket. Hard pass on *that* pipe dream.

Solving the problem of taking care of myself while also taking care of my kids continued to be like trying to solve a rigged Rubik's Cube with missing pieces and the sun shining in my eyes. For every step forward, it always felt like two steps back.

I FELT A SMALL WARM finger tapping on my closed eyelid and heard Ellie whisper-yelling into my face, "I had an assident Mommy and I hungee." The world outside was still dark. I looked at my phone, which glared 6:51 in my face. I needed to get myself ready for work and have both kids out the door for school and preschool, all before 7:30. It was already past go time.

I forced myself up, stripped the sheets off her bed, and then went into Oscar's room. I found him standing in the middle of it, pointing to the hallway and yelling. I picked him up.

"What do you need, buddy?" I said, searching his face, watching his hands. I asked twice more. I still couldn't understand. "Can you sign it?" I pressed.

More yelling.

"Slow down, bud. Mommy is trying to understand." I put my hand over my ear, attempting to stifle the rage I would feel if the screaming continued. Oscar tried to pull it away. I held tight. He slapped me in the face.

A moment later, the babysitter texted: *I'm sorry but I'm sick, and I can't watch the kids after school today.* CRAP. I needed to find someone. STAT. I started to text alternative sitters as I tried to shovel breakfast into three of our faces. All the while, the demands from both kids continued. Then I realized we were running late—something that now made my nervous system feel like it was being zapped by forty tasers.

Ellie refused the matching outfit I had set out for her because four-year-olds like autonomy and care not for the opinions of others. I wiped down her messy face and she yelped at me, jerking her head away in disgust. I bundled up the children, handed them granola bars to replace the toast they refused to eat, and buckled them into their car seats.

"Mommy has a phone call to make. Please be quiet just for a couple minutes, okay?" Oscar began to whine. "Please," I said, as we pulled out of the driveway. I dialed our last-minute babysitter. The moment the phone started to ring, Oscar's whining turned to yelling.

"I hear you, bud. Mom's on the phone. Please wait two minutes," I said. But he did not stop. I couldn't look into the back seat because I was trying to focus on the road and not annihilate our family in a small-town head-on collision.

Then Ellie started up. "Mom, Mom, Mom, Mom, Mom," she repeated. My blood began to boil as I left a garbled stress-ridden message on the babysitter's voicemail.

I tried to engage with Oscar without looking back at him, not wanting to drive into oncoming traffic. "What do you need, bud?" No clear answer. He just yelled, "Naaaaaa."

I am the grown-up. I am in control. Everything is fine. They need to learn to wait. Just one more minute until I can stop. Just breathe, I told myself. My empathy stores were so far in the red I could no longer access them. As we pulled up to the stoplight, my ability to talk myself down evaporated entirely. In its place was a tight, pulsing heat that crawled from my chest up to my neck. The chaos inside the car felt like a threat to my very being.

I could feel the weight of every unmet expectation, every little frustration, every minor inconvenience from the morning, all compounded by the last four and a half years of trying.

Ellie continued to kick my seat. "Mooooooommmmmmmyyyy," she whine-yelled. The stoplight ahead turned red. Before I knew what I was about to do, I slammed on the brakes. A switch flipped inside me. A primal, guttural sound that I had been holding in for what felt like a lifetime erupted.

I turned around, wild-eyed, looked into their unruly faces, and screamed, "STOP IT! JUST SHUT UP!"

I yelled at them about how I was doing my best, how neither of them listened, how I politely asked them to wait, how I was trying, how they only cared about themselves, how I couldn't play Nice Mom anymore, and how I'd had enough.

Once the words had left my body, my face grew hotter. My hands shook. My breath was quick. Cars behind me started honking. The light was green. I turned to face the road and pressed on the gas, shell-shocked by my own loss of control.

I pulled the car over to the side of the road and turned around to see their little faces, terrified and stunned. In Oscar's hands, I saw the granola bar, still in its wrapper. The packaging was crinkled up from him trying to open it.

The kids stared at me, silent. Afraid. Ellie's eyes were full of tears, like she'd seen a darkness she didn't know existed. I'd always been the one protecting Oscar and Ellie from the things they feared, big and small. Now that thing was me. I felt my own eyes well up.

Oscar looked at me sheepishly, holding out his crinkly granola bar and signing "help." I had forgotten to open the granola bar I gave him. He'd been trying to communicate the only way he knew how. And Ellie was trying to get my attention because she wanted to help him.

Ashamed, I took the bar from him without saying a word, opened it, and handed it back to him. Unsure, he took a quick bite of his breakfast, and I continued driving. The car remained silent, but it was not the kind of silence I longed for.

WHEN I DROPPED THE KIDS off at school and daycare, I pulled them close to me, gave them each a big hug, and said, "I am sorry for yelling at you guys. You didn't deserve that. Nobody should treat you that way. I am not perfect. I was really overwhelmed, and I am trying to figure out how to deal with my big feelings differently. I'm sorry for scaring you. I love you so much. You are good kiddos."

They hugged me back, nodded their heads, and waved goodbye. When I climbed into the car and sat down behind the wheel, I broke down. I was supposed to be the safe one, the adult, the one in control. But in that moment—and more moments recently—I knew I hadn't been the mom I set out to be. I just never imagined it would be so hard.

17

No Wonder

Objectively, I lived a good life. Certainly, the home we'd created for our kids was more stable than mine growing up. I'd escaped the cycle of poverty, met and married a gentle, kind, hardworking man, and we'd surrounded ourselves with other do-gooders in the world. Looking around, we had everything we needed to provide our kids with a strong, loving foundation.

But after I screamed in my children's faces because they wanted me to open a granola bar package, I decided it was best to do some digging as to what the actual flip was wrong with me. Was it moving so much that had screwed me up? Being a kid who frequented the low-income breakfast club? I considered other moms in my orbit.

My friend Darcy was one of the only moms I knew who'd grown up below the poverty line like me. We'd bonded over our shared experiences. As kids, we knew snacks like Dunkaroos were for the rich kids, that thrift shopping happened by necessity, not as a hobby, that birthday parties at McDonald's were *fancy,* extracurriculars were a privilege, and airplane trips were mysterious rich-kid activities. Yet, despite her upbringing, Darcy had put herself through college and settled down with a good husband and two kids. As a mom, she was one of the most grounded, calm people I knew.

When I asked if her childhood had affected her negatively, she said, "Not really. I mean, we didn't have much but at least we had each other. My parents did everything they could, and they were there for me no matter what. In some way I think growing up like that brings you closer together, makes you stronger."

OUTSIDE LIBBY: *nods*
INSIDE LIBBY: Does it?

Then there was my friend Anita, who'd had an idyllic childhood I couldn't comprehend. She lived in the same town with the same parents who'd worked the same jobs their whole lives—like some kind of Tim Allen–esque *Home Improvement*–fantasy family. They owned a big, beautiful house with an in-ground pool. Holidays were filled with family, traditions, and travel. Her parents supported her interests, paid for sporting extracurriculars, taught her about how the world works, and put her through college. When she told me she had great parents and every opportunity that she could have ever wanted, I couldn't help but feel a pang of jealousy.

And yet, as an adult, she was so hard on herself. No matter what she did, she never felt like she was good enough. She was fiercely independent, highly self-critical, and avoided conflict like the plague. After having kids, she struggled with depression and anxiety and hardly left her house. Despite what she presented to the world on the outside—that she took wonderful care of her kids—I knew that she was drowning on the inside.

"I'm a terrible mom. I can't keep up," she confided to me one day, a few weeks after her second baby was born.

"Could you ask your parents for support? They live close by, right?"

"I can't bring my kids there," she said. "I can't trust my parents with them alone. I've never told you before, but my parents used corporal punishment when I was a kid. My mom criticized me constantly. I love them, but I'm scared to leave them alone with my kids. I don't want my kids to experience what I did."

My friends' experiences were so different from one another's and yet, both so like mine—just in different ways. What did they have that I didn't? What made us the way we were?

THE FIRST SELF-HELP BOOK THAT I picked up on my own was *The Gifts of Imperfection* by some chick named Brené Brown, who I later discovered was a bestselling author and revered academic whose research on shame, vulnerability, courage, and empathy has radically shifted the cultural narrative around what it means to be wholehearted and well. *That's a mouthful. Gifts of imperfection.* Hmm. I thought it might be a crock, considering my tendency to be perfect and overachieve was what had gotten me so far in life. But I gave the book a shot anyway and wondered what sort of gifts she proposed imperfection had to offer.

Brené claimed that we internalize messages of shame as kids. Essentially, that shame causes us to become hypervigilant little perfectionistic freaks in an effort to keep the peace. These neuroticisms function to help us stay safe from the judgments and criticisms of the world (aka our parents). I'm paraphrasing here.

I considered her theory. I questioned it, because the women around me were good at having their crap together, too—and they seemed fine. Brené also suggested that we try to embrace our imperfections, adopt some self-compassion, and share our truth so that the shame doesn't fester and eat us alive. Again, paraphrasing. Play more, she instructed. Rest more, she encouraged. Be yourself, be authentic, she said gently. Her words felt good, but she didn't realize who she was talking to.

No disrespect, ma'am, but my *full self* is a bit of a train wreck, and I've spent too long working too hard at being a normal-looking person just to throw it out the window now. If I let go, everything would fall apart. I couldn't risk such insanity. There were too many people relying on me. It's likely that the real Libby was the terrible person who was raging at my family for no reason—so, being more of myself might not be such a good idea.

Inconveniently, Brené kept making me feel seen. Why *had* I built my life on grit and self-loathing? Why *did* other people's potential low opinions keep me awake at night?

"The irony is that we attempt to disown our difficult stories to appear more acceptable but our wholeness actually depends on the integration of all our experiences, including the falls," she writes. I thought I was the only one who did this. It seemed strange that someone would write a book for the general public that was so obviously meant for me.

Still, reading it didn't stop my body from feeling it was on fire when my children were whining. No help here! What was Brené getting at? As I dove deeper, I began to consider the difficult personal stories I used to tell at parties as if they were funny jokes.

Maybe, despite my intent to leave the cows, the moves, and the screaming matches in the rearview mirror, they were still following me down country roads and into my redbrick house with curb appeal and cute kids. Perhaps I was more screwed up than I once thought.

I COULDN'T EXACTLY PINPOINT ONE thing that had happened in my past that altered my way of being. In fact, I couldn't remember much at all. But a trail of google searches brought me to the Adverse Childhood Experiences test, more widely known as ACE. The test was created in the 1990s to measure the long-term impact of your childhood adverse experiences before you turned eighteen. The ten-question survey asks you about whether you witnessed or experienced things like physical, emotional, or sexual abuse; neglect; loss of a parent through divorce, death, or incarceration; and household substance abuse and mental illness.

Apparently, experiencing even one of these adversities can do long-term damage—especially if left unchecked and untreated. But the more adverse experiences you have, the more likely you are to develop physical, mental, and emotional health issues later in life. *Raises hand awkwardly.*

The website did warn me of the survey's limitations. Basically, we can't really understand the full context of someone's life by asking ten simple questions. I understood what they were getting at but took it anyway. I love a good quiz—and getting an answer as to what my problem was in less than five minutes sounded like a win I needed.

I was relieved to learn, before starting, that two-thirds of adults surveyed scored at least one adversity and most adults had more than one. *At least I am not entirely alone,* I thought. So, I clicked through the questions, eager to get my answer.

My ACE score was six out of ten.

Only 2.3 percent of the population have a score of six or higher. Two point three. I stared at the computer screen, bewildered.

My score explained so much and so little, all at the same time. I had a thimble of validation and a five-gallon bucket brimming with more questions than I'd had when I started. So, I kept searching for answers: during my lunch hour at work, while I waited in doctors' offices, and while we watched embarrassing amounts of *Peppa Pig* on TV. That's when I came across the words "childhood trauma."

I'd always believed that traumas were life-altering events like war, hurricanes, sex trafficking, and head-on collisions. But the article suggested that there wasn't always one event to pinpoint or some obvious experience that made the trauma clear. Apparently, ongoing traumas, especially throughout childhood, had far-reaching repercussions. The nuance and conflicting layers of stressful events, feelings, and people complicated things—making the trauma even more difficult to understand and heal from. But what does the internet know? I decided it was time to get serious—with books.

My therapist recommended *The Body Keeps the Score* by psychiatrist, researcher, and leading expert in trauma Dr. Bessel van der Kolk. I was shocked by what this man proposed. Essentially, it's in the title. Our bodies remember our trauma even when we don't, and those memories hijack our ability to function and feel things properly. Trauma reshapes our brains. He explained that often people think of trauma as an event or collection of events that took place in the past, but the trauma is actually the imprint left on the mind, brain, and body—from those experiences.

Trauma isn't the thing that happened. Trauma is how we internalize the event and live our lives because of it.

Like, if your wacko stepdad screamed in your face every time you made a mistake, the mistake isn't the trauma. The screaming isn't the trauma, either. The fact that you're now a thirty-year-old woman whose cortisol spikes every time you spill a glass of milk, even though no one is currently screaming at you—*that* is the trauma.

Or if you spent your childhood parenting your parents, being a responsible child who is skilled at regulating the emotions of adults is not the trauma. Your internal drive to fix everyone, do everything, be the bigger person, and feel responsible for everyone else's happiness, your stomach-curdling guilt and inability to ask anyone for help—*that* is the trauma.

So, the impacts of my experiences were infused into my very

being—whether I realized it or not. Was Dr. van der Kolk trying to tell me that "forgive and forget" doesn't apply? If I understood correctly, the implications of my childhood basically affected every area of my life and had been there long before I'd popped out some kids. There was so much I couldn't remember—things my body apparently could. But there were some things I'd never forget.

SHAKING, I STOOD IN MY bedroom of our new apartment with half-unpacked boxes behind me, shattered dinner plates down the hallway, and garbage strewn everywhere. I took another deep breath to brace myself, inhaling the fumes of Mom's rage. It was nighttime in the thick of winter. I had just come in from my evening job at Sport Chek, an athletic retailer who took me on in good faith despite my being new in town. I was sixteen years old and only a couple months into the semester at the new school I'd enrolled in halfway through the school year. We'd recently (and finally) left Karl at the farm and moved back to the city.

It was just Mom, Harry, and me, again. When Mom told us we'd be moving back to the city, away from the town where I'd spent my first two and a half years of high school, I wasn't thrilled. But a different school where I had anonymity, no bullies, and no history of being the weird kid whose cows ran away a lot turned out to be not so bad. I liked walking the hallways unaware of anybody's social standing. What I did not like was coming home.

The part-time job helped with that. Since the separation from Karl, Mom was not doing well. She'd given up work again and rarely left the apartment. When I returned that night, I went straight to my bedroom to relax. That's when I heard the kitchen cupboards slamming and knew it was happening again. *Not again.*

I walked down the dark hallway, past the bag of garbage Harry and I had been using the previous day when we cleaned our rooms and helped unpack boxes. Mom was standing in the kitchen, unpacking dishes and slamming everything as she went. I knew her manic, fury-filled eyes better than I knew myself. *This is a bad one.*

"What is going on, Mom? Is everything okay?" I asked, knowing the answer.

"No. We're moving back. I can't stand this city—and we can't afford to stay here. You never wanted to move here anyway so you should be over the moon that we are going to the country again, getting what you want, *again*," she hurled the words at me, like daggers.

I started to tidy the kitchen, knowing that sometimes that helped.

"Do we really have to?" I asked, calmly but genuinely. "I just got this job I really like, and I think I like my new school. I think I made a friend. We just moved. You said it would be better and it might be. Maybe there is a way we can stay?"

"We can't afford it, Libby!" she yelled. "All the money is gone!"

"Harry and I could help," I offered, not wanting to move again, not wanting to explain the situation to my friends again.

"You just don't get it, Libby!" she screamed. She threw the plate she was holding onto the floor, and it shattered at my feet like the hope I once had that things would get better. The heat in my chest rose. I looked away, trying to stifle my feelings.

"I don't have anyone, I don't have anything, I lost everything!" she yelled, louder with every word. "You have your friends, your church family, school, and a job. Nothing has changed!" Then another plate smashed.

It was true. She *was* alone. I knew this, which is why I did everything in my power to help. I was happy that Karl was in the rearview mirror, and still, I had nightmares about him. I didn't know what the future held for us. And worse, it felt like I'd lost Mom in the process. But she couldn't see that.

"I'm having a hard time, too," I said. I headed back to my bedroom feeling the heat rush to my face.

"You, parading around at a new school with new friends and a new job and living the life? I lost *everything*. All you lost was geography!" she yelled.

I covered my ears, wishing it would stop. I thought back to the mess that we'd just left at the farm, the one I'd been cleaning up for three years without so much as a thank-you. I couldn't forget the things Karl said and did to us at that farm, and how alone and unprotected I'd felt there, too. I'd been the one to help Mom finally leave him. I'd been the one to lend her my strength on the days she couldn't move forward. I'd been hurt, too.

I felt my temperature rise, my body start to shake, and a panic wash over me. I couldn't stay a moment longer. I had to escape.

I left my room, hearing nothing but the sound of my own racing heart. I ran out of our unit and the front door of the apartment building. Wearing nothing but jeans and a T-shirt, I went out into the freezing winter night as fast as my legs could take me. I ran down the street and around the corner until I was far enough away that I couldn't see our building. I couldn't feel the cold, not at first. Eventually I found a bus shelter. In it, I paced in circles. I didn't just want to leave home. I wanted to leave my family, leave my body, leave everything behind.

My chest was tight. My heart was pounding. Breathing felt like trying to suck air through a tiny straw. My skin prickled with heat. I couldn't focus. My muscles tensed, like I needed to run but I couldn't move. I felt trapped. Afraid. Fragile. I was having my first panic attack.

When it was over, I began to feel the cold. I looked around for my mom, hoping she'd followed me. Maybe she wanted to know if I was okay. I looked for Harry, too. Maybe he'd noticed I was gone. But there was no one. No one came, because no one ever came. I was, in fact, alone.

Eventually, I made my way back home. I stepped over the mess in my room and crawled into bed. The next day, as usual, Mom went on like nothing had happened. As usual, so did I.

AS I BEGAN TO LEARN more about how children develop, I couldn't help but go back to this memory and the others that were so much like it. The things I learned in *The Body Keeps the Score* heavily relied on research called attachment theory. In fact, everywhere I looked, there was a gigantic flashing arrow pointing back to this psychological and developmental research called attachment science. The theory was originally developed by psychiatrist John Bowlby and later expanded on by developmental psychologist Mary Ainsworth.

Long story short: They noticed major ties between the quality of the relationship (or lack thereof) between kids and parents, and the way those kids develop into adulthood. Over the course of decades, starting in the late 1940s, attachment theory became a foundational science that reshaped our understanding of early relationships and childhood development.

This widespread understanding of attachment seemed to explain why my nervous system always felt a hair away from being struck by lightning and why my hobbies consisted of swimming laps around a cesspool of self-deprecating thoughts.

How you are raised determines whether you are securely attached (read: healthy) or insecurely attached (read: unhealthy). There are various types and subtypes of insecure attachment, and no type is a monolith. But generally speaking, a securely attached person feels safe in relationships, trusts others, trusts themselves, and can handle emotions without completely shutting down or spiraling. These people sounded like unicorns. In contrast, children who develop an insecure attachment are set up from the start to struggle with some nasty concoction of the stuff securely attached people don't. What we need to become securely attached is a safe, predictable, stable relationship with at least one parent who meets our emotional needs. We need to know that we matter.

But if our parent is inconsistent, unpredictable, or absent, that teaches us that the world is not safe and that we're not worthy of love. Our developing sense of self gets distorted. How our caregivers treat us shapes who we become and how we function for the rest of our lives.

Dr. Gabor Maté, an expert in trauma, addiction, and healing, deepened my understanding of attachment by explaining the need for something my pal Brené Brown brought up: authenticity. In *The Myth of Normal,* Maté defines authenticity as "the ability to be in touch with and express our real emotions, needs, and desires without suppression or distortion."

Dr. Maté says that babies are the most authentic people out there because their connection to self hasn't been broken (yet). Babies come out attuned to their needs and their needs only, because their survival depends on their ability to listen to their bodies' cues. So, when they are hungry, thirsty, or sad that the boobies went bye-bye or their feet are cold, they don't hide it. They don't care if their crying annoys you because their number one job is to care about their own needs.

The problem is that our two core needs for authenticity and attachment get pitted against each other. In some kind of nonstop blindfolded baby gladiator warrior battle, attachment and authenticity go head-to-head. Moment by moment, the warrior babies are karate-chopping their way through life, unsure if they should allow their bloodcurdling screams to meet their needs but possibly piss you (their caregiver) off—or allow their rumbling tummies to scream at them so they can keep you content. This is a metaphor. Kind of.

Dr. Maté explains that when pitted against each other, attachment beats authenticity every time because without the attachment figure, the baby can't get any of their needs met. But technically, the baby *can* survive without being able to respond appropriately to its body's cues. Without an attachment figure (or connection), they literally cannot survive.

I can't remember a single thing from before the age of six, so I wondered, *Why does this matter?* Well, because it's not just about babies. As children, we develop our sense of self through all these experiences.

Obviously, no parent is perfect, but if children are regularly met with rejection, isolation, punishment, or neglect for voicing their needs, they eventually learn not to speak up. If our moms or dads—the people we are most reliant on to learn about the world from—are unpredictable, angry, dismissive, or consistently inconsistent, we become conditioned to prioritize our caregivers' feelings over our own. Reading the room is what keeps us feeling safe.

But consistently choosing connection with our parents over connection to our self ultimately screws us over. The more often our body's signals get ignored or overridden, the more disconnected we become from ourselves, the less we trust our own feelings. Disconnection to the self becomes a major source of dysfunction.

I knew disconnection well.

Throughout my childhood, I remembered the panicked feeling in my body whenever Mom—and eventually Karl—were upset. I could read Mom's moods by her footsteps, her breath, the way she flared her nose, the way she closed the door, the way she opened the fridge. I could sense the negative energy when I walked into the house. Something as simple as a bad mood would send me into overdrive, anticipating future needs, solving unspoken problems. Her body language alone made me readjust myself.

As a young person, like some kind of fear-stricken opossum playing dead until its predator passed, I became excellent at pretending bad things weren't happening when they were. I would mentally check out, hit pause on my stoic face, leave my body, float up to the ceiling, stare blankly, and wait for the chaos, perceived danger, or inescapable discomfort to pass. This kind of disconnection to self is called dissociation and it was just one of many ways I'd learned not to feel.

"You think you have it bad?!" I could hear my mom's words still ringing in my head.

Learning not to feel will get you through the day. Your parents are right. You are wrong. Their experience matters. Yours does not. Be quiet. Keep your needs to yourself. I internalized those feelings and made it my job to fix Mom's problems. If Mom was happy, I was happy. Well, not happy, but at least not on the edge. Learning to avoid the edge became my superpower.

We *suppress* to *impress*. The problem is that these behaviors become our default. What starts out as a perfectly natural coping mechanism becomes a maladaptive shitstorm of self-sabotage and hypervigilance.

Our nervous systems can't differentiate between our parents, partners, bosses, in-laws, friends, and the random lady at the supermarket. Severity aside, being raised in emotionally unsafe environments is basically People Pleasing 101.

So I care too much what people think. Is that a crime?! Surely, my love for keeping the peace could not be the reason I'm strung out and sometimes want to drive into oncoming traffic? Certainly, prioritizing the needs of others isn't a bad thing. No, but as I learned, my lifelong desire to be a good girl wasn't the valiant and enviable quality I thought it was either.

I swatted away the intrusive doom-spiral thoughts about how I was likely screwing up my own kids and tried to stay focused on my own experiences.

What I began to learn about childhood development explained so much about why I was the way I was. Why I couldn't sit down and relax to save my life; why, as a grown-ass woman, I still always felt like I was in trouble; why watching Greg do the dishes made me want to turn inside out; why I rage-cleaned instead of rested; why I struggled to be honest about what I wanted; why so often I said yes when my insides screamed no.

I'd rather push myself, accepting my own pain and exhaustion, than deal with the possibility of letting down others. Disappointment felt unbearable. Being agreeable kept me connected to those I needed most. I thought I was just a considerate person. Rather, I became a person who continuously chose to run on the fumes of other people's approval and then wonder why it wasn't enough.

My disconnection from myself didn't just make me a people-pleaser, it was at the center of so many of my other problems, too—the rusty wrench in the gears of my well-intentioned mothering. My trauma made me someone who relentlessly overcommitted and hustled to achieve goodness, belonging, and worthiness.

I became someone who lived life on autopilot, someone who assumed the church moms (and all the other moms) knew the best way to do everything and compelled me to try to do it all, too. I overthought everything, from the way I folded my sheets to the number of phone calls I made to the pediatrician's office. It wasn't just that I didn't have a concept of healthy or an example to learn from, it was that I couldn't trust my own instincts.

The standard for "good enough" was invisible to me, making it impossible to tell when I'd crossed over the line from neglect to overcompensation—so overcompensation became the norm. High standards and self-criticism became the norm.

Like many millennial mothers, I wasn't taught how to emotionally regulate. But my childhood experiences also made me someone who entered into fight-or-flight mode more often than the average person. Lateness felt like the house was on fire. Defiance felt like a threat to my very being. In the moment, calming down felt impossible. Despite my desire to be a safe, present, loving, regulated mom, the odds were stacked against me. I'd waltzed into motherhood convinced that my past made me resilient and gave me grit. Instead, I became someone who carried a five-ton weight of hypervigilance into every room I walked into.

I'd tried so hard to check the boxes of life because I wanted to give my kids what they needed and what I never had. But what they needed was to be raised by parents who made sure they were seen, loved, and known within a safe, predictable environment.

That was what my friend Darcy had. That was what my friend Anita and I hadn't had.

In the book *What Happened to You?* by Oprah Winfrey and renowned psychiatrist and neuroscientist Bruce D. Perry, the authors say we're asking the wrong question—"What's wrong with you?"—when we should be asking, "What happened to you?" Maybe I'd been asking the wrong question all along.

What happened to *me* had robbed me of the ability to hear my own voice—the one that told me what I wanted, needed, and felt. It had stolen the opportunity for me to truly know and trust myself, and conditioned me to believe and live as though I didn't really matter. What had happened to me set me up from the start to self-abandon. I suppose I just didn't notice, until it started affecting the people I loved most.

I realized, it's no wonder I was a strung-out basket case. Maybe I didn't need to keep swimming laps around a cesspool of shame. I wasn't a garbage person. I was a traumatized person and a loving mom, doing her best despite it all.

Still, something had to change. Because if I'd learned anything, it was that there was nothing—not clean floors, literature, extracurriculars, Pinterest crafts, home-cooked meals, speech therapy, or organic fruit—that could make up for growing up with parents who didn't make you feel safe and loved. Nothing could make up for a childhood consistently spent on the edge. So, now what?

18

Icebergs

In the three years after the panic attack in the bus shelter, I moved nine more times. Then, I got an offer I couldn't refuse. I was nineteen and in love with my British boyfriend, Greg, whom I'd met at summer camp a few years prior. We had been dating for just over a year when he suggested I move to England with him for a little while. I didn't have to think very hard about it before using what spare cash I had and booking a plane ticket across the ocean.

I didn't possess the usual reasons young people move abroad, like expanding my mind by exposing it to other cultures and food. I wasn't drawn to the UK by the architecture or the rolling hills. It wasn't even Greg's dashing looks or the way he said words like *beautiful* with a crisp t—although that was really *quite* lovely (I hope you read that like the Queen would've said it). I moved overseas because I wanted a new life.

And that's what I got. I moved in with Greg's family, who owned a redbrick house overlooking the river in Southampton—the same house where they'd lived for the entirety of Greg's life. Two pint-size British cars sat in their little English driveway. Greg's family were the kind of people who drank water regularly. They roasted their vegetables instead of boiling them and preferred to walk instead of drive. Dinner was eaten around a table where everyone shared about their day and nobody yelled. These people wore Oakley sunglasses on their ski trips in Switzerland, okay? *Switzerland.*

The family welcomed me with open arms. And me? I rested in their embrace. Greg's mom taught me how to make a piecrust and how nice it was to warm dinner plates in the oven before serving. His dad took us for walks in the English countryside and kept the back garden lush and orderly with such passion that he almost convinced me that gardening wasn't torture.

One of the first things we did was tour Greg's hometown, which sits at the very bottom of the country, somewhere around the middle, on the English Channel. We got down to the waterfront and saw an enormous cruise ship. Craning my neck to look up at the shiny white side of the ship, I was taken aback by its size. The people boarding looked like little ants I could squish between my fingers.

Southampton is where the *Titanic* left from. THE. *TITANIC.* The glistening, luxurious boat we learned about in the movie theater in 1997, when I fell in love with Leonardo DiCaprio and wondered with my nine-year-old brain why the car glass would fog up so heavily. *Was someone getting hurt?!* WHAT IS HAPPENING?!

To this day, I think of Rose whenever I'm met with the opportunity to use more than one fork and knife. Standing at the port that day in 2010, I thought about how—like Greg and I—Jack and Rose came from different worlds. It was hard to imagine that nearly a hundred years prior, people were boarding a ship to sail across the Atlantic from that very spot.

I'm sure you've heard this story before but let me remind you: They claimed the *Titanic* was unsinkable. When the 1,500-passenger ship departed the morning of April 10, 1912, to begin its trek to New York City, it was the largest and most luxurious ship of its time.

Icebergs were known to be dangerous, and that year there were more than usual. The captain, Edward J. Smith, and crew had been warned to be cautious of the icebergs, but Captain Smith ignored such warnings and cut through the icy waters with unusual speed. Filled with a false confidence, he overestimated what the boat could handle. Four days after the *Titanic* left port, the magnificent beast hit an iceberg. Three hours after that, it sank to the bottom of the ocean, taking the captain and two-thirds of its passengers and crew members with it. The saddest part was that the *Titanic*'s demise could have been avoided. They had been warned.

Good old Captain Eddy didn't intend to sink the ship, okay? He just thought she could plow through the ice, that she could handle whatever the ocean threw at her. But despite the captain's inflated sense of capacity, the *Titanic* sank, ushering those she had promised to keep safe, those she should have transported to the other side, down into the icy Atlantic waters with her. As it turns out, full steam ahead was not the best approach.

NOW, NEARLY A DECADE LATER, deep into spiraling, frantic research into childhood development and trauma healing, I recognized the impact of my choice to cut my way through the perilous waters of parenthood with brute strength, too. I'd gone full steam ahead on the drug of overcompensation and was paying the price.

Once I began doing the healing work, I realized that so many of my problems were symptoms of deeper, unhealed wounds. I was learning that what was on the surface wasn't what really did the damage—it was what was underneath.

Below my shiny exterior was a lost little girl incapable of dealing with stress. You know—that thing that you have to deal with 24/7 as a parent who gives a crap? I'd learned that the more stressed we become, the less access we have to the logical part of our brain: the cortex. It's science. Stress makes problem solving and emotion regulation harder. When our cortisol spikes, it's like someone plops a giant boulder between what we are feeling and what we logically know to be true. Our brain goes squirrelly, sending us into fight-or-flight mode, and it's hard to do what's normal or healthy or right. We literally cannot think straight.

This is true even for those parents who had magical childhoods full of love, affection, and unicorns. For the traumatized folks, we're more likely to perceive stress or danger to begin with. The smallest things send us over the edge. On top of that, regulating the additional stress is harder for us, too.

Here is what I'd like to know. What the actual fresh hell? How cruel is it that the people who endure insanely stressful experiences have the fewest regulation skills and the most toxic coping mechanisms that make their lives even more stressful?

I recalled the car-yelling incident with new eyes. Why, exactly, did I turn into Hulk-mommy? Well, I was overstimulated and tired—sure. The kids weren't listening. I was worried about being late for work. I was irritated about being slapped in the face. I was frustrated that I couldn't understand Oscar's request and worried about his future at the same time. It had to be factored in that yelling was the model I'd been given growing up. All these reasons and a million others were valid.

But with everything I knew now, I could see that those weren't really the reasons I was yelling. No. It was that I felt out of control. Despite physically being safe, I *felt* unsafe in my own body, pushed into fight-or-flight mode. My knee-jerk reaction was to yell because, subconsciously, I knew it was the quickest way to stop the external chaos and for my body to feel calm and safe. I was dysregulated and wanted to make the *perceived* threat stop. Unintentionally, I sacrificed my connection to my kids and their ability to feel safe—all so that *I* could feel safe.

Sometimes ships sailing the Atlantic think they see giant icebergs, and as you can imagine, it causes sheer panic. This phenomenon can be caused by superior mirages, which occur in cold conditions over the ocean. A superior mirage happens when layers of air at different temperatures cause light to bend, distorting objects or creating the illusion of objects that aren't really there.

This can make distant objects, like icebergs or other ships, appear larger or closer than they are, or even conjure up the illusion of an iceberg where there is none. My kids were like epic superior mirages. They looked like the dangerous icebergs, but they weren't the icebergs. Actually, they were the passengers on the ship.

That day—granola bar day—like anytime I lost my cool with my kids, I was plagued by guilt. But now, I could recall the apologetic words coming out of my mouth, sense the sorrow in my voice, and feel the desperation in my chest as I got back in the car and began to sob. *"I'm sorry for yelling at you guys. You didn't deserve that."*

As I replayed those moments in my mind, I realized I wasn't a bad, broken, impatient mom. I *was* trying. I might have frayed our connection, but I had also tried to repair it. I'd validated their experience and attempted to reconnect with them. I wanted, needed them to know that they mattered, could trust themselves, and were safe. I'd screwed up, but I'd done something about it.

For so long, I'd wondered if I would ever be able to break the cycle. Knowing what I knew now, I realized I already started.

I HAD A NEWFOUND COMPASSION for myself. What I didn't have was a fucking magic wand to fix future-me. When Christmas came, I offered to host multiple family gatherings again. I cooked the prime rib dinner Dad requested and tried to meet everyone else's expectations, again. I didn't ask for help, again. I was strung out and snappy with the kids, again—counting the minutes until they went to bed and then berating myself for it as I fell asleep. I'd overcommitted and then punished the people I loved most, again.

I'd have preferred it if my newfound understanding of the impact of being parented by unpredictable or volatile parents miraculously fixed my fried nervous system. I'd have loved to become a patience-toting mother-of-the-year.

But simply *knowing* that I could damage my children's ability to trust themselves and function in adulthood didn't change my moment-to-moment choices and long-established coping mechanisms. Understanding the validity of my stress wasn't enough to stop me from snapping over loud noises and my children needing me in the middle of the night, again. My good intentions couldn't douse the flames of my internal rage or magically create the patience I needed when I was a hair away from losing it. If anything, my newfound knowledge just piled on more pressure not to screw it up.

The pressure caused more stress. I couldn't just "calm down" because I wanted to. Who in the history of being told to calm down has ever calmed down? Literally no one. So, what was I missing?

Validate your kids' emotions, they say. *Make them feel known,* they say. *Let them borrow from your calm nervous system,* they say. What fucking calm, Linda? What calm, exactly, are they borrowing from? Coregulation sounds fine and dandy on paper, but frankly, singing kumbaya feels impossible when my four-year-old is having a world-class meltdown in the middle of the Walmart cheese aisle and my menstrual cramps are so bad I'm ready to rip my uterus out.

Life *still* consisted of numerable stressors that weren't going away anytime soon. I had to make them feel known, loved, and secure while feeling unknown, unsafe, and insecure *myself.* Kids need emotional safety and reliable parents who are regulated. *Cool beans, developmental psychologists who aren't living my life!* I wanted to raise kids who didn't need to recover from their childhoods. But how do you give what you never got?

How am I to re-parent myself while I'm cooking spaghetti nobody will eat because there are "bits" in it, scheduling endless appointments, folding the laundry, playing Barbies, going to work, coming home, shushing the kids because Daddy is sleeping, and trying to maintain boundaries with the woman who conditioned me not to have boundaries? How?

It's simple; just choose to be different. But it's not simple to break patterns that were burned into your neural wiring pathways over the course of almost three decades. Breaking cycles is not simple when there are endless tasks and humans who need your brain power, your body, your time, or some sick mixture of all three plus a smile. Healing isn't straightforward.

When you are already carrying more than you can bear and you've never had healthier behaviors modeled, it's hard to choose differently in the moment. Was I destined to ruin my kids regardless of how hard I tried? Because I was trying, and it didn't seem to be working.

I REACHED OUT TO DR. TANYA COTLER, a Canadian clinical psychologist who specializes in parent-child attachment and maternal mental health. I needed to know how people like me were supposed to make all these miraculous changes overnight and what would happen to our kids if we didn't. Unlike some of the parenting "experts" out there, Dr. Cotler doesn't shame parents into "doing better" or gloss over what kids really need. She's all about what she calls "holding both the parent and child in mind," which is fancy-person talk for: Both you and your kids' feelings and well-being matter. They are intrinsically linked.

"I'm trying to be patient and present. I'm doing my best to break the cycle. But the pressure to be perfect is too much. I don't want to screw up my kids. What am I missing?" I asked.

"Creating a secure attachment is not about a perfect performance in each individual moment, or any single behavior or choice. What matters is the overall pattern of connection that is built over time: moment to moment," she told me.

"Okay, but *how* do you do that? What do you say to moms like me who feel like everything is just too much? *Everything*, including the advice?" I pressed.

"That it's in her. That creating a secure attachment, ultimately, is the mother's capacity to feel alive, to feel safe, to feel known, to be understood, and to delight in her own self. You are going to best create that by figuring out what works for you and your child. It is a constant back-and-forth, and it's never at the same time, which is what makes it so hard. Still, it's in her."

IF GOOD OLD CAPTAIN SMITH had paid attention to the iceberg warning, maybe he wouldn't be at the bottom of the ocean. He might just be dead in a normal grave after a lifetime of ship-sailing successes. If he'd have acknowledged the limits of his ship and the uncertainties and dangers in the ocean, maybe he'd have seen what was coming straight ahead—and acted on it. But he was too busy trying to be Mr. Fancy Pants biggest-ship sailor. Turns out, ignoring the truth doesn't make it go away. It leaves you vulnerable to having your hull carved out—and drowning.

After the *Titanic* went under in 1912, there was a global effort to make sure it didn't happen again. Two years later, in 1914, the International Ice Patrol was established. To this day, it monitors the North Atlantic for icebergs and provides regular updates to ships to help them avoid dangerous ice zones. Once they became aware of how catastrophic icebergs could be, they created a solution. The people in charge did something new. Did every Atlantic passage go exactly to plan? Nope. But guess what? The ships didn't sink.

Despite what cynical Libby once believed, authenticity wasn't some pie-in-the-sky notion—it was at the crux of my problems.

Who was I, really? What mattered to me, really? Is it even possible to delight in oneself?

I knew that I needed to stay connected to my little humans to help foster their connection to themselves. But if anything was going to change about how I navigated the moment-to-moment choices in my day, if I was going to learn how to regulate, to be fully present, and to be safe, I had to connect with someone else—myself.

That involved paying attention. If I wanted to feel safe in my body, I had to learn how to access and feel my truest, most honest feelings. I needed what my kids needed: validation, compassion, safety, knowing, trust. If they needed to be heard, so did I.

I decided it was time to be radically honest with myself. So, I stopped ignoring the foghorn in the distance that I'd learned to tune out so long ago. I cut the engines, leaned over the rail, and listened to some version of my inner voice. Faintly, I heard her tell me the truth. It went something like this:

Lady, you're out here with your dang snowplow arms, trying to be everything to everyone, trying to please everyone but yourself. And you are doing it as if your circumstances and capacity aren't vastly different from the moms you compare yourself to. You've got complex trauma that makes your life harder, two fabulous kids who can suck the life out of you, and an unbearable mental load you carry alone most of the time. Why in the flying fuck nuggets are you out here trying to achieve perfection that doesn't even exist?

Slow down. Pay attention. Change course. Listen. Otherwise, you *will* drown, and you *will* take your kids with you. Your kids don't need it *all;* they need you, above water.

19

Sunshine

In the spring, shortly before the kids turned three and five, I was well into my healing journey. Dinner was on the stove because the kids were hungry and life doesn't stop because you're re-parenting yourself.

The incessant low hum of the fan above the stove grated at me as I pulled the tray of browning pork tenderloin out to baste it. The fresh salad waited on the island behind me to dress it. "I can help!" Ellie repeated every twenty-seven seconds, inches behind me and the hot oven door I'd nearly grazed her with, not realizing how close she was. "Please, give Mommy a few minutes alone, sweetie. I don't need your help right now," I said. Oscar was playing nicely, but loudly, in the corner. I was in a common place: overstimulation station.

By the time my husband came home to his hot meal on the table, I was spent. After we got the kids to bed, we sat down to drink a cup of tea together.

"Greg. Hear me out. I know I have been hardcore about cooking a wholesome meal every night of the week and having it on the table when you get home from work. But from now on, I'm going to make a schedule to eat at the same time every day. If you are here, great. If not, I'll put it aside for you to warm up when you get home. It's too much for me to coordinate everything. And I can't make meals from scratch so much. I don't have the energy and it's making me more stressed out than it is helping anything," I said.

"That's absolutely fine. Doesn't bother me at all. You should never feel like you need to wait for me or make something special just for me. You're with the kids most of the time. Do what's best for you," he said. *Was it really that easy?! All this time?* I thought.

The following day, I sat with the kids on a blanket in the backyard and we ate a cheese-and-crackers snack plate at 4:30 p.m. for dinner. We giggled. I left the dishes. They were a tomorrow-Libby problem. When Greg got home after the kids were in bed, I wasn't a basket case. I'd tossed perfection out the window.

YOU CAN'T CHANGE WHAT YOU can't or aren't willing to see. And once I saw my patterns and their ramifications, letting go became my full-time job. I didn't need to pretend I was fine when I wasn't or become an emotionless-robot-mom lady who overthinks every tiny interaction, disciplinary choice, or boundary with my kids. I needed to hold boundaries and space for their feelings and mine at the same time. I needed to let go of my ridiculous expectations and be okay with good enough.

Pouring what little time and energy I had into the emotional health of our home—instead of all the "shoulds"—is how I would manage my stress. It would not be about perfection but connection—the word at the center of everything I'd learned about childhood development, stress, trauma, and attachment. I'd make a daily practice of tuning in even at, and especially during, imperfect moments—to the kids, but just as importantly, to myself.

Nothing changed overnight. But I attempted to treat myself like I mattered, and I learned to live with the discomfort that choice brought. Self-prioritization feels unnatural when you've spent a lifetime believing that martyrdom is what makes you enough.

Accepting the truth about my circumstances and capacity was an important first step to mothering in a more realistic and regulated manner. Every day, I had to commit to the honesty gig and attempt to hear that little voice I'd blocked out so long ago. Truth be told, sometimes it felt futile.

With the consistency of a squirrel on espresso, I began journalling. I wrote down everything that I had to do that day, what energy I had to do it, and what feelings were coursing through my being. Sometimes it helped me refocus my priorities to cancel plans or give myself permission to put on an episode of *Peppa Pig* or take a long drive. With intention that took more work than I'd like to admit, I would pause during meltdowns before reacting. I'd take a deep breath when a child stared me dead in the face and screamed "No!" I tried noticing my blood pressure and asking myself, "Is danger imminent or does it just feel like it?"

When I'd find myself in a state of overwhelm, I'd ask, "Is this what matters most right now? What do I want or need? What do *they* need?" I became more curious about what the kids felt or why they were behaving a certain way—even if I didn't understand or agree.

I began to let go of the pressure to be the kind of mom I thought I was supposed to be and give myself permission to be the kind of mom I actually was. But *that* mom? She wasn't a full-time type A achiever. She was a certified type B and there was nothing wrong with that. She didn't give two craps about the state of her baseboards. If my kids got what mattered—a mom who was regulated enough to think straight—appearances meant jack all.

WE WERE BACK IN ENGLAND to visit family later that summer when we decided to take a day trip to the famous Jurassic Coast in the south of England.

I felt a tad disappointed that fog covered the roads as we drove toward the coast. I'd been hoping for a sunny day. But it was England, so therefore the forecast called for rain.

I packed our bag lightly. I didn't bother with over-the-top packed lunches with fresh fruit and ice packs on days out like this anymore. Let's be honest, I didn't bother with perfectly balanced meals at home anymore, either. Cucumbers and buttered noodles became my best friend. Good enough is good enough.

I also let go of the ridiculous expectation that I play with my kids at any free moment. I shook off the compulsion to keep my house Marie Kondo'd or give my kids a bath every single night. I put the TV on more often—and not just to get chores done but so that my children would stop talking to me for thirty-five minutes. Not five, thirty-five. Sometimes longer. Cancel me. I dare you.

I started to see the iceberg instead of the mirage. I acted on reality instead of my broken perception of it. Turning inward with curiosity helped me to recognize my triggers and do something about them. I started asking for breaks. I wore noise-canceling headphones. I warned my husband when my period was coming. The basics.

Each time I let go of an expectation that wasn't serving me, it opened up some space. Slowly, I found myself with more emotional bandwidth. More often, I even heard myself think.

I used some of the energy and time I got back to do things I wanted. And aside from occasionally still longing for a lobotomy and other unrealistic things, like my kids listening to me the first time I asked, I wanted naps. I wanted a new bra, a break from being the bedtime-routine parent, a kid-free dinner with Leah, and solo Big Mac sessions in my car while scream-singing to Taylor Swift.

I wanted something bigger beyond the house, too: to focus more on my career. Since dropping out of university after a year a decade earlier, I'd longed to go back. I'd worked for eight years in the education system, but I wanted to be more than an assistant. I wanted to be a teacher. I applied to university (college for the Americans) and got in. Come September, after our family's UK adventure, I would start working toward my BA, one night class at a time.

On the day of our outing, Ellie dressed herself, complete with a rat's nest braid directly in front of her face and an enormous multicolored unicorn headband on top. She was proud of her hard work, and I was proud of the fact that my concern for what people would think ranked a one out of ten.

As we pulled into the busy Durdle Door parking lot, I worried we might not make it to the seaside after all. England's notorious dark clouds swirled overhead, threatening to pelt us with rain. Greg and I had visited the breathtaking site years ago, long before Ellie and Oscar had arrived, but I'd forgotten just how long the trek was from the parking lot up to the cliff's edge and down the other side to the rocky beach with the picturesque blue water. When I saw the hill, I grimaced.

I anticipated feeling irritated by my children whining about the walk up all the steps. Could it rain? Possibly.

But I let go of the idea that our adventure would be perfect, and we forged ahead, prepared to admit defeat and pack up our bags and battered hopes without a fight if things went haywire. It was okay not to know the outcome. I would survive. Flexibility and stuff.

In past summers, I'd taken day trips because I thought I had to, because I thought I needed to be the magic maker, the tradition protector, the joy facilitator, and the full-time obligation keeper. But that day, we trekked to the sea purely because we wanted to. Go me.

We made our way up the long, steep gravel path, the boys out in front, Ellie and me in the back. The sky began to gently spit on us. I crossed my fingers that the specks of water would stop. Eventually, we reached the top of the path and remembered why we'd decided to return to the Jurassic Coast in the first place. Holding the kids' hands with a death grip, I looked out over the cliffs across the stunning sea.

The bay was filled with bright blue water, boats, and optimistic swimmers. White cliffs cascaded down to the white pebble beach. A wide path wound its way along the crest and carried on for miles until it was out of view. Emerald grass stood tall on either side. Directly in front of us, 142 wonky steps led the way to Durdle Door, the gigantic limestone arch we'd come to see that sprouted out of the turquoise water.

I thought people were insane to be flip-flopping in the sea on such a chilly day, but then again, they were British, which meant they didn't feel the temperature like the rest of the human race. It was still a little gray overhead when we began our tight-gripped descent toward the white pebbled beach. Ellie looked up at me, nervous. I looked down at her, assured.

The farther we went down the steps, the more the clouds began to scatter and flee like they had never been there in the first place. By the time we reached the beach, it was a brand-new summer's day, not a cloud in the sky. It felt like we'd been transported to some kind of tropical destination. The fact that the kids weren't complaining felt like maybe we had entered the fifth dimension. If there had been wood within reach, I'd have knocked on it. "Can we play in the water?!" Ellie had asked eagerly.

We hadn't brought towels or bathing suits for the beach because the forecast was cold when we'd left home. We'd only planned to come down, take a few pictures, and leave. But the sun was perfect, so I accepted that we weren't perfectly prepared, and we stayed.

We rolled up our pant legs and set out to locate a resting spot. The unruly pebbles jabbed our feet as we made our way toward the sea and searched for a vacant sliver of beach. Apparently, all of England had had the same spur-of-the-moment idea that day. There were ill-prepared people everywhere: misfit families, starry-eyed couples, merry friends, single old men, and mischievous teenagers. Half of them sported underwear as they lay on the beach, soaked up the sun, or jumped into the water, seemingly in no hurry to go anywhere. Everyone appeared relaxed. Weirdly, I was, too.

We went to the water's edge and started to throw rocks in. Ellie laughed hysterically. She'd always gotten a little bit nutty around water. She loved to go in the backyard and play in the rain at home. She lived for studying drizzle on car windows and giddily watched storms from our front porch. And the kid jumped in puddles like it was an Olympic sport. Needless to say, five-year-old Ellie asked to swim in her undies that day. The past, uptight version of me would have said no because she'd have been stressed about Ellie getting her clothes wet, stressed about the time, stressed about looking underprepared, stressed about the fact that no one else was stressed. Instead, I said yes.

Oscar played by my feet. We splashed each other and built little pebble mountains. I watched him delight in the simplicity of rocks and water. We threw stones. The glee on his face melted me. I talked to him about the ocean and England and dinosaurs and how rocks are made and what animals the clouds looked like. Often, I longed for my three-year-old to talk back. But that day, I let that worry go and I opted for his simple presence.

Ellie was clinging to Greg, arms around his neck, legs around his waist. As he walked deeper into the sea, I heard them both cackle as the cold water washed over them. I watched them, unencumbered by bags, or tears, or towels, or expectations, or a scowl on my face, or the stress in my voice.

I breathed in the fresh sea breeze. The tension my body usually held wasn't there. In its place? Ease. Joy. Was this delight what I'd been missing while I'd clung to my expectations all these years? Regardless, being present for the sight of my family in front of me was like medicine to my weary soul.

I'd spent so much time surviving, fixating on getting it "right," that I often struggled to see what was directly in front of me. I hadn't been able to conceptualize a time when I'd feel light again, unburdened by to-do lists or my own failings. I had spent so long trudging up the daunting hill of motherhood, looking down at unpredictable terrain, fretting over my lagging pace and the ache in my legs—always fearing the impending doom that might be waiting for us on the other side of the cliff or in the clouds up above. The stress just made motherhood harder. It robbed me of so many moments, too.

In doing so, I failed to both show up for my kids how I wanted to and missed out on the beauty around me.

Ironically, letting go is what helped me to pay attention to what matters most. That's when I quit force-feeding myself patience and try-hard stamina. That's when the slow trek toward regulation and presence actually progressed. As it turns out, real regulation can't be manufactured. It takes work from the inside. Noticing the icebergs had helped me notice the sunshine. Hearing my own voice had helped me to hear my kids' laughter. I began to experience the goodness of mothering again. And more? I realized I knew more than I gave myself credit for. In fact, I began to suspect that the answers I'd been looking for everywhere else might have been inside of me all along.

20

Rainbows

Four months later, when Grandma Pearls came to visit, she brought gifts. And I don't just mean the gift of her presence, the roast dinners, afternoon childcare breaks, and early-morning "Let's let Mommy and Daddy sleep longer" operations. Beyond all that, she brought physical gifts. One of the gifts was a book for each of the kids. Anyone with a brain knows you need to bring two of everything to two-kid houses.

They were personalized books, the ones with the name of the child as the main character. The storyline went like this: Santa comes to your house and he's in trouble; he needs *you* to help save Christmas, and because of *you,* magic in the world is restored. Obviously, the books were a slam dunk with both kids. Every day for a week we read the stories to the kids at bedtime—many times over. They giggled along, never getting sick of the same story. I am telling you, there are books that will be seared into my brain until the end of time for this reason. Repeat, repeat, repeat. Not too dissimilar from the work I had been doing with Oscar for nearly two years of speech therapy.

At three and a half years old, my sweet, sensitive, and smart little boy was still struggling to speak. I had yet to hear him utter his own name, never mind speak up at preschool. We communicated with a combination of single syllable sounds, sign language, and picture communication systems by then. Our strategies were better than nothing, but the back and forth, the depth, the questions, and the ease? It was nonexistent.

Twice a week we went to therapy, and multiple times a day, every day, we practiced his sounds. Sometimes he would learn a new word, say it once, and then not say it again for many months. He would say two sounds—but couldn't pair the sounds together to make one small word. When we weren't practicing, I was on high alert—prepared to problem solve or translate for anyone who might need to know what he was saying.

During Grandma Pearls's visit, she watched as I continued Oscar's regular speech therapy with him. I saw the sadness in her eyes as she bore witness to his struggle. Alongside my own progress, I was still wound in a knot of anxiety that Oscar might never speak. I'd poured myself into helping my son and already begun preparing for what kindergarten in September might look like.

My thoughts constantly revolved around his future while I navigated the present and felt unsure if any of it was enough. I was full of grief over the questions that never got asked on car rides, over his concerns that never got addressed, the nursery rhymes I never heard him sing, and the jokes I never got to laugh at.

ON THE SEVENTH NIGHT OF Grandma Pearls's visit, after I'd read *Oscar Saves Christmas* approximately one billion times, I snuggled into his bed and told him I would read it one last time. He pretended to read along, mimed the action words, laughed on cue, and pretended to be surprised by the storyline, again.

And then, I heard him say something that was more than just a sound. Something else came out of his mouth. There were two syllables—and that was a big deal, especially if he could say them close together. There were a handful of two-syllable words or sounds that he'd mastered in therapy. One particular word, "open," he had been practicing for months, and he had clearly said it earlier that week. The next day, he'd tried, but the progress was lost.

So, I asked him to say the word he'd just uttered with delight again.

"Osss . . . kaaa," he said, in the sing-song voice I'd been reading the book in. He pointed to himself as the word came out with a big goofy grin. I tried to maintain normalcy.

"One more time, bud. I want to make sure I am hearing you correctly," I said with a hope-filled smile. I wanted to cheer, scream, or yell, "You did it!" But I didn't want to overreact or pressure him.

"Os-kaaa," he said, beaming.

He said his name! My heart all but exploded. For the first time in three and a half years, my son spoke his name. Progress was possible. He did it!

I called downstairs to Greg, Ellie, and Grandma Pearls. They ran up the stairs, and I tried my best to act cool. "Say it again, bud!" I said. "Oskaa," he said, beaming in shy adoration of himself. I pulled him in, wrapping his little body in my arms and telling him how proud of him I was. I looked to Grandma Pearls and then to Greg, and that's when I broke.

My eyes filled with tears as the past few years flickered in my mind like a movie. I saw him in the back of the car silently staring out the window as I asked about his day. I saw him at the zoo, frantically gesturing at something and then screaming in frustration when I didn't guess what he was pointing to. I pictured countless meltdowns where I held him tight, trying to regulate the storm of emotions. I saw him looking to me with tears in his eyes at the park when other children were ignoring him.

I saw him practicing in therapy, frustrated and sad. I saw him in the hospital bed when he'd been sick for days, unable to tell us how he felt. I pictured us building snap cubes together, silently, wondering what he was thinking about. I saw us playing with dinosaurs and me doing all the talking during pretend play. I saw myself combing through articles online, emailing specialists, and begging for answers while friends told me not to worry.

At the dinner table I pictured him eager to share a story with the rest of the family, realizing he couldn't. I saw him on Halloween, making noises instead of saying "trick or treat," and on his birthday, signing "thank you" instead of speaking it. I noticed others looking at him endearingly while I felt an ache for his voice. I squeezed him tight and told him I loved him before saying goodnight. I paused at the door and glanced back, with equal parts pride and hope.

In the weeks and months that followed, Oscar began to verbalize new sounds and say words that we didn't know he thought. He even recalled memories from years past when he couldn't speak. The work remained difficult, but it was effort we could finally see the benefits of. Finally, we got to know what was inside of his genius little head.

I eventually realized I'd worked double time in hopes of helping my son to speak. When you have a kid with extra needs, it makes finding the line between motherly sacrifice and maternal neuroticism even harder. It's easy to let our kids' progress become the yardstick for our worth, feeling like we're carrying their future in our banana-peel hands. Worry and hypervigilance become your trusty sidekicks, taking the wheel for so long that you don't even realize it's happening.

Oscar's progress helped me to further ease my impulse to stop breathing whenever uncertainty loomed overhead. You don't realize just how long you've been holding your breath until you finally breathe again.

Motherhood hadn't become all sunshine and rainbows by any stretch of the imagination. But there was sunshine and there were rainbows—and I needed them for what was ahead.

21

Dishes

Wearing my oversize-Lululemon-sweatshirt-leggings-and-mom-bun uniform, I walked onto campus on that first crisp September evening, feeling like some kind of academic phoenix rising from the ashes of mom life. My major? Sociology. The class? The only one available on the evening that I could make it out of the house: Sociology of Sexuality and Gender.

That first class went by in a blur. I was like a kid in a candy shop, ready for my brain to activate again. A few weeks later, we got to the goods. I took my seat alone near the front, like the devoted, hard-of-hearing mature student that I was. Unlike my fellow students, I was stoked to be in class. They simply could not appreciate how wonderful the outside world was when you've been nap trapped and perpetually splattered in bodily fluids of some kind for five years.

"In the home you grew up in, who had two parents?" the professor asked.

I looked around the auditorium packed with early-twenty-somethings who probably hadn't heard the words "mommy come wipe my bum" that day, and three-quarters of them put up their hands.

"Keep your hands raised if you have two parents who work outside the home," the professor said. Most of them did.

"Keep your hands raised if both parents do an equal amount of the chores at home," the professor went on. Most of them put their hands down. *Shocker.*

"Raise your hands if it's your mom that does most of the work at home," she went on. Most of the kids put their hands up. I say kids, because there were only three of us who looked a day over twenty-five and the professor was one of them.

"Statistically, women are more likely to carry two-thirds of the unpaid labor at home, even if they work outside the home," the professor told us.

"Tell us something we don't know," I whispered under my breath. The two young cool-looking girls sitting to my immediate left looked over and laughed. I'd said it louder than planned.

"Sorry, I'm a mom," I said.

"Awwwww," one of them replied, looking at me like I was a cuddly mama polar bear in the zoo with cubs at my feet.

Their names were Annie and Farah. To my delight and surprise, each week when I went back in my ratty sweatshirt and leggings, they smiled and waved me over. I wondered if they'd picked me as their third wheel as some kind of sick joke. Were they writing down all the cringey millennial things I said so they could cackle at them with their roommates after class? Maybe I was a social experiment. Regardless, I soaked up every second of their Gen Z gossip that had nothing to do with laundry or where paper towels were on sale. Those few hours each week were a gift.

We continued to learn about how society decides what jobs people should do based on their gender.

"The gendered division of labor is the systematic allocation of different tasks, responsibilities, and roles in society—based on gender. Women are often expected to handle unpaid domestic work and caregiving while men are typically associated with paid labor outside the home. It reinforces traditional gender roles, leading to economic, social, and psychological disparities between men and women."

That's a mouthful. Economic, social, and psychological disparities. Sounds dramatic, I thought. But every time I saw or talked to my mom friends, the level of exhaustion they felt *was* dramatic. Like my coworker Laura, who worked full-time as a teacher, just like her husband. He cut the lawn and repaired the cars, but she did everything else at home. His jobs were more occasional and nonessential for keeping everyone alive and functioning. His jobs also just so happened to be the kind he could do *solo*. Meanwhile, her tasks were . . . the opposite? She was responsible for doing all the daily tasks that kept the family alive and their worlds turning—often with two kids at her feet. "We didn't decide it would be like this, it just happened," she'd said to me. Doing everything just "happened" to a lot of moms I knew.

My friend Ashley, who'd once told me being a stay-at-home mom made her happy and that leaving her husband home with the kids so she could go out felt like too much work, had recently confided that she was unbearably lonely and not sure who she was anymore.

Mostly, I thought of Bianca, who'd gotten married and supported both herself and her husband financially while maintaining their home while he was unemployed. When his career finally took off and they had babies, she continued to care for the house and the kids like she always had, assuming her traditional gender role. One day I texted her.

ME: Want to come over for tea one night this week?

BIANCA: Sorry I can't. Life has been so busy lately. I can't catch a break and there is no one to watch the kids.

ME: Can their father watch them?

BIANCA: No, he doesn't really babysit.

INSIDE LIBBY: You mean, watch his own kids?

OUTSIDE LIBBY: *Really? Oh.*

BIANCA: Yeah. He works so much, and plays a lot of hockey, too. He's busy and isn't involved at home with the kids. He doesn't do diapers or anything, says it's my job. Honestly, it's too much work to figure out childcare.

I was shocked. I knew lots of women carried the majority of the work at home, but I didn't realize it was stopping them from having a life.

Over the years my friend became less involved in her own aspirations, interests, and even our friendship. I rarely heard from her and she left the workforce, too. A few kids and a few years later, she found out her breadwinner husband had been cheating—for the whole marriage. He'd not only advanced in his career but was also in control of all their money and used that power dynamic over her during the separation. He took everything. She had to start all over again. I wanted to castrate him.

Years after their separation, she was still fighting to get a fair cut while trying to build a new career and life as a single mom. Then she was diagnosed with an autoimmune disease that is highly linked to chronic stress. Her own body, overwhelmed and confused, had started attacking itself, mistaking healthy cells for threats. The result was constant inflammation, relentless fatigue, unpredictable flare-ups, and a body that no longer felt like her own. Every day became a balancing act between managing her symptoms, maintaining her strength, and holding together the life she was fighting so hard to rebuild.

My friends were textbook examples of *economic, social, and psychological disparities . . . physical ones, too.* I learned that chronic stress and emotional suppression in women lead to plenty of physical health conditions like migraines, hormone imbalances, digestive issues, and autoimmune disorders. *That checks out,* I thought.

In class, the conversation expanded beyond women's roles in the proverbial kitchen. I learned how plenty of jobs, including bank tellers, teachers, and office administrators, used to garner higher wages and higher respect when they were fields that were male dominated. When those same jobs became "women's work," the roles were deemed less valuable and it lowered the rate of pay.

Work that women do is seen as less valuable whether it's paid or not. Statistically, the domestic work women do adds up to an extra five years of work over their lifetime on average compared to men. Whether the moms I knew worked outside of the home or not, the majority carried most of the load at home and felt invisible doing it. People don't appreciate how many balls you are juggling until the balls start getting dropped.

I certainly didn't understand the disparity of expectations between genders until I railed against them. It was when I'd begun to lower my expectations that I noticed how much higher they were for women to begin with: the small, constant ways Greg was praised for things I was just assumed to take responsibility for, the adoring looks he got when he took the kids to the park, the applause he got for doing the dishes. Gender norms explained why I was "lucky" he folded his own laundry but I was expected to fold everyone's. No one batted an eye while I put my career aspirations and basic needs on hold so I could run the house for five years while my husband worked. But when I went back to university for one night a week? I was "lucky."

Our social conditioning explained why moms who grabbed McDonald's for dinner were "lazy" but McDonald's dads were "fun." Dads get a gold star for taking kids to appointments, but moms are seen as selfish if they can't get the day off work to do the same thing. What moms are expected to do, dads are exceptional for doing.

Moms are seen as *naturally* gifted at organization, multitasking, dishes, housework, and caretaking, and dads get a free pass. Listen, if you call shoving everything into a closet because I don't have time to put it away before company comes over *natural*, then sure, I'm a natural organizer. Otherwise, I call BS.

My new friend Rachel helped me feel confident in this assertion. We met in the parking lot of our kids' preschool. She invited our family over for a BBQ the following weekend. When we arrived, there were toys all over the backyard and the kids ran off to play. She didn't apologize for the mess. Her husband cooked frozen burgers and served them on paper plates with a bagged salad on the side.

"This is so refreshing," I said to her.

"What? Burgers on paper plates! We aren't fancy," she replied, laughing.

"No, I mean, coming somewhere that I don't have to pretend to have my life together. Spending time with another family where the husband *actually* parents and participates at home."

"Hey, they're his kids, too!" Rachel said. The men were playing with the kids on the trampoline while we drank our tea on the porch.

My new friend made me realize how long I'd been mothering around well-meaning women who unintentionally contributed to my feeling like I had to keep up and carry it all—the dinners where the men almost never entered the kitchen, the holiday planning that almost never included men in the chat, the beach days where moms were on high alert while dads had a beer. Despite having an involved partner, in groups it was easy to fall into the norms. Being around another family like ours started to shift what I saw as normal.

I knew I had it better than lots of moms, but I began to see just how low the bar was for men in general, and how pressured I felt to carry on like it wasn't.

Despite being burned-out, many of the moms I knew made excuses for their partners doing jack all at home and playing golf or video games all weekend. Women were constantly referred to as nags or the old ball and chain and were simultaneously expected to be the household project manager. The most essential work at home to keep our lives afloat and bolster our families' ability to thrive seemed to be the exact things that limited *our* ability to thrive as moms.

"Feminism has helped change the laws and some of the social expectations, but there is a long way to go still," my professor said near the end of one of our classes. Feminism? According to people in my churchy or traditional circles, feminists were just angry, radical, bra-burning women who hated men, wanted to kill their babies, and wanted to take over the world.

But the feminism I was learning about took shape because women were being oppressed and simply wanted the rights men had. Things like being seen as whole human beings who can vote and work. The feminists we learned about simply wanted to level the playing field, regardless of gender, so that everyone could have fair treatment and opportunities regardless of what was between their legs.

Feminists aren't encouraging girls to be boss babes who refuse to put on an apron and cook dinner. They are giving a voice to people who, for centuries, have been told there is only one way to be. Feminists want social change so that women have rights and *don't* have to burn their bras or have to scream to be heard. Feminists don't just want what's best for girls, they want what's best for everyone—and that requires changing how people think about and treat people of all genders.

Like with any label, the word "feminism" seemed to come with baggage and misunderstanding. The people of faith I knew said the word like it was dirt in their mouths—like feminists were a symbol of everything that was wrong with the modern world. But then my friend Krista handed me a copy of *Jesus Feminist* by bestselling author Sarah Bessey, and the stories inside shifted my perspective. Turns out, there were plenty of women in the Bible who did kick-ass things—who led, taught, and challenged injustice with courage and love. I started to wonder, *What other Jesus-y truths had been toned down, twisted, or blown out of proportion by the church subculture I'd been immersed in?*

Regardless, I came to understand that at its core, feminism is the belief in equality. And that's something I could get behind. As I began to see it, I couldn't separate feminism from my desire to see our work as moms—whether paid or unpaid—as valuable. Eve Rodsky, author of the *New York Times* bestseller *Fair Play,* calls the gendered division of labor "the last frontier of feminism." Because while we have the right to work, being paid less and supported less make attaining equality pretty hard. When having babies means women's financial, emotional, physical, and social lives are radically altered and men's remain nearly intact, that is not equality—no matter how many "rights" we have.

Equality isn't just about getting to work in the same office as men, but also about having an equal opportunity to sit down like your partner and eat the steaming soup you prepared without getting up fifty times while it gets cold. It's the equal opportunity to go out with friends without having to write a step-by-step guide for your partner called How to Look After Your Own Damn Kids. The right to work only gets you so far when childcare, paid leave, and other systems in place make working harder for women than for men. The "choice" to stay home becomes less fulfilling when you find out you aren't deserving of a break because of it.

Before our semester ended, Annie and Farah invited me to their study session for our final exam. I took a break from our studies to grab some lunch, and when I returned, they were filming themselves . . . dancing? *Weird,* I thought. But I like weirdos. I could never film myself dancing, never mind in public like that. But good on them.

They caught me watching.

"TikTok," Annie said.

"It's a dance," Farah added.

Their arm movements *did* look alarmingly similar to clock hands, so I concluded that TikTok was a clock dance and moved on with my life. We finished our study session later that day and a few weeks later I passed my exam with flying colors. The semester ended with my mind turning, eager to start the next course, a little sad that I wouldn't be getting my Gen Z fix with Annie and Farah over the break and feeling a little less guilty about going back to school in the first place. Maybe I wasn't the lucky one for having a partner who provided and was involved with his kids. Maybe he was the lucky one.

A FEW WEEKS LATER I hosted a Christmas potluck for a group of our friends and their families. There were easily forty people, and I loved the hustle and bustle. Every family had brought a dish or two. By every family, I mean every mom. We, the moms, had planned a simple but fun gift exchange for the twenty-some-odd kids among us. We, the moms, warmed the food up in time, supervised the kids, executed the gift exchange, and then made the coffee. We, the moms, did all the things nobody overtly discussed doing because we, the moms, were used to doing that.

Once the food and gift shenanigans were over, the men went back to the sunroom to hang out, the kids continued playing, and the moms sat in the dining room trying to drink our coffee. The dishes were waiting. And I, newly irritated by the normalcy of men checking out on such occasions, waited, too.

I watched my friend stand up and head for the kitchen. The same friend had cooked two separate side dishes for our Christmas potluck, purchased and wrapped three gifts on behalf of her children, coordinated her family in ugly Christmas sweaters; she'd also helped serve the meal, supervised the kids, and also made the coffee.

"I'm going to get started on the dishes," she said.

"No, you don't need to do that," I said.

I didn't want to make the dishes an issue, but it was our party, too, I thought. A fire had been lit in my belly and I'd been losing the ability to shrug off moments like this. Now I could see that what was happening was part of a much bigger problem. I considered saying I would do it because it was my house and she needed to take a break. But truthfully, I needed to take a break, too.

"The guys can do the dishes. They've been chilling this whole time," I suggested. The women looked at one another in half agreement and bewilderment. My friend looked at me, uncomfortable. She didn't want to rock the boat.

"It's honestly no big deal. It's fine," she insisted. But it wasn't fine. Just because it was normal didn't make it fine. My desire to drink my coffee with my friends was bigger than my desire to stay likable to all the men drinking beer. Greg did the dishes in our house a lot, but I knew that the pressure of doing what other men do is real, because the pressure of doing what other women do is strong, too. I asked myself how things would ever change if no one changed. Then I got up.

I walked to the sunroom and said, "Hey, boys, could you do the dishes tonight?"

They looked at me, trying to figure out if I was joking. I didn't laugh. Then they looked at one another as if to say, *What are you guys going to do?* A few of the other moms came in to talk to their partners.

I went back to drink my coffee. Soon after, the husbands did the dishes together. Did all the men participate? No. Did all the women agree with me? No. Did the dishes get done perfectly? No. Did we change the course of gender norm history at group functions with one single potluck? Certainly not. Changing social norms would take a lot more than one awkward conversation. But did we get to drink our coffee hot? Yes. Yes, we did.

22

The Contract

Mothers have martyred themselves in their children's names
since the beginning of time. We have lived as if she who disappears
the most, loves the most. We have been conditioned to
prove our love by slowly ceasing to exist.
What a terrible burden for children to bear—
to know that they are the reason their mother stopped living.

—GLENNON DOYLE

Is dancing in public a thing now? Like planking?

A few months had passed since the potluck. It was almost spring break in 2020, and I was running a reading group at the back of the seventh-grade class where I was working that day. I turned to see some girls in the corner dancing. I was also close to the end of my second semester at university. I'd taken two night classes this time, with the newfound knowledge that I wasn't brain-dead after having children like I worried I might be.

"What are you doing?" I asked the girls.

"We're practicing a dance. It's from TikTok," they replied.

"I thought TikTok *was* a dance. You're saying it's *from* TikTok?" I asked.

They laughed in unison, confirming my suspicions that I was officially older than the trees they'd climbed in first grade.

One of them explained, "It's an app with trends, songs, and sounds where you learn dances, post them, and other people copy them."

"Ohhhh . . . so random people can see these dances?"

"Yup!" another girl chimed in, proudly.

"You shouldn't go on there. It's not safe," I said, hearing myself sound like a lecturing grandma.

Then spring break came, and with it, the shocking news: a mystery virus, rising death tolls, tent hospitals in China, New York on lockdown. Schools shut down for two weeks—an extra break, school officials said. *We'll take the chance to slow down,* I thought. A few days later, I decided to find out for myself what TikTok was all about.

The first video I saw was of a couple doing a synchronized dance like the ones I'd seen the girls do. *Cute*. Then, a funny skit. Then, cute animals. Then, a grown man in his truck having a lip sync battle with another creator. *What is this nonsense?! Someone please explain this to me!*

This . . . was not Instagram, my favorite app to scroll when I wanted to feel like an ugly, boring, good-for-nothing mother. This was not Facebook, where I went to compare how I was doing in life next to people I'd met once at a Christmas party in 2009, or where I learned of the peculiar opinions of people I used to respect. This was different. And there was much less dancing than I thought there would be.

Within a few days, the algorithm had figured me out. For the first time in my life, I could relate to people on the internet. I felt seen. Suddenly I wasn't the only mom I knew with complex childhood trauma, an offbeat funny bone, or an appetite for social discourse. Other adults were silly like me and wanted to discuss the things I was actually interested in? People were doing silly dances and saying all the stuff no one says out loud? That's a big yes from me. *These are my people,* I thought.

TikTok was the perfect distraction from what felt like the world falling apart. The first video I posted was an abomination to the app and I've since deleted it for the sheer level of cringe and poor lip-syncing that made no sense. (You're welcome.) I tried to learn dances and failed miserably, so I pivoted and attempted other things. Eventually, I found subject matter that I was passionate about: motherhood. I shared about how I cried in the bathroom, how the kids never stopped asking questions, how lonely the job felt, and how hard it really was. Relatable mom content became my thing, and I decided that TikTok would be my little corner of the internet where nobody in my real life would find me. That is to say: I had no concept of the beast that is TikTok.

As @diaryofaweirdmom, suddenly, I wasn't alone. My comments section filled with moms who, like me, were ready to check in to either a mental hospital or a monastery. The women were tired of Pinterest moms who swore that making sensory bins was fun and easy when we all knew they took sixty-seven hours to prepare and six seconds to destroy. The moms were tired of being told to enjoy every moment. The more I shared, the more confirmation I got that everything my professor was talking about regarding the impact that gendered expectations had on moms was more far-reaching than I could have imagined.

My comments section shed light on the lived reality of other moms. Of particular interest were the American moms who got diabolically inhumane amounts of unpaid maternity leave and even less social support than we did as Canadians.

I went back to work a week after giving birth because I couldn't afford to take more time off and I can't keep up. I felt like a horrible mom.

I gave up my career to raise my children, but my husband just left me, and I have no way to support myself. I have a ten-year career gap and nothing to show for it.

My employer told me that since I became a mom, I didn't give 110% anymore and overlooked me for a promotion. I've worked so hard to get here. I even came back after five weeks when I could have taken longer. Now I can't even afford daycare.

I haven't had a break from my kids in four years, but my husband goes out every other night after work.

We lost our house because we didn't have enough money to pay for unexpected medical bills for our special needs child.

My whole paycheck goes to childcare. I want to stay home but we can't afford it. I am the only one with medical insurance in our household.

WHAT THE FUCK, USA?!

Thousands of women started pouring into my inbox every single day, telling me that they felt lost, broken, completely drained, and unable to take breaks. They felt stuck. It really wasn't just me. Our collective conundrum confirmed everything I'd learned in the class I'd just finished. The primary data was at my fingertips. Deep in the pandemic trenches, amid an influx of content that highlighted the very real burnout epidemic of mothers, it was clear: As a maternal collective, we were not well.

But wait. What do kids need most? Emotionally regulated parents who are present. I thought we would all begin to agree that moms need more support. Surely, we were all equally stunned by how the system was breaking women and the effect it had on their children. The pandemic was making clear, so surely, we have to agree something needs to change!

I accepted that not everyone was in the online bubble I occupied. There were a lot of problems in the world. But the lack of care for mothers in general became more glaringly obvious by the day. Instead of the support I anticipated when I shared about my mental health or the mental load, I received angsty judgment—and not just from men or childless people.

Stop complaining and get back in the kitchen.

I feel sorry for your kids having a mother like you.

You wouldn't be so depressed if you loved your kids.

I raised six kids. It's not that hard.

Women and men from all walks of life were triggered by my honesty or vulnerability. I learned for the first time what it's like to arm-wrestle internet trolls. Let me tell you: It is not fun. Among many seething, hurtful comments on my videos, there was always some variation of this: *Well, you signed up for this.*

Did I, Chad? Really?

OVER THE COURSE OF THE next year and a half, my desire to have fun on TikTok and show up as my unfiltered self transformed into a deeper desire to be honest about my experiences in motherhood so I could show moms everywhere they weren't alone. I changed my handle to @diaryofanhonestmom and joined Instagram, too.

For every single "you signed up for this" comment, there were hundreds of women saying, "I can't do this anymore," "Thank you for saying this," and "You're the first person to put words to what I've been too afraid to say out loud."

One day, after reading my comments section, I'd had enough. I sat on the edge of the bed with my messy mom bun and recorded a spur-of-the-moment video rant about the rage that moms feel. I was tired of women being pathologized for being angry when it was clear that there was a 75,000-foot mountain of worthy reasons to be pissed. As soon as I posted it, the comments swelled:

> Exactly this, please send it to all the husbands.
>
> Signed, a mom that's DONE.

A few months later, I got an email from the producer of the *Tamron Hall Show*. They'd seen the video, and they wanted me to come to New York and talk about it on the show. Me? Talk about mom rage on *live* national television? This must be a mistake.

A few weeks later, Greg and I flew to New York. We were picked up in a shiny black car from our all-expenses-paid hotel and driven to the studio. The makeup artists covered my face in full glam, and I waited backstage in a long-sleeve white bodysuit and forest green polka dot skirt. I paced the small square floor of the green room with my name on it and told myself not to stress-eat all the snacks they provided while Greg and I waited.

When it was my turn, the producers cued me up. I walked on stage like a high-profile weekday morning television appearance was a completely normal thing for a regular sleep-deprived mom from small-town Canada. In reality, I was sweating. A lot. While filming my segment, the producers played my TikTok video that had since accumulated more than 1.4 million views.

> Maybe it's not [air quotes to convey supreme sarcasm] "mom rage." Maybe it's "mom is doing everything for everyone and having less of her needs met than anyone else in the house, all while society tells her to calm down and shut up because this is motherhood and you chose this" anger. That anger is valid and necessary. We need to stop treating moms' anger as if it's a mental health issue. Moms are allowed to be angry about things that are unfair and unequal. A lot of us are tired and resentful for good reason. And society has given us an impossible standard to achieve. Work like you have no kids and mother like you don't have a job. Carry the entire mental load, be the default parent, and never need a break. Simultaneously having all the work, you will be undervalued by society and the people in your house. And then be gaslit by society into making you feel like you are overreacting for being upset. You are upset because you're exhausted, and you are tired because it's tiring. It's not a character flaw—it's a social issue that needs to be fixed.

Tamron wanted to know if I was surprised by the response to the video. I told her that I was not. Then I told her some version of this: Nearly two years had passed since I'd started sharing about all the hard parts of motherhood. Moms are tired of doing everything for everyone. Moms are tired of being expected to hold all the cards and stop complaining when it is literally breaking them. We've got good reason to be mad, and being treated like we don't makes us even angrier.

Society needs to do better. If there was anything I was certain of, it was that my head was attached to my body and that moms were fucking pissed.

"THERE MUST BE SOMETHING IN THE WATER," my pastor would joke on Sunday mornings, six years before I landed myself on live television. The congregation would all laugh along like the sentiment explained our fertility and zest for scrumptious babies. I'd thought our baby parades were evidence of the joy and fulfillment that motherhood would bring.

And certainly, they were. But now, I could see the baby parades as something else. A foreshadowing of what so many modern mothers come to experience: hollow applause, impossible ideals, and the unspoken expectation that we'd sacrifice ourselves until there was barely a self even left. The parades may have looked a lot like pedestals back then. But now, they looked more like empty cardboard boxes.

I spoke with Dr. Sophie Brock, a motherhood sociologist and researcher, and she confirmed my suspicions: There *was* something in the water. Just not what the pastor thought.

In my conversation with Dr. Brock, she unpacked the damaging effects of what she calls the "perfect mother myth"—the pervasive and completely bonkers idea that there is one perfect way to be a good mom. It's the conflicting and unrealistic expectations that literally none of us can fulfill anyway.

You know: the "natural-birth-only, breastfeeding, meet-all-the-kids'-incessant-needs-while-ignoring-yours, organic-vegetable-steaming, crafty, be-fun-and-don't-forget-your-mother-in-law's-birthday-gift" mom. You've got to look like a Stepford wife, but don't let anyone see you trying too hard—*that's unnatural!*

Of course, the definition of "perfect" is always changing, too. So, we best stay up-to-date! Aspire! The messages weren't even always as explicit as the ones I'd been hearing at church: *Motherhood is the most amazing thing that will ever happen to you* or *Being a mom is the most fulfilling thing you will ever do.*

The cultural norms around what make a good mom are everywhere. We're fed messages about what motherhood is from all angles, what it looks and feels like, what's acceptable and what's not. These "perfect mom" memos are woven into the stories we read, the films we watch, the TV shows we're obsessed with, the conversations we have online and in our parents' living rooms every day. We don't even realize it's happening because it's always happening. We're literally swimming in it.

We're told to do well not to *be* well. Performance, perfection, and achievement. Strive for excellence in academics and sports. Stay busy. Buy bigger, go faster, be shinier, and make sure you downplay the work so that it looks easy.

These relentless, powerful messages don't just exist in our group chats or in the shame we carry for not measuring up—they shape the very culture, systems, and structures we interact with every day. They influence public institutions in ways that often reveal how little we collectively value motherhood—determining who matters, whose time and skills are valued, and ultimately, who gets to thrive versus who moves through the world with a five-ton weight around their ankle.

I considered Eve Rodsky's words: "We treat men's time like diamonds and women's like sand." I had. Despite Greg being a better partner and dad than many of his peers, despite his telling me not to shush the kids while he rested or plan my life around his needs, I did it anyway. I focused on his need for sleep because without consciously acknowledging it, his shut-eye seemed more important than mine—even though I was the one spending most of my waking time raising actual humans.

I felt grateful when he took the kids out alone. I felt bad when I left him home with the same kids and responsibilities I had every day. So many of the things I did to care for my family I contorted into acts for myself. I squashed and molded my life, my hopes, dreams, my Costco trips, my evening walks, and career choices around his, just like women have been doing for men for centuries. Then, when I was breaking or—goodness forbid—wanting more, I wondered what was wrong with *me*.

I'd been trying to fill my cup for years, not realizing that the society I was mothering in had handed me a Styrofoam vessel with a massive hole in it. Like the millions of women who began to follow me, I'd let the rigged system that was breaking me tell me my burnout was all my fault, instead of seeing and questioning the system itself.

It's not just moms paying the price—it's their kids, too. Kids need caregivers who aren't chronically stressed, who can be truly present and mentally well. But the very society that tells us to take care of ourselves is set up to get in the way of our ability to feel whole. The system is rigged.

My unplanned catapult into internet virality taught me that I wasn't crazy. Society might roll its eyes and side with internet trolls who say "you signed up for this," but when I decided to become a mother, I certainly don't remember agreeing to the fine print I was drowning in each day.

WHEN I FIRST CHOSE TO go back to university as a mom, the decision to pursue teaching came down to passion and convenience. Passion because I could use my story, experiences, and skills to make a positive impact on children. Convenience because the work hours fit into our family's lifestyle, my kids' needs, and Greg's unpredictable schedule. But by the time I graduated with a degree in sociology and accepted an offer to start the master's of education program, much had changed. The unexpected trifecta of my journey into trauma healing, late-in-life academia, and unplanned TikTok virality caused me to see the world through new eyes and finally ask myself what I really wanted.

Throughout my life, I'd often done what I thought everyone wanted of me, what made life easier for others or what I knew would please the masses. I put myself last because I wanted to be good. Now I just wanted to be honest. I no longer wanted to help kids by being their teacher. I wanted to help the people who have a more profound impact on children than anyone else on the planet: their moms.

It would be risky given that I had no idea how or if I would be able to create a stable income from my work online. But everything inside of me knew I had to take the leap. So, just weeks before my master's program began, I pulled my enrollment and quit my job as an educational assistant. I hired a web designer, got myself an agent, and told everyone in my life I'd changed my mind about becoming a teacher.

The truth is that I was sick of moms coming last and being told by everyone else what it means to be a good mom. I hadn't signed society's stupid contract, and it was time to stop living like I had. So, I set it on fire, rewrote my own contract, and invited other moms to do the same.

23

Gardening

Sharing my truth on social media gave me access to people and information I wouldn't have found otherwise. Niche people, like moms with complex trauma, highly sensitive children, British husbands, or people with a deep hate for pretend play. Okay—that last one was most moms. The online world confirmed that I was not crazy, helped me locate my people, and pointed me to resources in plenty of other categories of my life.

For example, I learned that there was a reason (outside of being a mother) that I was experiencing life as an overstimulated, distractable, impulsive, roller coaster of a human being at baseline. Moms discussing their ADHD on social media were the first ones to suggest that my ever-evolving passions, inability to wear itchy clothes, and deeply feeling nature weren't simply personality traits. My suspicions were later confirmed by the psychiatrist who asked, "How on earth have you been able to function up until now?!" and then promptly gave me a prescription for a stimulant that would reduce the noise in my ever-racing brain.

My ADHD diagnosis altered how I saw myself, which pushed

me to have some self-compassion for the ways I'd struggled to function for over thirty years. I gave myself more grace for my scattered brain and felt prouder of my creativity. Now I knew *why* I was such a basket case sometimes and a productive delight at other times. Score.

Another thing I didn't expect? To find other Christians who looked at the church and the state of our reputation as a group and thought WTF?! My relationship with God and the people who introduced me to Him had been a cornerstone of my life ever since I'd committed to not saying "fuck" so much back in my teenage hobby-farm-from-hell years.

The Christians I knew were loving, kind, gracious, and generous. They'd given me couches to sleep on when I had nowhere to go, warm meals, and prayers in the hardest times. Their actions hinged on what the most important part of our shared faith was: loving God and loving others. All these things made it easy to push my growing questions aside.

But the mind-boggling soapboxes of my fellow believers during Donald Trump's first term at the height of the pandemic made my questions harder to ignore. And not just regarding what women were supposed to be doing with their lives. But why did we give money, time, and pulpit energy to certain issues and not others? Why weren't gay people loved like everyone else? Why weren't the most loving people I know outraged about racism and poverty? Why did they advocate so hard against abortion rights, immigration, and sexuality but fall silent on gun violence, the mental health crisis, or child welfare? Why did they care so much about the "harm" done by trans communities and hardly bat an eye at harm done by clergy? Where was their passion for the common good, and why was everything about winning some kind of you-versus-me battle?! Were these really my people?

Years before the pandemic, before the word "feminism" entered my vernacular, I'd begun to critically examine the beliefs, messages, and practices I'd long held dear. But I often felt alone in my wonderings and ended up more confused and ashamed for asking questions.

But then, I watched Jen Hatmaker—a bestselling author who'd once been a fixture in Christian bookstores, whose work had carried me and countless other women—be shamed and cast out for affirming the LGBTQ community. And now, on TikTok, I found creators like Ashley DeSanno (@lotsamiles) and KC Davis (@domesticblisters) unraveling the current and past problems with our religion's ties to oppression and the hypocrisy that was rampant in our circles.

Other women, real people online, helped me feel safe to question, too. There was a term for what I was doing in figuring out what I really believed and why: deconstruction. Once again, I wasn't alone.

There was more to it than politics, too. "I learned from a young age that my heart was deceitful, sinful, and not to be trusted. It made me someone who felt like I was never good enough no matter how much I tried, but that I always had to try," one creator shared.

"I was taught to trust God no matter what. But it left me vulnerable to be taken advantage of by people who claimed to love Him and unable to listen to what my inner voice was telling me," posted another.

"*I give myself away, I give myself away, so You can use me*—lyrics from a worship song I used to sing. It's no wonder it's taken me until age forty-five to undo my martyr complex and struggle to say no," the next video pointed out.

For years, I'd heard these and countless similar messages on repeat. *Wait a minute,* I thought. *Did my unhealthy patterns and beliefs about myself come from my religious experiences, too?*

As it turned out, lots of Christian women spent their days under a cloud of shame for not measuring up, in a choke hold of over-commitment and servitude in the name of God. Self-erasure, as it turned out, was a common theme among us. *What am I teaching my kids?*

Over time, I realized that all those years ago, when I was so young and vulnerable, my desperation for connection and belonging had blurred my ability to decide for myself what I believed and how to live it out. I'd blindly suctioned to a faith community that gave me structure and some form of conditional acceptance but robbed me of my ability to trust my instincts and believe I was inherently good inside. I'd assumed they knew best.

I'd worked so hard to trust myself again. Now among a million other things, I knew that other people—even those with pulpits—didn't always know better.

Two things could be true. The people who loved and shaped me would forever hold a dear place in my heart *and* their messages messed with my head. They helped me *and* hurt me. Our religion has caused irreparable damage to plenty of groups of people *and* I still believe in a God who loves.

I could keep my faith in God *and* let go of what beliefs and labels were no longer mine. I no longer needed to rely on others to tell me what "loving others" looks like. As it turned out, my questioning was not a sign of flawed faith but a sign I was a human being with a brain.

Another two things: The community I found online made it safe to wonder *and* it terrified me to think that some of the very people I'd built my life around might not be my people after all.

IN PART, RECONNECTING WITH MYSELF over the course of the pandemic—locked in my house, away from the people and places that had once made me feel like I needed to contort myself into a box I did not fit—was a blessing. Swirling around the petri dish of my own thoughts, arm in arm with the women online who reminded me I was not alone in my motherhood struggles, my trauma, and my now-clear vision of how society screws us over, was exactly what I needed. The concoction of those circumstances boosted my confidence to be unapologetically and authentically who I was in the world.

Unfortunately, social media also gave me a megaphone to declare who I was to the world when I was just learning to listen to my inner voice myself. If I'd had any choice in the matter, this great awakening would not have coincided with being catapulted into the public eye. Eleven out of ten, do not recommend. (To the people who know me in real life—that must have been a confusing time for you. Whoops.)

My social media following was growing by the thousands daily, and I had absolutely no idea what that meant or how to deal with it. With pandemic-style homeschooling in the rearview mirror and both kids out the door by 8:30, I figured I would have more than enough time to be a content creator. Wrong. Each night I'd find myself inundated with work: answering droves of emails, responding to comments or DMs, editing content for a shifty brand that altered our collaboration timeline at the last minute, updating my website, preparing for a speech, looking up more terminology about the creator industry, learning how to run a small business.

I'd work until near midnight, when my eyes would no longer stay open, and then I'd get up and do it all again the next day. Everything about my work was new to me: the business lingo, the public speaking, the interviews, events, branding, websites, digital marketing, contracts, agencies, sponsorships, blogging, SEO, and PR.

Something else that was new to me? Being in such high demand to people who hadn't entered or exited my vaginal canal. Despite wanting to make sure the moms in my DMs were all seen and heard,

I couldn't keep up. Somebody needed something from me, always. If I had a battle with my people-pleasing and boundary-less ways before, now it was a full-blown war.

I'd never been popular, okay? In school, I moved so often, I rarely stayed long enough to make a couple friends, never mind excel into coolness. Prior to my internet explosion, I lived a regular life and *that* was already hard enough to manage. I was only just beginning to feel a sliver of balance at home as a mom, when my new life on social media spun back into a different brand of overwhelm—one that now involved thousands of unread notifications each day, and no way for my ADHD dopamine-seeking brain to prioritize them. Work–life balance? LOL.

I was invited to all kinds of events, from conferences to PR launches to influencer get-togethers. After being holed up at home with my fun-loving crotch goblins for four years, and then holed up at home during a pandemic for two more after that, putting on nice clothes and going out into the wide world sounded excellent. But that, too, was a lot.

The fanciness and the unspoken expectations made me feel like the new kid at a high school dance, where you don't know what to wear or where to stand or where to look or whom to talk to or if anyone really likes you. Cady Heron, anyone? Except somehow *lots* of people know you and plenty *about* you. Looking around, I thought, *I am not like the people who get invited here. I don't belong here.* And yet, I was there, at their tables and in their pictures tagged on social media. Some new people became amazing friends I have to this day.

Others wanted something from me: a tag, a shoutout, status, information, gossip, a business deal, or a connection. Like the business coach I met, who'd empathized with my struggle navigating this new world and offered to help me by talking to me once a week for two months—for the low price of $20,000. *Hard pass, Belinda.*

Or the agency that promised to look out for my best interests but tried to pressure me into promoting a gambling app to stay-at-home moms—even when they knew the whole intention of my platform was to help moms. "Oh, but you could frame it as self-care! It pays really well!" they said.

INSIDE LIBBY: Gambling as self-care? WHAT?! Hey, moms, I know you struggle to even take a shower without feeling like the worst mom on the planet, and you feel guilty because you couldn't afford to throw a special birthday for your kiddo, but I've got something for you! Just download this fucking app and sacrifice the money you don't have to gain an addiction that will make your life worse and steal away what little time you could otherwise spend on real self-care. Link in bio!

OUTSIDE LIBBY: No, thank you. I won't sacrifice the trust I have built with my community and their well-being, no matter how much they pay me.

I was inundated with new relationships with people who claimed to love me or stand with me or give me opportunities I'd never had before. But in exchange for what? The authenticity I'd worked so hard for? No, thanks, mate. I'd finally begun to see myself as a human outside of being solely a mom; I'd finally begun to know myself and be myself. Now, here I was in a brand-new career that everyone also glorified, wondering the very same thing I used to—am I a person to them?

THE BUSIER I BECAME, THE more I needed my real-life friends. But that, too, had become tricky. I wasn't just changing in private—letting go of the need to host every family holiday gathering, the urge to rage-clean my house, or let my kids show up to church in mismatching outfits with Nutella on their faces because I couldn't be bothered to fight them on wiping it off. I was changing in public, too—sharing my strong opinions on the interwebs for all to see. Balancing my passion for helping moms with my passion for not losing my people was not a skill I planned on needing.

The dynamics of my real-life relationships began to shift. It wasn't always big obvious conversations; often it was a slow backing away—family avoiding certain topics at get-togethers, friends being less vulnerable about their issues, acquaintances making less eye contact. People got weird with me in implicit, confusing ways that I tried hard not to read into but couldn't not. Some relationship tensions were more obvious.

Of particular note was my friendship with Rachel, the mom from preschool whose husband shared in parenting their children. After our BBQ family date, Rachel and I had become fast friends. What started off with a few coffee dates quickly moved to seeing each other multiple times a week, then to texting all day every day and oversharing everything from our pelvic floor health to our traumas to our love for cheese and fart jokes. Her friendship brought laughter and silliness to my life I'd long craved. My new friend seemed to understand me and align with me on more things than any one person ever had.

She was extremely thoughtful, too. During the pandemic, Rachel would deliver small gifts to entertain my kids and hot coffee to my doorstep to let me know she was thinking of me. She would send me messages telling me how amazing I was, how great my style was, how good of a mom I was. I'd never had such an adoring friend. Nor had I ever spent so much time with a friend. Was it that we were local? Was she just the perfect friend?

Rachel's overzealous compliments began to slowly morph into semi-mean jokes aimed at herself. I laughed along at first, being a fan of self-deprecation. But her jabs became bigger and then evolved into explicit comparisons between us that made me uncomfortable. The more I tried to offer compliments or reassurance, the more she would double down on herself.

When my life got busier with my internet explosion, all the previous little red flags multiplied. At first, she appeared to be my biggest supporter. But one day one of her comments left me feeling unsure.

"Oh look, you've got ten thousand followers, people who want to be just like you. Guess you don't need me now!" she said. I reassured her that nothing could replace online followers and that I needed her just as much. But small, questionable comments continued.

We still saw each other regularly—but it was no longer enough to satisfy her need to feel important in my life. When I would reach out, she started taking days to respond in what felt like an intentional punishment. Time would pass and then she would pretend everything was okay, or she'd ask why I didn't come after her more. Our friendship began to feel like a test that I couldn't pass. Like I was supposed to chase her to prove her significance in my life—but I couldn't even keep up with my day-to-day life. No matter how much reassurance I gave her, it wasn't enough. I decided it was time to talk.

"I'm sorry I've been so busy," I told her one day. "I hope you don't take it personally. I'm really drowning over here. I'm not sure what to say when you make comments about me not needing you. I try to show you that you are important to me. But I don't know what to do when you don't respond to me. This is hard for me to say, but sometimes, the way you communicate—or don't—really hurts. I'm trying really hard. I'm not sure what to do."

I took a deep breath, looked at her genuinely, and hoped to hear some kind of compassion or a suggestion on how we could work through our issues.

"I'm not sure what you are talking about. Do you even have proof that I do that? Maybe I am just busy. Obviously, you don't care about me as much as I care about you. Nothing I do is good enough. I don't know what you want from me," she replied.

I was shocked. I had to prove that she was wrong? What about everything else I'd said? I decided that instead of going back and forth in a "who did what," I would just set an expectation and boundary that I hadn't before. Maybe that would help. Clear communication. That's what I'd been working on in other parts of my life, too.

"I still want this friendship. But I cannot give as much as I once gave. I think it's important to have clear and healthy expectations. So, I would love to hang out once every week or two. I am excited to. Between my and Greg's schedule I can't do more than that—it's just not realistic for me. It's not personal. I'm just overwhelmed right now. I hope you understand."

"I guess I'm just not that important to you," she said.

I walked away feeling worse than when we'd begun the conversation, more confused, too. Little by little, I'd found myself feeling responsible for her feelings and self-esteem, like I said or did something wrong—no matter what it was. I went home with an old familiar feeling. Was I . . . crazy? Where had I felt like this before? Oh yeah. Mom.

SINCE BEGINNING MY HEALING JOURNEY, the tension I felt between who I was, what I needed, and the way I behaved with my mom had blared in my ear like a foghorn. I saw how much of my energy our relationship pulled from me and my kids.

The more I tried to advocate for myself and my needs, the more those boundaries got pushed, the more my insides screamed at me. Like when I asked her not to lament over her health concerns or family drama in front of the kids, now four and six years old—but the topics always ended up being broached anyway. I could get over that. But I'd also asked Mom not to pick up the kids because of her balance problems and my fear of an accident. It was a safety concern. But she would roll her eyes in frustration. Her dismissal of my boundaries always layered the guilt on thicker.

Mostly, I was concerned about my mom's inability to tell the truth. Throughout my life, I'd lost the ability to trust that my mom was being honest. I knew that this tendency came from her desire to be liked and accepted, to tell people what she thought they wanted to hear. I'd learned to take her words with a grain of salt—promises of gifts, trips, help, or behavior change. I'd accepted that this was part of who my mom was when it affected *me*. But when it came to my children, I drew a line.

"One of these days, you kids can come over here and we will have a slumber party! Wouldn't that be fun?!" Mom said to Ellie and Oscar one day around the kitchen table. The kids cheered.

I knew it wasn't possible. Later that day I talked to her. "Mom, please don't make false promises to the kids. They don't know any better. It's not fair to them and it's confusing."

I didn't want our kids to get their hopes up for anything that was not a reality—from birthday gifts to sleepovers and everything in between. I didn't want dishonesty modeled to them as an acceptable way of being. Mom promised she would change. But a few weeks later, it happened again—in an outright lie.

"Mom, Grandma told me not to tell you, but she is going to give us extra candy for Halloween," one of the kids said to me one day after a visit. It was innocent enough, but cultivating a trustworthy relationship with my kids, without secrets, was a core value of mine. I called her.

"Mom, please don't tell the kids to keep secrets from me. I want to trust my kids and have them trust me, too. If you continue to lie or normalize dishonesty, I won't be able to continue our relationship as it has been."

The words felt extreme. Guilt washed over me. Over time, I realized that I was enmeshed with my mom—a term I learned in therapy to describe when personal boundaries are so blurred that you lose sight of where you end and someone else begins. You often confuse their feelings with your own, taking on responsibility for them. I'd been doing it for years. And despite all the work I did to set boundaries, I couldn't help but feel the pull to go back to her. She was my mom, after all.

THERE ARE TWO MAIN PROBLEMS with listening to your inner voice. One: She always tells the truth. When you're living outside of your values or when your unmet needs are left dangling around, she doesn't shut up. Two: When you choose to heed her words, align your values with actions, and become your authentic self, the inner work eventually comes out. If it was up to Outside Libby, I'd have gone my merry way, lowering my expectations, and hoping my growth didn't bother anyone else. Unfortunately, it was not up to Outside Libby. Repairing my people-pleasing ways inevitably had to impact the very people I'd worked so long to please.

Despite the growth I'd experienced, it seemed I'd become stunted—suffocating under the overgrowth of other people's expectations. Like in a garden, they were blocking my sunshine and crowding my soil. I realized I had some gardening to do, some weeds and flowers to cut back. Begrudgingly, I grabbed my gardening tools and consciously let the inner work come out.

I tried hard to assert myself with kindness and clarity in many areas of my life. At home, I was more direct about my need to cook dinner without twenty-seven noises happening at once. At church, I stopped singing along to songs that made me feel like I was a piece of human garbage who could never get anything right. I said no to work commitments I used to say an obligatory yes to. I stopped volunteering when I was overloaded. I fought the pull to answer DMs all day and focused on my family instead.

I started leaning into what I loved and leaning away from what I didn't. I accepted help when I needed it. I stopped replying "Lol no worries" when I did in fact have many worries. I stopped saying yes when my body was howling a gut-wrenching no.

I did my best to show up as my authentic self, online and offline. With great gusto, I tried to stop apologizing for everything, to speak my truth without my voice shaking or becoming catatonic at the thought of disappointing people. My need to justify my every thought and action to the world began to dissipate. With practice, I honed the skill of communicating my needs. I stopped being a doormat.

Eventually, it became impossible to ignore the area of my life where I was the biggest doormat of all. One day when I was gardening out back, I agreed to let Mom watch Ellie and Oscar at our house. When I came inside, I asked how everything went.

"Great!" Mom said. "No big issues!" She looked at them with a sort of bemused look I'd seen before. They both nodded in agreement, smiling. I took her home later that day without issue. But that night, when I tucked up in bed with the kids after our story time, I asked again, "How did it go today with Grandma?"

One of them began to cry. "Grandma told us not to tell you because you would get really angry at us and at her . . . but we spilled a cup of water. She got angry and said if you found out we wouldn't be allowed to see her anymore!" they told me.

I was confused. Spilled water was not a concern to me. "Did the glass break? Did someone get hurt? Is there a stain?" I pressed gently, wondering what could possibly make me angry about spilled water. I kept my face calm, making sure they could tell I wasn't upset. "No, it was just a plastic cup of water," they said, timid.

"Thanks for telling me, sweetie. You aren't in trouble," I reassured them.

They both looked relieved.

I called Mom. "Did you tell the kids not to tell me about the spilled water?" I asked.

"No. That's ridiculous. I would never say that. It was just water, Libby. No need to get upset. This is exactly what I was worried about." Then she carried on about how everything was always her fault and how I was blowing it out of proportion.

"Mom, you know I don't get upset over spilled drinks. I'm upset that you lied to me. That you told the kids to lie to me. And that you made them feel like they would be responsible if their choice to be honest impacted how much they saw you! They are kids, Mom."

"I didn't say any of that. Are you sure they aren't making it up?" she said, clearly upset with me.

I took a breath. This was the moment I'd skirted around, time after time, for years. These were the moments when I made excuses and let my empathy override my knowing. I promised myself that if my boundary about telling the truth was crossed again, I would follow through. I had to follow through. After spending a lifetime feeling responsible for the happiness and well-being of the woman who had brought me into the world and raised me, I drew a line in the sand.

INSIDE LIBBY: Mom. I need a break. I can't keep doing this. I asked you to keep your word and to model honesty to my kids. This is the opposite of that. Please don't contact me. I will let you know if and when I'm ready to talk again.

OUTSIDE LIBBY: DITTO, GIRL.

I hung up the phone, feeling that familiar mix of guilt and pride that I'd come to know when being true to myself. I'd chosen my kids. I'd chosen my peace. I didn't bring up the conversation to my kids again. They held no responsibility. I ached for them and simultaneously knew it had been the right thing to do. Only time could tell if and when we would see Grandma again.

In the weeks and months that followed, enormous waves of grief washed over me. The kind that swallows you whole and makes you feel like you'll never be okay again. Who was I without her? I wasn't just grieving the end of my relationship with Mom, but the acceptance of what never was, what wouldn't be, and all the time and energy I'd poured into trying to force it to be.

As it turns out, protecting my children was the kick in the butt I needed to clear my throat and speak up about what I needed and what my kids deserved. Along with many other things, they deserved a mom who didn't let other people make her feel insane. I'd spent so long shape-shifting to be accepted, even by the very people who'd caused me harm, that I didn't realize how much I had been doing it—until I wasn't anymore.

My desire to give two shits about what most people thought continued to dissipate. I could see more clearly now than ever before. After multiple attempts to mend my relationship with Rachel in a healthy way that always seemed to get turned back around on me, I pulled away from her. I saw her manipulative behavior for what it was and recognized that my own desire to make her happy regardless was unhealthy, too. It takes two to tango. Allowing myself to chase her or try to prove something was no longer on my bingo card of life.

I mean, I did spend a hot minute lambasting myself for being drawn to the kind of people who confuse enmeshment for love. I stressed about my work life and all the new people pulling at me, wondering if I could ever trust my own judgment of humans again. But then I screwed my head on straight and reminded myself: unlearning takes time.

I didn't realize the box I'd crammed myself into until I stood up straight and my back stopped throbbing. Over time, the roller-coaster gut feeling I'd lived with for so long subsided. Then I felt something new. Peace.

Brené Brown writes, "True belonging is the spiritual practice of believing in and belonging to yourself so deeply that you can share your most authentic self with the world and find sacredness in both being a part of something and standing alone in the wilderness. True belonging doesn't require you to change who you are; it requires you to be who you are."

It sure felt like the wilderness. In attempting to undo a lifetime's worth of self-denial, I had to face the real consequences of choosing to disappoint others rather than disappointing myself—of belonging to myself, first. Like all those hours I'd spent bent over in the gardens at the farm, tending to the weeds of the beautiful, stupid little garden called my life was grueling.

My messy, nonlinear growth was lonely work that sometimes made me think my honesty had ruined everything. With every step toward finding and listening to my voice, I felt like I was stepping away from everything I'd ever known. The surer I was of myself, the less sure I was welcome at the tables I'd once set. My biggest fear came true. I lost some people.

But when I looked at myself in the mirror, I realized that what I saw on the outside finally matched what was on the inside. I knew who I was. I was a deeply feeling, intensely loving, passionate advocate for well-being. I was an impulsive, creative, and distractible person who was traumatized but healing, imperfect but accountable, funny but also depressed. I believed in Jesus, social justice, love, forgiveness, and boundaries. I was a gentle parent who struggled to feel gentle. I was a caring friend, wife, and good enough mother. I was a strong, smart, kind woman who told the truth and expected the same in return.

Even without the people I thought would always be there, even without everyone's approval, I had worth. I was enough. I didn't have to pretend anymore. I may have lost people, but what I found was something better, something I didn't even realize I'd been looking for.

I found myself.

24

Safety

The first time I met Abby it was nothing to write home about. She neither intimidated me nor thrilled me. A mutual church friend had introduced us because Abby was new to town. She rolled up to my house one evening shortly after I put the kids to bed. When I opened my front door, I recognized her as a typical mom in her thirties: black leggings, an oversize sweatshirt, brown Blundstone boots, and her hair in a messy bun. She looked put together but tired like the rest of the moms I knew—which was a magical relief.

I appreciated that Abby was likely looking for friendship, but I was not. I was already too busy with the friends I had, but I remembered the feeling of starting fresh and figured it couldn't hurt to be nice to the new girl—with caution. Since realizing my inclination to attract opportunists and people who played mind games like a magnet, I struggled to trust my judgment of character. There was also the glaring issue of being recognized everywhere I went as "the Honest Mom from Instagram." This is not a selling feature for making new friends that one might imagine.

Did Abby know who I was? Follow me online? If she did, how

much did she know? Did she just think I was that funny mom who did silly dances and made relatable jokes or had she read my trauma blogs? Has she seen me cry on the internet? I could accept that I wasn't everyone's cup of tea, but meeting people whom I knew nothing about and who potentially knew a great deal about me filled my body with emotional liquid nitrogen.

All options were awkward. I was awkward. But I forced myself to keep on my two-day-old leggings and tidied my house just enough to make sure there was somewhere to sit. People lived here, after all. I needed to be myself.

"So, you're a teacher? What do you teach?" I asked her, already knowing the answer to her question.

"Fourth grade. I love it. Though I might change grades next year," she responded. "How about you?"

"I used to be an educational assistant!" I said, noting we had something in common and that I was from the real world. Then I said, "But now, I'm a content creator—by accident. It's a long story."

She smiled and nodded. "Oh, cool." She said this as if I'd just told her I'd had Cheerios for breakfast—neither fazed nor overly impressed with my Insta-fame. Green flag. I exhaled. Over a cup of tea, I learned that my new friend-candidate lived around the corner, had kids the same age as I did, and had a deep love for strolling around HomeSense looking for new organizational contraptions with a Starbucks in her hand. Again, regular suburban mom stuff.

Abby had quiet teacher-y type-A energy. Since starting my healing journey, I'd gotten better at accepting well-functioning women like her as "just another way of being"—rather than as a reminder of all the good stuff I am not. Abby shared that her son had struggled with speech in his early years. It was nice to meet another mom who'd once banged her head against the wall looking for answers while the world told her to "just wait and see." She seemed normal, but in truth, there was nothing about our encounter that was electrifying enough for me to imagine forging a long-term relationship. I determined that Abby might be a nice person, but I didn't find myself desperate to hang out the next day. Time would tell.

Over the next several months, we passed each other in town, I saw her at church, and we attended some mutual friends' events together. Our husbands and children met uneventfully. Abby wasn't lacking in vulnerability, but she certainly didn't trauma-dump on me or love bomb me from day one, either.

Every few weeks, we went for walks around the neighborhood together, bundled in parkas and hats. I joined her for her HomeSense browsing sometimes, too. Having another like-minded mom close by was certainly handy for last-minute hangouts.

I texted her sporadically to see how she was doing, and she responded in her own time, honestly but succinctly. I tried to remind myself that this likely wasn't a sign that I was annoying but that she was a working mom, like me.

Abby wore some combination of black, white, cream, and muted pink most of the time—the same rotation of colors in her home decor and family's outfits. Her vibe was "put together but not fancy." I was still very much a person with a love for haphazard colors and trends. We were different.

I got to know my new pal slowly—in part because I, too, was very busy and therefore had to cancel plans more than I wanted to. Such as one particular night.

ME: I know I said I could come out for a coffee tonight, but I have so much to do, I don't think I will be my best self if I come.

ABBY: No problem, you've got to take care of yourself.

Two weeks later.

ABBY: Hey, I've got another meeting at work tonight, so I won't be able to hang out.

ME: Don't worry about it. I'll be fine. Hope the meeting goes well! <3

We went back and forth for months on end canceling on each other. Abby asked me not to apologize and I asked her to forgive me for apologizing so much. I didn't feel slighted by her cancellations, either. Sick kids, busy schedules, and work commitments happened. The more she canceled, the less I felt like I needed to push myself to meet up even if I was "technically" available. Overwhelmed was a good enough reason. Tired was, too. Abby made me feel safe to say no.

We said yes, too—to coffee, to walks, and to double dates. We said yes to a few weekends away. We also said yes to talking until midnight in the hot tub together and driving to Walmart for groceries in exhausted silence.

Over time, Abby became a steady person in my life who helped me choose home decor, who knew what I took in my tea, and accepted my kids' hand-me-downs. I offered fashion advice, convinced her to try karaoke, and listened when she needed to vent. We were a slow burn, unlike the firework beginnings of other friendships I'd had over the years.

If other relationships were a gigantic rickety roller coaster at a brand-new theme park without safety permits, Abby was a modest, steady steam train at the petting farm that followed its schedule to a T and never left the station without checks and balances: predictable, secure, safe.

IN THE FALL, OVER A year after we'd met and months after I'd said toodle-doo to my codependent relationship with my mom, I got slammed with work. Abby and I went a few months without hanging out. The Christmas holidays were the busiest months of the year for marketing—holiday sponsorships and promotions, brand events, and conferences galore. Managing it all on my own wore me out, and just when I thought it couldn't get busier, at the start of December, I got a call from the hospital saying my dad had just arrived in an ambulance.

On the drive there, I remembered the last time I'd received an emergency call to come see him at the hospital—when he'd had a heart attack a few years prior. I'd arrived to discover my 6-foot-5 and 250-pound dad only partially covered by what looked like a green minidress in the hospital bed. He looked at me, gestured to it, and laughed.

"DOOO YOUUU TAKE ANY MEDICATION?" the doctor blared directly into my dad's hearing-aid-less ear. His hearing aids were dead—and in his pocket. My dad had looked at me like *here we go again.*

"My dad is deaf," I said. "Whether he is wearing his hearing aids or not, he needs to see your face and read your lips. No amount of yelling will get through."

"We know," one of the nurses said, as the doctor continued to yell directly into his ear like he was a complete idiot. I stepped in and interpreted where I could and answered where I couldn't. Everyone seemed to sigh in relief. Well, everyone except Dad.

He waved me over, pulled me close, gave me a bristly mustache kiss on the cheek, and boomed, "THIS GUY'S A PAIN IN MY ASS," thinking he was whispering, pointing at the doctor. I didn't blame him. When you can't hear, people look at you and treat you like you have no brain. Being hard of hearing myself, I understood this on a personal level. As my dad's daughter, I understood this for his sake on a much deeper and wider level. Seeing him stubborn, strong, and loud told me he was going to be just fine.

Now, years later, when I arrived at the hospital to interpret for him, I expected Dad to be the same large, deaf, funny, stubborn man that he always was. But he wasn't. He was half-conscious and unaware of who I was. He hadn't had another heart attack. This time, his kidneys were failing. Seeing him so unaware and vulnerable made the pit in my stomach grow. I'd hoped to visit him more in the last few years, but with the COVID lockdowns, I couldn't risk it. The long, lonely months had made his already quiet life go practically silent. Could that be why Dad's health had declined? Guilt crept over me like a fog—damp, chilling, and blinding. Had I caused this?

COVID hospital restrictions meant only one family member could visit per day. In Dad's case, "visit" also meant advocate. Despite my overwhelm, I volunteered to be that voice for him. Throughout December, I went to the hospital daily. In between work commitments, kid activities, school drop-off, and holiday prep, I made the drive to the city. He became more coherent and started walking and playing cribbage again. The doctors informed us he had surprised them and no longer needed to be considered for dialysis. By the end of the month, he'd improved significantly. He was a tough bugger and was going to be fine.

We wanted Dad home for the holidays, but his doctors decided to keep him a few extra days to be sure. I visited Dad on Christmas and asked him if he'd like me to get the nurses to hook up the TV for him. All month he'd declined my offer, but finally he gave in. The next day, I called to inquire about the TV hookup.

The nurses' station informed me he'd been transferred off that floor because there was an outbreak of COVID in his ward. I waited nervously while they transferred him to the new ward. When I got through to that phone line, the nurse told me he wasn't there anymore and asked me to hold the line while they transferred my call somewhere else. The line clicked. "Hi, you've reached the ICU, how can I help you?"

My heart plummeted. I felt sick. What?! The person on the other end of the line explained that earlier that morning my dad had gone into cardiac arrest. Harry and I rushed to the hospital to find Dad hooked up to what looked like every machine imaginable. “It’s only a matter of time. We can’t do anything else,” the doctor said. A couple days later, wearing head-to-toe PPE, I held his big, warm, motionless hand in mine. It was time to say goodbye.

Eventually, we gave the doctor the go-ahead to unplug. I felt Dad’s hand grow cold, and the machine stopped breathing for him. I said, “I love you,” even though he couldn’t hear me. I signed “I love you,” even though he couldn’t see me. And just like that, he was gone. The silence was deafening. Harry and I left the hospital, stunned. How had it happened so fast? How was our dad . . . dead?

He’d missed out on so much, for so long—during the pandemic, in the years before, when new motherhood made visiting difficult, and all the years before that, too. My heart ached for my dad, for how hard his life had been, for how the system had failed him, and possibly how I had, too.

On the drive home, I wanted to call someone, but whom? Greg was with the kids. Harry was driving home. Mom was in the rearview mirror. Dad’s family wasn’t involved in our lives. Abby and everyone else were enjoying time with their families over the holidays. I was alone.

Since finding myself and losing people I thought would always be there, so much had changed. I’d convinced myself I was fine with it. Or maybe I’d been too busy to process or grieve the changes to my relationships until *this* loss. Now, with Dad gone, it felt like the gravity tethering me down to earth had suddenly dissipated.

At home, I collapsed on the cold bathroom floor. Greg picked me up and brought me to bed. Like a child, I lay there, soaking my pillow with tears.

Dad had made me the executor of his will and I took charge of the funeral planning.

In my mind, this was yet another confirmation of the fact that I was the only one I could rely on. I'd been telling myself this since before I'd started selling our furniture in yard sales on Tuesday mornings at the age of eight. I was a fixer, a take-care-of-business-er. I raised the cows and raised my hand whenever there was a problem in my vicinity. I'd married young, popped out kids young, and taken care of my parents young. For as long as I remembered, I'd been the responsible one. Despite my growth, it seemed that life still required me to be the grown-up.

"I just want someone else to hold the cards, to be in charge. Why does it always rest on my shoulders? Why do I have to do it alone?" I lamented to Greg one evening as I was writing Dad's obituary and making lists of what needed to be done.

"I know it's hard, Libby," Greg said, pulling me in with a hug, tucking my hair behind my ear. "But please know you don't have to do it alone. I am here for whatever you need. Other people have offered to help, too." I felt his good intentions, but he couldn't understand the gravity of my aloneness. He had parents. He didn't feel the weight of being the most adult-adult he knew. He didn't know what it was like to hold up the sky.

NEW YEAR'S EVE ARRIVED. WE'D been counting down the days till spending the evening with Abby's family, but I didn't want to burden our friends with my fresh and unpredictable grief. She must have known, because I received a text.

"Just want you to know that we are here for whatever you need. You can cancel New Year's if you want. My kids will be okay. But if you want to get together, we would love to see you. Don't worry about bringing anything. Invite Harry and Amanda, too. Your call."

I checked my phone to see my longtime friend Krista in my inbox: "Hey, I know it's a lot having to plan your dad's funeral. Can

I help by scanning your dad's old photos and making a slideshow?" Maybe my friend couldn't fully understand my grief, but she showed up for me. For several years, Krista had walked and talked with me, watched my kids when I had appointments, and took them before and after school on a moment's notice. We shared meals, collected one another's advice, and mulled over what we wanted to be when we grew up while our kids played at the park. When I thought about it, Krista had been there, a lot.

In addition to supporting her husband (my grieving brother), Amanda checked in with me daily—she brought cookies, sent funny memes, made dinner, and made decisions. Like she had been for over a decade, Amanda was there, quietly supporting, laughing, and putting up with my roller coaster of healing and change. Becca, my childhood best friend, stepped in, too. Despite her own life being in shambles, she texted when she heard about Dad: "Let me help you with work. I'm far away but I can respond to emails and do scheduling and other administrative work for as long as you need."

Becca handled it, like she'd been doing for years—from helping me move from house to house through my chaotic teen years to flying to England when I decided to get married. When I became "successful" and other friends got awkward, Becca embraced my new trajectory and celebrated me.

Leah proofread my eulogy so I didn't say anything stupid. Harry acted as my sounding board, helped empty Dad's apartment, and supported me in making many of the hard decisions. Grandma Pearls sent flowers. Roger sent encouraging messages from across the pond where he was visiting when it happened. Church friends showed up with snacks and distractions.

It was a small funeral of about thirty people sparsely scattered in the congregation at my church. I was pleasantly surprised to see so many loved ones in the same place—friends, family, people I'd never met, and people there just for me who had never met Dad, either. I walked up to the stage to give my eulogy. As I took the microphone and told stories about my dad, I watched the faces of our people connecting, caring, and sharing in my pain. In each of their faces I saw a reflection of the beauty of my dad's life along with so many of the ways they'd shown up for our family.

While the gathering of humans that day may have looked somewhat empty, the room was full of love—both seen and unseen. I thought of all my people and I was overcome with a sense of being held together and held up—as if the faces in the crowd were collectively shouldering the weight of my grief, of my dad's memory, and of me.

Maybe I did have to be more self-reliant than the average thirty-something. But maybe I wasn't as alone as I'd thought, either. Sometimes, I suppose, the love I was surrounded by was hard to see, which made it easy to double down on my independence and fear of relying on others. Perhaps, feeling lonely didn't mean I was alone. I did have people—wonderful, complex, busy, caring, funny, imperfect, thoughtful people. And if anything was certain, it was that I needed them.

UNFORTUNATELY, NOT EVERY FRIEND WILL show up exactly how we want, when we want. The friend who saves you during your postpartum season might not make it to your dad's funeral. The friend who gives great parenting advice might drop the ball on your birthday. Friends can't all be roll-on-the-floor funny or available around the clock. Not every friend is up for a neurodivergent deep dive into the history of pyramid schemes (honestly though, they are missing out). Not every friend wants to eat Big Macs in the parking lot or binge-watch *Love Is Blind* while the small humans entertain one another.

I struggled to trust people.

This much was obvious. Childhood trauma, finding myself later in life, and being catapulted into the public eye all at the same time—in an industry known to take advantage of vulnerabilities—certainly didn't help. But the love I'd felt when Dad died reminded me the answer was not to bury myself far away from anyone who could ever break my trust or let me down. I couldn't keep pretending that I was the only person I needed while also resenting it.

I wanted to know I could continue to be true to myself while still leaning on other people. Because while nobody is perfect, nobody should have to carry a pair of shears and a backpack of Roundup around to stop themselves from being smothered out of their own fertile soil. I didn't want to keep getting hurt. So could I reevaluate my perceptions of what healthy relationships looked and felt like? How could I learn the difference between a dandelion and a daisy? Who was safe and how would I know?

My new pal, Abby, seemed safe. But why? I thought about it. At first, when things were slow, it made me wonder if she even liked me. But I realized she was trying to figure out if she could trust me—she was testing the waters, inching closer over time. Something about this slowness was safe. The gradual interconnectedness gave us both an out if we weren't jibing. She wasn't being mean; she was being normal, healthy. I reflected on my other longstanding relationships, with Greg, Leah, and my sister-in-law. They, too, had been slow starters.

Safety wasn't just about time, though. I'd been initially surprised when Abby gave me grace for canceling plans, for saying no, for missing texts—or even disagreeing. She hadn't taken it personally and it made me feel like I could breathe. Over time, the more she expressed her needs, it helped me to do the same without overthinking what might happen.

We could be disappointed without making each other responsible for fixing the other's feelings. When I told her I was sad or feeling insecure, she had this strange ability to empathize with me without jumping in to save me. It helped me feel like my feelings wouldn't be a burden—like being transparent or vulnerable wasn't going to cause a conflict. The more often she let things roll off her, the less I let my stomach turn into a mess of knots when I had to share a need. Abby wasn't boring. She was grounded, consistent, predictable. She was fun without putting the "fun" in dysfunctional. When I achieved a milestone, she celebrated. When I fell into a pit of despair over my worries about ruining my children, she listened. When I spent time with other people, she told me to have fun and meant it.

I could trust that she said what she meant and meant what she said. "I'm not mad" never meant "In two weeks I'm finally going to tell you that I am mad." "I miss you" didn't mean "You're a bad friend." There were no emotional puzzles for me to solve. As it turns out, kids aren't the only ones who need to be allowed to have feelings without judgment.

All the work I've read on attachment, relationships, healing, and well-being says some version of this: Human connection is what we were made for. We need safe human beings like we need food and water.

What made me feel safe? People who told the truth and let me do the same.

Experiencing repetitive safety, security, and belonging with real people doesn't just make our lives better, it heals what is broken. For those of us with trauma, safe relationships are even more integral. The more often we have healthy relational interactions, the more our brain learns that the world is not a flaming pit of fire and knives.

These experiences teach us a new way of being. In doing so, we can spend our energy on learning new skills instead of relational hypervigilance. We become more secure and learn to trust ourselves. *That* trust is built slowly, in real relationships, with real people, over time. As it turned out, emotionally safe people weren't just "nice to have," they were the cornerstone of my healing, the main ingredient that would finally allow my inner child to unclench.

Once I let go of unsafe people and understood why the safe ones were so important to me, I made a decision. I wanted relationships with people who were self-aware. Power in realness, not in numbers. Connection, not perfection. Are you insecure? Me, too. Let's call it what it is and find a reasonable solution together instead of hiding behind deflection tactics. Tell me when my silly comment about your height hurt your feelings or how it felt when I didn't put my phone down as you walked into the room. Voice your needs. Be real.

I deserved to break bread with the kind of friends who called me out when I was being neurotic but who did it with kindness or the kind of humor that softens the blow instead of rips me wide open. I deserved women at my table who could say "that's not for me but you do you," who don't expect me to maintain the emotional temperature of the room.

I needed the kind of people who didn't make my digestive system want to empty itself on the floor when we had a conflict to resolve, who didn't make me guess what they want or need, and then punish me when I'm wrong. I needed people who lit up for my success and grieved for my losses. Ones who let me into their mess and let me speak truth to them, too. I needed people who were fully and entirely themselves and wanted me to be my full self, too.

I *did* need people after all—safe, honest ones. In truth, that's all I ever needed.

25

Human

I couldn't help but notice the contrast between how my mom's lack of honesty became the final push that led me to draw a line between us, and how choosing honesty for myself became my path to healing. I always wanted to know why she couldn't do the work to be my safe place. In the time and space I had away from Mom, I began to unravel the tangled mess of answers.

Mom's mom, Grandma Eileen, was born in 1931 to blue-collar Irish immigrants. They were real-deal Catholic. We're talking devout—cover your shoulders, birth control is a sin, homemaking is your calling, and you better follow the rules so our family doesn't get judged or kicked out of church—Catholic. Discipline and religious duty were the name of the game, and shutting up about bad things that happened was one of the golden unspoken rules.

Eileen left school after tenth grade, married my grandpa at eighteen years old, and a year later, popped out a baby. Normal stuff for the 1950s. She took care of the house and supported her parents, too. Normal. She struggled with her mental health during postpartum. Normal. When her mental health deteriorated even more, they sent her to a psychiatric hospital for months of social isolation away from her new baby and loved ones. She endured several rounds of shock therapy. After her little institutional stay, Grandma went home as a new mom to bake apple pie, put rollers in her hair, and keep up appearances at church. She went on to pop out four more babies back-to-back and kept hush-hush about her brain problems, too. Normal stuff.

I only learned about this part of Grandma's story once I was a mom myself. I wanted to know more, so I called my aunt and asked what she knew about Grandma's postpartum stay in the psych ward. "She didn't talk about it much. She didn't even tell me until I was an adult. I don't have any details. Sorry, I don't have much to tell you. Nobody talked about that stuff," my aunt said.

The mental health conversations that we have these days were simply not being had when my grandmother was raising her children. Betty Friedan was honest though. In 1963 she published *The Feminine Mystique*, which put words to the quiet plight of the 1950s housewives and mothers who felt like they were dying a slow unfulfilled death inside.

She gave voice to the women who were told that popping out babies, baking bread, and collecting Tupperware like it was going out of business was the path to fulfillment. Prior to Friedan (whose work I am certain my Catholic grandmother wouldn't have touched with a ten-foot pole), there was no language to talk about that unseen despair and its consequences.

Despite looking the part on the outside, many women found themselves lacking in purpose, autonomy, identity, and often mental stability. But without the vocabulary and the safe spaces to talk about it, what do you get? Shame and silence. More problems.

Doctors recognized how big of a problem it was for women to be so destitute, so they did what doctors do: prescribed mind-numbing pills and treated the surface symptoms—headaches, fatigue, sleeplessness, anxiety. Women are just crazy and hormonal, *amirite?*

In the fifties and sixties, tranquilizers were being prescribed by the millions to housewives. Shock therapy wasn't uncommon, either. Michel Foucault—a French philosopher who made a career out of challenging power structures, institutions, and society—explained how the treatment of women with mental illness affected them: Women who were "locked away, subjected to the authority of doctors, and kept in confinement [were] marked with a stigma that follows her even after release.

"The asylum was not just a space of healing, but one of control, reinforcing the boundaries of acceptable behavior for women. The trauma of shock therapy, of institutionalization and of the horrific way women were treated as objects to be corrected, rather than humans—had lasting effects on women's mental health, even if they left the institution 'cured.'"

Well, hi, Grandma. Hello, trauma. No wonder she went home to pop out four more babies back-to-back after her little institutional stay. What else was she to do? Once all five babies were out, my grandfather fell in love with the neighbor and ran away to start a new life. That left my grandma, in the early 1970s, without an education or sustainable career, to raise five kids on her own. Shock therapy, social isolation, secrecy, subservience, sacrifice, submission, and scorn? Normal stuff. Bucking up and shutting up are just what one does when raising five kids as a single mom with no education, no money, and a history of untreated mental illness.

Honestly? I don't understand how you live through those things and not go certifiably insane—not that we use pathologizing terms like that anymore. Let's say it another way. Considering the culturally normative pressure to maintain appearances in the face of unbearable circumstances and the lack of resources or language to get help—that didn't leave a woman like my grandmother with many choices.

Still, it was no excuse to let out the valve of red-hot feelings she suppressed in public onto the most precious five humans inside the four walls of my mother's home. Was it healthy for Eileen to project her unhappiness and trauma onto her children? Well, no. Was it normal? Well, certainly more common and acceptable than I'd imagine it'd be than to call the doctor or the priest and say, "I'm not okay."

And so, my mother's childhood was fraught with trauma, too. My mom was an early teen when her dad ran off with the neighbor. Aside from being a child of divorce and part of a generation of authoritarian parents who believed in corporal punishment and lived by the "children should be seen and not heard" notion, she was subjected to her mother, who had become a master manipulator of her children.

My grandmother chose her eldest daughter as her confidante and emotional support. My mom was the middle child and the only other girl. While my aunt received special treatment with affection, new clothes, and time together baking or going out, Mom was left behind to figure out life on her own, a second-class citizen. Mom's eldest sister was given the responsibility of keeping tabs on the younger ones, too, making Mom and her siblings simultaneously loathe their sister and long for their mom. Mind games were par for the course. Accepting what little love or material items were given to you, even if it was a fraction of what your sister got, was just what you did.

"She took care of us. But I just remember Mom lying in bed when we got home from school. She still did things, but she wasn't *really* there. And she was angry, so unpredictable all the time," Mom told me once. "My brothers teased me relentlessly. My sister was the favorite. I was invisible. Nobody liked me."

As a single mom with waning mental capacity and unbearable responsibilities, my grandma became known for her toxic behavior, manipulation, and next-level narcissistic traits that deeply traumatized and ultimately drove away her children. First of them was my mom.

As a teen, Mom dealt with her difficult home, desire to be seen, gain control, and meet her needs in one of many classic traumatized-people ways: by lying and stealing. That only led to more problems and even less reason for her mom to give her the connection, attention, and guidance she needed.

When my mom was fifteen, her mom had had enough of her lying and stealing and told Mom she was no longer welcome at home. After Mom was kicked out of the house, she began sleeping on friends' couches, in storage lockers, or amongst whoever would take her. With no money, education, or stability, her life spiraled. My mom became a master at shaping the truth to cope. Her maladaptive coping mechanism—like my people-pleasing—was how she attempted (and ultimately failed) to create safety for herself.

Mom became nomadic, searching for anywhere to belong. Between leaving home at fifteen and turning twenty-five, she moved countless times, wrote countless false checks, told countless lies, went to jail, went to a home for at-risk young adults where she briefly dated a deaf man, moved away, married, became a widow, and eventually landed back in the dating pool with that deaf guy: Dad. Harry and I came along and so, motherhood began.

"I'M SO PROUD TO BE YOUR MOM."

"You can trust yourself."

"Your feelings make sense. I believe you."

"You're allowed to say no."

"You're not too much, you are just the right amount."

"Your opinions matter to me."

"What do you need from me?"

"It's not your job to fix things."

"Nothing you do will make me stop loving you."

"I don't always have the answers. I'm not perfect."

"I'm sorry."

These were phrases that my children heard come out of my mouth almost daily—many of them I'd longed to hear growing up. Certainly, Mom and Grandma hadn't heard them. I was giving what I never got. I'd become the safety I craved.

With hard work I learned how to attune to my kids' emotions, regulate mine, and be present for their lives. Love wasn't merely a feeling I had or words I said, but something I aimed to ensure my kids felt unconditionally, every day. Even on my hardest days, I parented them with humility, self-awareness, and honesty.

I didn't intentionally shame, blame, or gaslight my kids. If I messed up, I apologized. I did the inner work and cared for myself so that I could be there for *them*. In doing so, I *chose* them. Breaking the cycle was both bone-weary hard and the most important thing I'd ever done.

I *chose* to be different than my mom and her mom before her. And I *was*. But was it as simple as a choice?

Even with remaining stigmas, we're the first generation to openly talk about mental health. We have more rights than any generation of women who came before us. We are the first generation of women who have access to higher education and outpace men in attaining it. We've gained access to birth control, healthcare, social services, and freedoms that our grandmothers could only dream of.

Culturally, we no longer subscribe to the notion that "children should be seen and not heard." It's normal to listen to our kids, even if we suck at it. It's no longer considered normal for moms and dads to spank kids for not listening—or, at least, corporal punishment is now extremely controversial. Authoritarian parenting, while still common, is on the way out—thanks to bundles of research and advocacy from experts and other professionals alike. Together, we are finally acknowledging that kids are people, too.

With all social media's downsides (and there are many), we're also the first generation that can connect with women who share our experiences—and those who are completely different. Online, we have access to people who help give us language to describe overstimulation and the mental load. They provide stories that help us understand our triggers and give us tools to regulate. Other women are finally giving us permission to lower our expectations or take care of ourselves.

The healing power of that cannot be understated. We have access to resources and information that past generations couldn't even imagine. Therapy is becoming as normalized as getting your teeth cleaned. The research we now have on addiction, mental health, and healing simply didn't exist fifty years ago—not in a way that regular people could *actually* use.

We call out abusive men now. We have shelters and safe spaces for women who need to leave. We have language for the wage gap, weaponized incompetence, emotional labor, burnout, toxic masculinity, and the patriarchy so we can make sense of what the hell is happening to us. This vocabulary and camaraderie have given women power to change culture and create essential support networks. They sure gave me power.

The more I learned about why I was the way I was, and the ways society *still* screws modern-day mothers over, the more my eyes opened. If my mom and her mom had had those tools in this culture, who knows how their lives and their children would have turned out. If *my* mom had had a mom who was safe, secure, and whole, who knows what healthy coping skills she might have passed on to me, what steady foundation she may have been able to create.

We are all products of our circumstances, socioeconomic status, environment, history, neural wiring, and events that occurred far before we could think full sentences. Whether we acknowledge it or not, our ability to heal and change is inextricably linked to these factors. Our mothers and grandmothers didn't lack the conscious awareness to change because they didn't care. I began to believe that a major reason so many of them didn't "do the work" was because they were raising their babies in a different time.

I came to accept that Mom wasn't selfish or unloving. Her actions had nothing to do with the love she felt for me. My mom's inability to show up as a safe person had everything to do with not being given what she needed from the beginning, too.

For so long, I viewed my healing journey as a choice that I'd made—one that my mom hadn't. It *was* a choice. I *was* different. But I had to admit that the circumstances of my life played an undeniable role in making change possible. I had access to the honesty of other moms, and it made breaking the cycle of generational trauma a little easier. Being a good mom was never as plain and simple as making a choice. If it were that easy, every mom throughout the history of time would've nailed it.

Even with all the privileges I had that previous generations didn't, I was far from a perfect mom. I still made mistakes that kept me awake at night, smothered by a heavy blanket of guilt—for knowing better and doing worse.

Meanwhile, the messages on social media continued:

Thank you for this video, it's helping me to heal & I am a better mom because of your work.

Your videos have changed my marriage and how my partner and I see the work I do at home.

This makes me feel less alone.

Your content is a life raft for me.

I never realized it was overstimulation I struggled with before this.

That book you recommended changed my life.

I don't know what I would do without you. You are helping us all become better moms! Your kids are lucky to have you!

What a farce, I thought to myself one night as I was scrolling, after I'd shortened the bedtime routine again and yelled upstairs, "PLEASE JUST GO TO BED!" *If only they knew that I still snap at my kids when I'm overstimulated sometimes. I still tune out the* Minecraft *chatter because it makes my brain melt. I still make promises to play in five minutes and then forget for the rest of the day. I still dissociate when I'm stressed out. I say "that's great, sweetie" without looking up from my laptop, and I shoot critical looks when my kids make simple mistakes. I say "you're fine" when they aren't because I need them to be. I still worry about if I'm doing it right.*

Despite my progress, I was still a deeply flawed human. I gave myself grace for my mistakes and told other moms to do the same. But since cutting ties with my mom, I'd begun to wonder, *What about grace for her? Does withholding it make me a hypocrite?*

FOR SEVERAL MONTHS AFTER BREAKING contact with my mom, we did not interact. Nearly a year passed of fighting the urge to call, to give in, to gaslight myself. Mom had attempted her version of an apology but apologies hadn't always equated to change in the past, and I was tired of being hurt or disappointed.

But over time, I could tell she was trying—differently than

before. So with the kids' birthdays coming up, I agreed to visit her and communicate what my boundaries were again. When we arrived, I could see that Mom's apartment was clean. She gave me the space I'd asked for. She'd quit smoking, too. On the bookshelf was a book on healing trauma. On the fridge, a reminder of her therapy appointment coming up. There were cupcakes and two wrapped presents on the table. On the wall, a Happy Birthday banner. Mom sat down with folded hands and looked around the room, seeming kind, timid, and respectful. For all her faults, I'd missed her.

I peeled back the wrapping on the cupcake while Mom asked the kids questions about how school was going. Ellie and Oscar unwrapped their gifts while we sipped our tea. Afterward, as Mom watched the kids play, I could see her holding back tears. But they weren't tears meant to manipulate or control. They weren't "this is about me" tears. They were happiness and gratitude tears. They were "this means so much and I really don't want to mess this up" tears.

When the visit ended, the kids said thank you for their presents, gave her a hug, and we went home without incident. And I went home with a softer heart. Our time apart had helped me see my mom as the hurt girl she was. But this time, not in a way that felt like my responsibility. This was different.

After that visit, I didn't dive headfirst into codependent fixing, fawning, and compulsive caretaking because I was bored on a random Tuesday. I didn't pick up every time she called or share my deepest longings. Whatever *this* was, it was going to be messy.

There was no going back to our enmeshed past and no knowing what the future held. I'd been on the merry-go-round of promised changes long enough to trust the voice inside me that said *go slow*.

I couldn't ignore the harm Mom had caused me, or the ways her traumatized tendencies had ripped my wounds open throughout my adult life. I couldn't ignore the reality that my own wounds fed our dysfunction.

I didn't regret protecting myself and my children, either. In fact, time and space had helped make boundaries easier to hold, Christmas and backyard visits easier to relax into. In moments of uncertainty, I grounded myself. We began to learn a new way forward where perfection was not required but honesty was.

Turns out, you can love a person without being responsible for them. You can set boundaries with the people you love. Sometimes, it's the most loving thing you can do.

I'd told myself in the past that I'd forgiven and forgotten. But the truth is, I don't think I ever really had. My body never forgot—and maybe it never will. But holding on to the immense, complex pain that my mom had caused was only holding me back.

I could no longer, in good conscience, continue telling mothers that we were imperfect humans deserving of grace while refusing to extend that same grace to the woman who had raised me. So, in a quiet corner of my heart, without her asking and without a grand gesture, I forgave my mom.

I DON'T BELIEVE THAT FORGIVENESS is compulsory or that reconciliation is always possible or even healthy. There is no excuse for abuse or childhood neglect or willful ignorance. And if you've suffered tremendously at the hands of the people who were meant to protect you, I'm so sorry. You didn't deserve that.

Understanding why our parents did or didn't do something or couldn't show up isn't about making excuses for them. It's an explanation. The explanation doesn't mean they didn't wreak havoc on who we became and how we exist in the world. It doesn't stop us from being more likely to struggle with confidence, trust, control, boundaries, mental health, addiction, and chronic health conditions. It also doesn't excuse or erase the damage. Explanations don't mean we should excuse past or present toxic behavior or allow emotionally unsafe people into our lives just because they're blood. Explanations matter because they help us understand.

Explanations also help us to see our parents' personhood, not just their parenthood. And isn't that what we want for ourselves, too? To be seen as people, ones who aren't perfect and shouldn't be expected to be? That's what I want. A world where mothers are no longer reduced to one-dimensional narratives that deny our humanity, complexity, and history. If we want to stop the world from expecting perfection from us regardless of whatever crap sandwich we are handed, we've got to stop expecting it from one another, too. Giving and accepting grace helps us not to hide from our mistakes *or* be defined by them, either.

I know that no matter how hard I try, I'm going to screw up—not because I am bad, but because I'm human. I want to raise kids who aren't shocked by that fact. I want to raise kids who know that being imperfect doesn't make you unlovable, who offer themselves grace because they have seen it modeled. I want to raise children who know they are good enough and believe in the goodness of others.

If you have a broken relationship with your child, it is never too early and never too late to say, "I screwed up, you didn't deserve that, I am sorry." Giving grace and taking accountability is the best gift we can give our kids. It's how we reconnect and create safety again. And that is a gift I wish my mom had had, and every generation before her.

ONE MORE QUICK DEAD PERSON story. My grandma passed away a few years ago, after a decade of the family thinking she was *just* about to die. I am telling you, that lady *held on*. By the time it happened, most of our family were no longer in contact with one another. The funeral was clouded in sad, stiff Catholic tension. After the service, about fifty people gathered for lunch in the church hall where beautiful, hilarious, good stories were shared about her life.

One old lady who had been friends with my grandma since they were children stood up. At the end of her story, her eyes welled up with tears and she said, "You know, she was just a little girl, walking around in a grown-up's body. I guess that's what we all are."

26

Rubik's Cube

The summer the kids turned eight and ten—practically elderly—we vacationed in France. We've never been the type to use "summer" like a verb, so this trip was a big deal. It's just, when Greg and I got married in England fifteen years prior, we'd road-tripped around France afterward on a budget-friendly quasi-honeymoon. It had been a great adventure filled with sunshine, croissants, beaches, gelato, and baguette-wrapped hot dogs that reminded me of Pogos. "If we ever have kids, we should bring them here when they are old enough," I said to him.

So, we did. Upon arrival, we gave both the kids fifty euros each to spend how they liked over the two weeks. We hit Paris, Bordeaux, Carcassonne, Nice, and plenty of villages in between. On one of the long stretches of road, we took a break at a bustling truck stop beside the foothills of the Pyrenees. After much deliberation, Oscar decided to purchase a Rubik's Cube from inside the store. I wasn't overly impressed that he chose to spend nearly a third of his money on a toy from a truck stop he would open once and never play with again, but I kept my mouth shut. He is his own person.

The first few days of Rubik's Cube ownership, Oscar did a lot of what I do anytime I try to solve one: fart around with it, grunt in frustration, try again, realize he was getting nowhere, then throw it on the seat of the car. But then he'd pick it up and try again. In truth, it served as the perfect fidget for long car rides.

"Can I watch a YouTube tutorial?" he asked one afternoon as we were lounging, recovering from a hot morning in the sun. At first, I said no, because I wanted him to learn the old-fashioned way. Kids these days! But then my brain logged on and I remembered that learning from other people is normal. Also, I like quiet time.

The tutorial binge began and, as you do when your child is obsessed with something, I learned a lot by proxy. Fascinatingly, solving a cube is like learning to code. For each scramble, there are sets of steps or there's an algorithm to follow to solve it. Each step-by-step sequence is used to solve different sections. When solving a cube, you have to learn and remember specific sequences for aligning colors and solving edges, or corners. You begin to recognize what each mess is and which steps are required to set it straight.

Oscar watched endless videos of YouTubers solving cubes. The learning was helpful. He even followed step-by-step guides, slowly copying each move with intense focus until a small section unscrambled. Without a tutorial, he struggled. Back to YouTube. Countless videos played in the background of our Airbnb on the French Riviera.

But at some point, he realized that memorizing the algorithms did jack all without developing muscle memory through hands-on repetition. The videos became redundant. If he wanted to solve his own cube, he just had to practice. Solo.

One day at the beach, Oscar finally got to work. The goal? Unscramble one side of the cube with one set of steps. He had no such luck. Over and over, he tried to execute the knowledge he'd absorbed, but partway through, he'd make one wrong move and be forced to start again. Feeling defeated, he'd take a break. Eventually, I'd catch him in the rearview mirror, twisting the cube with fervor again.

Practice. The point of practicing is that with each attempt, you understand the cube's mechanics more deeply, developing the ability to spot patterns and anticipate outcomes without having to think so hard. Muscle memory eventually takes the reins. This repetition is essential because, over time, you learn to adjust your approach and solve for different configurations more intuitively. But at first, every single twist and turn feels painfully slow. Every potential mistake feels like an unraveling. Every setback feels like complete failure.

Still, he persevered. Over and over, in cars, on benches, standing in line to buy a baguette, in between scoops of gelato on the beach, and lying in bed at night, he practiced. For days, it seemed as if he was getting nowhere, until one day, he solved a side. He ran to the vacation rental's balcony to show me. We celebrated with a high-five and he ran off to re-scramble the cube before trying again.

Once he mastered solving one side, he began to try to solve more sides consecutively. The more he practiced on *different* scrambles, the more quickly he could assess which algorithm or set of steps he needed to take, simply from looking at the cube. Of course, the more progress you make, the more stressful it can become. Solving one part of the cube "unsolves" the other pieces around it because the puzzle's layers are interconnected. Annoying. But while the roller coaster of hope and frustration remained, he was learning. Without his noticing, his technique was improving.

Eventually, Oscar learned to accept the regressions that came with taking steps forward in solving his cube. He began to trust that no matter what the cube looked like, he was making progress overall. What once felt like his demise turned into "whoops, I've got to do this other sequence now."

Eventually, I could no longer keep up with how quickly his

hands moved on the cube or how little he had to think. Then one summer day when we were back in Canada, a month after he'd first bought the toy, I was quietly passing time in the backyard when I heard him come running, complete cube in hand.

"I did it, Mom! Look!" Oscar called to me, face full of pride, holding his solved Rubik's Cube out for me to see.

"That is amazing, buddy! You worked so hard on that. I am so proud of you!" I said, smiling, as I turned the cube over in my hand. *What an accomplishment.*

AS FOR ME, I'D FINALLY begun to feel like I'd made progress on my own Rubik's Cube of motherhood. I could speak my needs without becoming catatonic. I could lay down boundaries and hold my ground without wanting to peel my skin off. Leaving the house alone didn't plague me with guilt. Greg and I had worked hard to make our household dynamic fairer, and among other monotonous tasks, laundry was Greg's job now. We're talking from conception to completion here, people. Greg also became the family admin—emails, appointments, kids' activities, and calendar management were his domain. (Bless his neurotypical soul.) I could take off for a weekend or leave the room for a poo without making a list.

Then, a miracle. Greg changed departments at work. Twist, twist, click. For the first time in almost a decade, my husband stopped working twelve-hour rotating day-night shifts from hell. We became one of those mysterious Monday-to-Friday families I'd always wondered about. Finally, another parent to consistently share the bedtime routine with. Our family could eat pancakes together *every single Saturday*. We could have traditions! My ADHD brain could finally anticipate the daily routine and support. The domestic load no longer made me feel like I needed a lobotomy.

In time, more positive changes cascaded into our lives and made my experience of motherhood shift into even more orderly, color-coded terrain. Time alone, guilt-free. The ability to finish thoughts and finish meals while they were still hot. After years of wanting to set the kitchen on fire whenever someone dared speak to me while I attempted to cook food nobody ate, I enjoyed cooking again. Increasingly so, I could show up as the mom I wanted to be.

And yet, life still threw plenty of punches. Upon our return from France, reality hit. My semi-tidy cube began its descent into chaos territory.

Deadlines. Pressure. Family sickness. Managing a full work schedule without childcare while Greg worked Monday to Friday during the summer? Impossible. Trying to balance rest, play, and productivity? A joke. Then, out of nowhere, someone I'd held dear for almost a decade blindsided me and unleashed their own pain on me. The betrayal was immediate and visceral. I couldn't eat, sleep, or think straight for months. The circumstances surrounding the events triggered a domino effect of problems and unearthed countless past hurts that left me feeling vulnerable, broken, and afraid for the future. *Will the people I love most always hurt me in the end?* I wondered. Cue the rapid downward spiral.

I dragged myself back to therapy and, in a moment of unhinged luteal-phase honesty, I let out my frustrations.

"When is this going to start working? I've learned so much. I try so hard. Looking at my life from the outside, I can see that it's good. But it doesn't always feel that way. I'm just so tired of taking one step forward and two steps back, ever searching for a finish line and camping at the start instead. There is always something. Nothing is working."

Annoyingly, my therapist did what good therapists do: She listened and validated my feelings. Then, she asked me to consider if what I said was true. Had I made as little progress as I felt? Had anything changed?

Ugh. When our session ended, I ruminated. *Was* I the same person who struggled to exist outside of motherhood, filled with guilt or pressure no matter what she did? Did anything I tried to do make a difference? Would the work ever end? Is everything always going to come undone?

UPON ENTRY TO CLUB MOTHERHOOD, I'd gone on a quest to solve my own mad-making puzzle. When attempting to discover how to be a good mom and whole person at the same time, I'd looked out first to all the other mothers around me and then into the self-help world. Assuming everyone else had the answers, I'd gleaned their knowledge, watched their tutorials, read their books. I'd learned about authenticity, perfectionism, people pleasing, attachment, and beyond.

But as I looked over at my son racing to beat his own record for the thirty-seventh time that summer, something clicked. The wisdom of self-help gurus and their well-meaning advice *had* helped—but they aren't what changed me.

Leah didn't drag me by my ankles into therapy. My professor didn't ask my friends' husbands to do the dishes. Glennon Doyle herself did not rise from the pages of *Untamed* to advocate for my needs and carve my martyr mentality out from my very being. Dr. Shefali did not coach me when Ellie drew a *Lion King* face in permanent marker on the wall of our living room. Brené Brown did not hop on a flight from Texas and force me to be vulnerable with my friends or make chicken nugs instead of a roast dinner because I was tired. *I* did. It wasn't the therapy or the books that made change possible. It was me. I wanted to know when all the therapy would start to work. But I'd *been* working.

If I hadn't picked up my little messed-up Rubik's Cube, sought help, and stuck with my attempts to solve it, I might still be hopelessly wrestling with it, floundering in my feelings, and incapable of knowing any of the next right steps. But, like Oscar, I dared to try.

With every messy attempt, without noticing, I was learning a new way of being in the world. I absorbed what worked and what didn't. Little by little, the wisdom and tools I picked up along the way were embedding themselves into my subconscious and changing the way I engaged with my problems. Now, I was better at noticing patterns and using what I'd learned. Things like ignoring the "shoulds" in my brain and tuning in to what my gut is telling me I need—like alone time in a dark room, a snack before I bit someone's head off, or a break from my own phone addiction. I became better at lowering my expectations around birthdays and Saturdays and friendships and perfect pancake batter. Note: Costco mix is where it's at.

With infuriating practice, I noticed which decisions made parenting more challenging and what combination of choices pushed me toward growth, healing, and wholeness. I figured out how choosing rest sometimes made my whole day or week a more regulated one, and how other times, it spiraled my to-do list and caused more problems. I figured out how to be firm about rules with my children while holding space for their real feelings about their mother's inconvenient boundaries.

Mistakes were made. Life got scrambled by other people or the universe or my own unhealthy habits that still took the reins. But that's how I landed more opportunities to try again. And yes, maybe I had a tendency to figuratively chuck my proverbial cube into the imaginary back seat because I was sick and tired of life being so relentlessly difficult. *Sue me.* Like solving cubes, it's easy to forget how far you've come when things still look messy. Yet, I always picked it back up and tried the next right thing.

Understanding and intellectualizing didn't solve my problems. Practice, despite the setbacks, did. There was no shortcut. I learned to listen to my inner voice, even when it was uncomfortable. I spoke my truth even when my voice shook. I learned how to navigate the difficult consequences.

If I hadn't done the work, I might've missed out on fully experiencing the goodness of life. Like having safe people nearby who allow me to be fully, imperfectly, and weirdly myself without judgment. I could have missed the chance to be present while making paper snowflakes with my kids or to engage in work I loved because I was slaving away on useless housework I felt obligated to do. I might have missed the chance to watch Ellie splash in the waves or hear Oscar say his own name. If I didn't pay attention to my needs, I could have missed out on the goodness of a fried chicken sandwich shared over bouts of laughter with friends I wouldn't have met.

I might not have finally taken the step to go get hearing aids, either. Now my ears could behold sounds they never used to, like Oscar's thoughtful questions and Ellie's giggles in the back seat, or rain falling on our sunroom roof and the red leaves crunching beneath my feet on my crisp fall morning walks.

The thing is, for every glorious sound I enjoyed, I also had to put up with noises I'd rather not experience. Like *SpongeBob* blaring from the living room TV or handfuls of cutleries clanging on the table. These noises made me want to gouge out my inner ear. But that's the deal, isn't it? We don't get to mute the hard and only hear the good. They are two sides of the same coin. Paying attention requires us to see, hear, and feel the complete spectrum of human emotions—the good and the bad.

Kids whine. Parents die. Husbands ask dumb questions. Overstimulation melts our brains. But shoving our feelings into pretty shoeboxes doesn't make them go away. Practicing boundaries with toxic people won't stop those blessed souls from taking up oxygen. There is nothing on the face of this earth that will save us from the reality that raising kids well and simultaneously *being* well is just fucking hard.

Ironically, facing that truth is what led me to experience the full magic of motherhood. Without starting the work of being honest with myself, I might have missed being present for the life I fought to build and the children I've worked so hard to raise. I would have missed Sunday Dinner, too.

MANY MONTHS BEFORE MY "will therapy ever start working?" spiral, back when Greg changed jobs and life started following a more predictable weekly pattern, our friends Abby and Noah invited us to have dinner with their family.

"Don't bring anything. We're just going to keep it simple," Abby texted.

Years ago, I might have spiraled. *Will the kids get along? What if her house is cleaner than mine? What if we don't agree on everything? What if I am a disappointment of a human being?* Maybe, I'd have said no or an insincere yes.

Instead, I said an unquestioning, full-bodied, YES.

That Sunday, the kids played happily while Abby and her husband, Noah, shared the preparation of a simple spaghetti dinner. They split the dishes, too. Spending time around another family who shared the load like we did was a welcome surprise. Over our meal, we exchanged our highs and lows. Then our family went home to a clean kitchen with full bellies and hearts.

A few weeks later, Greg and I invited our friends to our place.

We hosted back and forth like this until eventually Abby asked me a question I'd been longing to be asked for a decade, back when I was frazzled and alone at home with two small children every other weekend, back when we were new in town, when I scrolled Facebook, and when I watched my friends fill their lazy Sundays with their big, beautiful families, week after week.

We'd just finished dinner. The kids were in the basement playing a game and she turned to me, eagerly, and asked, "Do you want to make this a regular thing?"

My face answered before I could say the word. "Abso-fricken-lute-ly."

And so, Sunday Dinners were born. We kept expectations low for everyone. Sometimes Greg and I served nothing but frozen chicken nuggets and French fries. Other times, we ordered in. Nobody rushed to clean their house, lay out the perfect table settings, or fluff the pillows. There was no quiet comparison, judgment, or competition.

The rhythm, routine, and kinship Sunday Dinners provided us each week became a part of the fabric of our family's village quilt. Each week, I looked forward to Sunday Dinners. Our kids did, too. Living in community with good, honest, safe people is as valuable to me as oxygen and unbroken sleep. Our garden of humans? It was smaller now. But healthier.

Our shared meals didn't neatly cure all our parenting woes. Sure, the food was yummy. And half the time labor-free. But it wasn't about the meal or the table settings. Sunday Dinners were not just about dining with friends who had kids similar ages to ours that happened to live nearby (though I know this is much like winning the lottery). They filled buckets I didn't realize had been empty. Our gatherings connected us, gave us perspective, buffered us from isolation, and strengthened us all to face another week.

Now I could see that the birth of our little tradition was the result of every hard-won lesson I'd learned since I first picked up my rigged Rubik's Cube all those years before. Sunday Dinners, like the other recent wins in my life—the laundry I didn't do or the guilt I no longer felt for having human needs—was a representation of the slow, imperfect progress I'd made. Every baby step. Every agonizing setback and brave step forward without any guarantee of progress. Every lesson I didn't realize I was embedding into my psyche, changing how I moved through life.

Countless lessons. Like how unclenching my jaw and letting the process be ugly allowed things to happen that would have happened anyway. Like the truth that moms deserve full cups whether we are pouring out of them or not. Or that, despite my inflated sense of capacity, I am not, in fact, the *Titanic* but a mere fishing boat who will surely go under if I don't pay attention to the icebergs all around me.

I learned that using my voice gets me invited to some tables and barred from others, that emotional safety is more important for our kids than getting into Stanford, that cycles end with "I'm sorry," and that all humans suck sometimes—even me. (Well, I already knew that one.)

I learned that I have ADHD and that . . . wait, what was I saying? Oh yes! Sunshine and rainbows! They are pretty and bright and fun and easier to spot when you slow down and look up.

I'm sure we wouldn't have gotten the same magic out of our shared meals if I hadn't begun to heal. Those lessons are what made Sunday Dinners even more delicious and the hardships of life more manageable.

THE SUNDAY AFTER I BROKE down in therapy, it was our family's turn to host.

"Hey, Google, play 'Ain't No Mountain High Enough,'" I said, as Ellie pulled the ingredients for dinner from the fridge. We danced around the kitchen as I sliced the lemons, fresh dill, cucumbers, and peppers. I smothered the chicken in fresh olive oil and oregano and set it in the fridge to marinate. Good things take time. Dancing helps. I was preparing a fancy meal because I had the energy. Creating lovely things reminded me there is beauty in the world. This is corny and true. I moved slowly and intentionally. Fun fact: This practice helped calm my nervous system. On the menu? Chicken souvlaki. My favorite.

Once I finished all the preparations for dinner, our company arrived. The smell of roasting lemony garlic potatoes wafted through the door. The kids ran outside to play and the adults caught up on life. Our friends held space for my wounded heart, and I held on to their reminders that I'd been through hard things before. Sometimes, that's all we need.

As it turns out, there was never a world in which I aligned my little colorful squares, tossed the Rubik's Cube over my shoulder, and walked into the sunset victorious. The scramble is unavoidable. I don't think I'll ever feel calm while more than two devices are playing on full volume at once or *not* call myself an idiot when I forget an appointment or step on LEGO pieces, again. Some qualities and habits just get baked in, I'm afraid.

Society has a long way to go before it honors mothers like it should. I don't think the patriarchy will be falling down anytime soon. I'm sure the folks responsible for enacting public policy will not wake up tomorrow and suddenly realize the life-altering importance of supporting mothers and families. I don't know if it will ever be considered normal for fathers to do dishes at a potluck or for moms to go on child-free trips without someone saying something stupid like "But what about the kids?"

Honestly, I don't know much for certain, but I do know that the beauty and pain of being a mom is indescribable.

I know that so many things can be true at once.

I know that being a good mom will always be hard because it matters and that being able to be honest about all of it has made me more grateful for the opportunity than I ever imagined possible.

There's a lot I can't change. I accept that.

I also accept that it's my job to figure out what I *can* change to make it easier. Sometimes that fact makes me want to scream into the abyss. And you know what? Maybe I will. I don't need anyone's permission anymore. I listen to myself now.

27

Summers

People will forget what you said, people will forget what you did, but people will never forget how you made them feel.

MAYA ANGELOU

"You only get eighteen summers!"

This is a quote that gets circulated on social media every year. I'm pretty sure the words are meant to encourage parents to soak up the glorious memories while their kids are still sweet little dependent darlings. One might think I could get behind the sentiment. Instead, every time I see this reminder, it makes me want to strap my phone to a rocket ship and launch it at the surface of the sun. As if we need more pressure.

And yet, nearing the end of the summer, when it popped up on my feed, I still felt a pang of guilt stab me in the ribs. And so, I reflected on our sunny season. The incredible privilege of a sun-kissed French road trip for my kids could not be denied, obviously. But in that moment, all I could recall from our adventure abroad was the stress of travel and the heat that boiled my brains into an irritable oblivion.

One particular day was unforgettable. We'd driven five hours straight down the Atlantic coast of France to a little village called Lit-et-Mixe, where Greg spent his summers camping as a child. While we were not prepared to camp, we decided to include the stop on our adventure for the sake of nostalgia and the beach. The village sat in the middle of nowhere. It was so remote there were no nearby hotels, so I booked one of the only VRBO rentals available for the three nights of our stay.

Upon arrival, hungry, ready to pee, hot and tired, we found our accommodation: full. Every weary traveler's nightmare. Other guests were staying in our place, and despite our attempts to contact the owners or knock on the door, nobody answered. I googled our options. I asked locals who didn't speak a word of English. I tried everything I could think of and then broke into sheer panic. Where would we stay?

The kids waited in the back seat of the car while I kindly spoke, then pleaded, then argued with the VRBO agent on the phone. Thirty minutes passed. Then another hour of her assuring me that she'd find a solution. She did not. We were stranded without options unless we wanted to abandon Lit-et-Mixe altogether and drive another two hours to find beds that night. *Hard pass.*

After two-and-a-half hours on the phone, I hit my limit with the lukewarm customer service lady. I'll admit it was out of character, but I snapped. Did I yell? Yes. Am I proud of it? No. Was there a collection of colorful f-bombs thrown around that my children were not used to me using? Absolutely. After I hung up, I melted down in the front seat of the car. Eventually, Greg found a trailer park and booked us into a caravan rental that we were absolutely not equipped for. Sleeping bags, anyone? Defeated and operating with oatmeal for brains, I gave in. We unloaded our luggage into the little, partially air-conditioned trailer without sheets, paper towels, and toilet paper. It felt like our vacation was imploding.

Eighteen summers. We had the chance to give our kids the trip of a lifetime and make our newlywed selves proud. Now, freshly triggered by the Instagram gods, that nightmarish scene and the rest of my imperfect, stress-ball moments during the summer were all I could think of.

A few days later, Greg, Ellie, Oscar, and I were out for breakfast at our favorite local eatery. The kids colored while Greg and I drank our hot coffee—one of the wonders of having middle-size children. *Hooray.*

I spotted a mom and her toddler walking back from what I assume was a bathroom diaper change toward the table beside us. The little one tripped over her own feet and landed on her hands and knees on the ground before bursting into tears. "Mommmmyyyyyy," she cried. The mom swooped her up, carried her back to their table, kissed her hands and knees, and rocked her. The toddler rested her head on her mom's chest, the mom hummed to her, spoon-fed the child fruit salad, and watched her own food get cold. *I remember what that was like,* I thought.

Then, as I watched them, I felt uncomfortably similar to the old ladies in the Walmart checkout a decade earlier who longingly watched me with my whining kids. The ones I wanted to throat-punch when they told me how fast it all goes.

I looked over at my middle-size kids and for a moment I could picture the little scrumptious versions of them so vividly. Oscar, who used to come running to me the moment he bumped his knee, now spat out "I'm fine, Mom," whenever he grazed a limb. Ellie, once glued to my side, now begged me to walk to school alone. Both kids, once absolutely obsessed with me, waking me up at the crack of dawn, wiggling, giggling, unable to contain their excitement for a new day, now woke up without needing me whatsoever.

They were becoming more independent. I was not responsible for being everything to everyone all the time anymore. I had wanted this stage so bad. So why were my eyes welling up looking at this mom and her baby? I should be happy!

I *was* happy, the happiest I'd been in years, overall. But I couldn't help but wonder and worry that my kids wouldn't remember the years I devoted all my energy to the bath times, bedtimes, breakfast times, story times, playtimes, and snuggle times that went on and on and on. I feared they'd forget the way I cut their Nutella on toast into puzzle shapes, or created magical homemade cardboard contraptions, how I gave butterfly kisses, or signed "I love you" as the school bus drove away.

I fretted that they'd only remember the empowered years I went after my dreams and let go of holding all the cards, that they'd only remember when Dad was the default and wonder if it meant I didn't care. I knew it was silly, but I couldn't help but think they might forget the years my life revolved around their moment-to-moment desires, fears, food aversions, and fevers. The way their legs straddled my hip, the way they looked to me for assurance and applause for front lawn cartwheels.

Eighteen summers. What if they only remember my worst moments? The days I felt incapable of being present? What if they only remember the parts I wished I could change? What if they don't remember our delicious memories or how much I love them?

Did I feel unimportant because my children were no longer a part of my shadow? Or had I reached that weird point in motherhood that I thought would never come, the moment I realized just how fast it all went; how beautiful it was to be so viscerally needed and kind of miss it? I think I did.

The truth was that sometimes I did want to go back and be there again, to the thick of it, with their squishy cheeks, mispronounced words, their robots, dolls, their "I wuv yous," and puddle jumps. I ached for the times when the solution to nearly all their problems was a long cuddle with Mummy.

I didn't miss the overwhelm, the wet coughs I caught in my mouth, the tantrums, and the blood-curdling screams about bananas I opened the wrong way. I didn't want to experience the insanity of the sleepless nights and my own unmet needs for another moment. I sure didn't want another baby.

But sometimes, the truth is that reflecting on the past caused a tidal wave of grief to wash over me. I mourned for the memories *I* couldn't remember or be present for. I grieved the loss of time, the songs I didn't hear because I needed to tune them out to survive, the stories I only pretended to listen to because I was disassociated or depressed. I imagined the moments I didn't get to fully enjoy because I was just so tired, eye-glazed, and desperate for rest.

In my most honest nostalgic moments, I think I'd give anything to hold my own babies one more time, to be needed again—except this time, with rested eyes.

ON THE LAST NIGHT OF summer break, Greg, Ellie, Oscar, and I tucked up into my bed to read a story. As we wrapped up, I asked the kids to share their favorite moments of the summer.

"When you said yes to staying up late at the drive-in!"

"When we had a picnic on the trampoline!"

"The day we had a family campout in the basement!"

"When you threw me in the pool!"

"Making the cardboard fort in the backyard!"

"Back-to-school shopping!"

"The bike ride where we got caught in the rain!"

"France!" one of them said.

That's kind of generic, I thought. Was it the crepes in Cannes or the gelato in Monte Carlo? Was it frolicking in the Palace of Versailles or the Seine river cruise that did it? We'd covered so much ground over three whole weeks. I was curious as to what stood out.

"What about France?" I asked.

"That beach where you played in the waves with us," Ellie said.

"Oh yeah! Remember, we built that awesome sandcastle with a moat?! That was the best day," Oscar chimed in.

A knowing smile spread across my face. "I remember," I said.

It was the day we checked into that damn trailer park, when I was worn out and filled with rage. We tried to make a small attempt at salvaging the day with a trip to Greg's favorite beach. We parked beneath the towering pines, their mossy scent thick in the air, sun flickering through the branches. The needles crunched under our feet as we passed the beachgoers leaving for the day before we got to the bottom of a hill. With towels in hand, the four of us climbed the massive sand dune that led to the beach. Our legs burned. Our sweat trickled. And then, there was the Atlantic Ocean, vast and wild. Windy in that way that filled our kids—and a nostalgic Greg—with giddy beans.

On the beach, we set up our towels. The sun was still warm but not quite warm enough for this cautious mom to throw herself into the crashing waves. My deep and irrational fear of large bodies of water may have also played a part in that choice.

I was happy to sit out while Greg and Ellie galloped into the choppy waves and began splashing like maniacs. I laid down and gazed at the ocean while Oscar happily dug in the sand. I took a few deep breaths, letting the evening sun soak into my skin. The sound of the waves eased my shoulders down. The sight of my happy, safe family filled me with gratitude. *What a view.*

Twenty blissful minutes passed before Oscar asked me, "Mom! Want to dig a massive hole and bury me in it?" "Absolutely I do." We got to work with our bare hands. Once we dug deep enough that he could neatly fit inside, he hopped in. "Want me to cover you?" I asked. He nodded enthusiastically. I piled the sand over every part of his body until we could only see his head. Greg and Ellie giddily came back to shore shortly after we finished and Ellie yelled out, "That's amazing! Can you bury me now?"

Oscar jumped out of the sand and together we began to dig a hole big enough for Ellie. Greg picked up his phone and pointed the camera at us. "Smile!" he said. He moved to another angle. "One more!" and snapped a few more pictures. Together we took turns burying each other and then built a massive sandcastle complete with a round moat and a flag in the middle.

"Mom, want to come play in the waves? They are awesome!" Ellie said. I hemmed and hawed. But I was covered in sand and remnants of stress that needed to be washed off, so I gave in. Despite my fear, the waves *did* look fun.

"I'll race you there," I said, and booked it to the water. We splashed until the sun set, and our cheeks ached with joy. Once dusk set in, we hopped in the car, rolled the windows down, and cranked the French radio. I let the coastal wind blow through my tangled salty hair all the way home. Well, all the way to the trailer park.

My kids didn't give two craps about the fanciness or charm of France. To my delight, they didn't seem to recall the visceral stress or the curse words I dropped in the front seat of the car. Ellie and Oscar didn't mention my time-sucking workload once we arrived back in Canada; the TV I plopped them in front of for hours on end, or all the times I said no.

The memories that stood out for them? Both that summer and so many of our seasons before—they were simple. They didn't require long stretches of time, feverish planning, or wads of cash. Often, their mentions were nothing more than happy accidents or activities squashed into seven-minute windows of time at the end of a busy day.

Luckily, their happiest memories didn't require the lack of unhappy ones, either.

What did their favorite memories have in common?

My full-bodied presence.

Mine do, too.

UNFORTUNATELY, I CAN'T CONTROL WHAT my children will remember when they grow up. I can't control the storms they will endure, how they'll interpret everything I did and didn't do, nor can I control the choices they'll make once they are out of my reach. Alas, *that* was never my job.

My task has always been to love them and raise them well. To create independent people who know and trust themselves. Not needing me like they used to is simply a bittersweet result of that work. I know now that there will always be moments where I long to relive the wonder from their littlest years.

But I *can* continue to fight for my wholeness so that I'll be the kind of person they *want* to be around, even when they *don't* need me. Then, I won't have to chase the echo of their childhood laughter down a hallway. Eighteen summers? Please. I want long-term genuine connection, not obligation. A strong foundation. Giggles about teenage crushes. Tears shared at concerts. Inside jokes, good wine, and holiday dinners together that nobody has to pregame for or recover from. A lifetime of love and shared memories. *That's* the dream.

For now my focus isn't on memories. It's on living full life in the present.

Undeniable worth. Ferocious joy. Palpable peace. Nourishing work. Consistent good-enough-ness. Bone-deep belonging. Unapologetic authenticity. Hot tea and hopeful books. Belly laughter in backyards. Naps under shaded trees. Dancing in kitchens and vineyards and cars.

I deserve it all.

They're my summers, too.

Acknowledgments

One final truth? Words cannot convey the depth of gratitude I hold for all the people who have made this book a reality. Still, I will try.

To Greg, my husband, best friend, and life partner. You have carried me through endless storms over our decades together. You've witnessed every messy, evolving version of me and remained steadfast, loyal, and unwavering. Thank you for loving me, for building this incredible family with me, and for staying committed to the work of making our lives beautiful and whole. Thank you for allowing me to share my version of our story and for carrying everything while I brought it to life. This book would not exist without you. I love you.

To my children. Thank you for leading me back to myself and reminding me what matters most in life. Thank you for your grace in all the imperfect ways I have mothered you. Thank you for allowing me to share parts of our lives and for your endless patience, love, and support as I wrote these words. You are my reason.

To Veronica Goldstein and Rebecca Gradinger, thank you for believing in me from the very beginning, for seeing the value of my work, and for your endless support and encouragement to tell my story and trust my own voice.

To my editor, Aubrey Martinson, and the entire team at Crown—Chantelle Walker, Julie Cepler, Tammy Blake, Annsley Rosner, Dyana Messina, Joyce Wong, OJ Singh, Yang Kim, Dan Novack, Andrea Lau, Christopher Andrus, Eldes Tran—who made this book a reality: Thank you for taking a chance on me and holding my hand through the process of becoming an author *eeeek.* I'm so grateful for the way you have championed this book, supported my voice, and helped bring it into the world. Your expertise, steady guidance, and behind-the-scenes magic have made all the difference.

To Libby Burton, who saw the heart of this book before it had a spine. Thank you for recognizing its potential, for helping me see the strength in my own storytelling, and for guiding it toward what it was always meant to be.

To Samantha Rose, for coaching me through the process of writing this book and being my rock. Thank you for holding both me and my truth in your hands as you encouraged, edited, and helped me shape this story. You are a godsend.

To Elissa Joy Watts, for your incessant optimism, unwavering support, and unmatched wordsmithery. You have made me a better writer and renewed my hope in new humans again.

To Hilary Swanson, who coached and cracked me open at the beginning of this journey. Your passion, support, and guidance helped me make this book what it is.

To Christine and Roger, thank you for raising your son to be the man and father he is, for all the support you offer our family, and for all the ways you've modeled love throughout the years. Our family, my mothering, and this book would not be what it is without you.

To my brother, Harry, and Amanda, you've been a wonderful uncle and aunt to these kids, great friends to Greg and me, and much needed encouragement on this wild journey of *being a person who is writing a book.* Thank you for riding the waves and always sticking by my side.

To Becca, my lifelong friend and ride-or-die, consistent lifesaver: Thank you for all the ways you have supported my personhood, motherhood, and career so that I didn't entirely lose the plot. You held up the sky when I could not. Endless gratitude for you, my friend.

To Krista, for being my gateway drug to feminism, for being my first and most consistent example of a woman who champions women, puts love into action, follows her dreams, and allows herself to be messy in the process. Thank you for being a friend and village member. I could not have written this book without all the threads of you in my life.

To "Leah," for being the first mom I could be honest with, an example of what motherly love looks like, and a friend who has helped me become who I am today. I hold so much love and gratitude for you.

To "Abby," for showing me what safety looks and feels like in friendship, for being my village, for reading too many versions of this manuscript, and for stitching me back together all the times I fell apart writing it.

To Dr. Tanya Cotler, Dr. Sophie Brock, Eve Rodsky, Anna Malaika Tubbs, and Laura Danger: Thank you for your time and expertise as it pertains to this book and also my own motherhood. Thank you for your work in supporting mothers and making the world a better place to be a mother.

Lindsay, Jacquie, Cait, Jaimee, Kalie, Jess, Jocelyn, Julie, and all the friends these pages can't contain: Thank you for being badass women who support other women, friends who show me what love is, mothers who inspire me, and humans who are fully and authentically yourselves and allow me to be the same. Your support has impacted this book more than you know.

To my team who kept me afloat while this book took over my

brain and life but specifically: Jaime Schmidt-Little, your steady, reliable, and compassionate support made my writing possible. Jen Swartly, what can't you do? I'm endlessly grateful to have had your support in a season of business that I struggled to stay above water in. Thank you for helping me to stay true to myself, for always being four steps ahead, and knowing just what I needed when I needed it.

To my online community, for entrusting me with your stories, vulnerabilities, and for your support. There is no chance this book would exist without you. Every day, you inspire me, encourage me, and push me forward to be a better mother for my children and to make the world a better place for women to be mothers. From the bottom of my heart, thank you.

To the women authors whose stories, expertise, and courage have shaped me into the woman and mother I am today: Brené Brown, Jen Hatmaker, Glennon Doyle, Sarah Bessey, Kate Bowler, and others. I would not be who I am, or how I am, nor would this this book exist without you. Thank you for enlightening me, creating a path, and for helping us all to be more whole humans.

Finally, to my mom, who has been there since my first breath. I love you. Giving me your blessing to share some of the most difficult parts of our story takes indescribable courage and grace. This very act alone is a testament to the work you have done to be the most honest version of yourself. I'm grateful to have you in my life and for all you have done to be a good mother, despite the setbacks and traumas you also endured. I hope you know the gravity of the power our story beholds to help other mothers heal and to become the moms they were meant to be. Thank you for beginning to do the work and allowing me to shine a light where there was once darkness.

To all the mothers doing their best with what they have, falling and getting back up again, and telling the truth: I see you; I am you. Thank you from me, from your children, and from your children's children. It matters.

Notes

1: Mmm, Raisins

11 **"increasing stress and declining mental health":** Mary Whitfill Roeloffs, "Surgeon General Urges More Governmental Support for Parents Amid Mental Health Struggles," *Forbes*, August 28, 2024, https://www.forbes.com/sites/maryroeloffs/2024/08/28/surgeon-general-urges-more-governmental-support-for-parents-amid-mental-health-struggles/.

12: Shoeboxes

111 **30 percent of moms who struggle with postpartum mental health:** Laurel M. Hicks et al., Assessment of Canadian Perinatal. Mental Health Services from the Provider Perspective: Where Can We Improve?" *Frontiers in Psychiatry* 13 (2022), https://pmc.ncbi.nlm.nih.gov/articles/PMC9537741/.

111 **blinding rage were gigantic flashing arrows:** "A Fact Sheet From the Office on Women's Health," *Office on Women's Health*, October 17, 2023, https://womenshealth.gov/mental-health/mental-health-conditions/postpartum-depression.

17: No Wonder

150 **"The irony is that we attempt to disown our difficult":** Quotation and paraphrased ideas from Brené Brown, *The Gifts of Imperfection: Let Go of Who You Think You're Supposed to Be and Embrace Who You Are* (Hazelden Publishing, 2010), 6.

150 **The test was created in the 1990s to measure the long-term:** Zachary Giano et al., "The Frequencies and Disparities of Adverse Childhood Experiences in the U.S.," *BMC Public Health* 20 (2020), https://bmcpublichealth.biomedcentral.com/articles/10.1186/s12889-020-09411-z#Sec4.

151 **2.3 percent of the population have a score of six:** Ibid.

152 **Our bodies remember our trauma even when:** Bessel Van Der Kolk, *The Body Keeps the Score: Brain, Mind, and Body in the Healing of Trauma* (Viking, 2014).

156 **They noticed major ties between the quality:** Inge Bretherton, *The Origins of Attachment Theory: John Bowlby and Mary Ainsworth* (American Psychological Association, 1992), 759–75, https://psychology.psy.sunysb.edu/attachment/online/inge_origins%20DP1992.pdf.

157 **"the ability to be in touch with and express":** Quotation and paraphrased ideas from Gabor Maté with Daniel Maté, *The Myth of Normal: Trauma, Illness, and Healing in a Toxic Culture* (Avery, 2022).

159 **The problem is that these behaviors become our default:** van der Kolk, *The Body Keeps the Score*, 44–50.

161 **what they needed was to be raised by:** Colleen Doyle and Dante Cicchetti, "From the Cradle to the Grave: The Effect of Adverse Caregiving Environments on Attachment and Relationships Throughout the Lifespan," *Clinical Psychology: A Publication of the Division of Clinical Psychology of the American Psychological Association* 24, no. 2 (2017): 203–17, https://pmc.ncbi.nlm.nih.gov/articles/PMC5600283/.

161 **the authors say we're asking the wrong question:** Bruce D. Perry and Oprah Winfrey, *What Happened to You? Conversations on Trauma, Resilience, and Healing* (Flatiron Books, 2021).

18: Icebergs

166 **Stress makes problem solving and emotional regulation harder:** Amy Arnsten et al., "Everyday Stress Can Shut Down the Brain's Chief Command Center," *Scientific American*, April 1, 2012, https://www.scientificamerican.com/article/this-is-your-brain-inmeltdown/#:~:text=The%20work%20showed%20that%20neurons,stronger%20hold%20over%20our%20behavior.

167 **A superior mirage happens when layers:** "Fata Morgana Mirage," Farmers' Almanac, accessed June 2, 2025, https://www.farmersalmanac.com/fata-morgana-mirage.

170 **"Creating a secure attachment is not":** Tanya Cotler, clinical psychologist specializing in parent–child attachment, interview by the author, Toronto, via Zoom, 2025.

170 **"That it's in her. That creating a secure attachment":** Ibid.

170 **the International Ice Patrol was established:** The Editors of Encyclopedia Britannica, "International Maritime Organization," *Encyclopedia Britannica*, February 11, 2025, https://www.britannica.com/topic/International-Maritime-Organization.

21: Dishes

186 **"The gendered division of labor":** Candace West and Don H. Zimmerman, "Doing Gender," *Gender & Society* 1, no. 2 (1987): 125–51, http://www.jstor.org/stable/189945.

188 **that is highly linked to chronic stress:** American Autoimmune Related Diseases Association (AARDA), *Autoimmune Disease: The Facts,* 2021, https://autoimmune.org/.

192 **"the last frontier of feminism.":** Eve Rodsky, *Fair Play: A Game-Changing Solution for When You Have Too Much to Do (and More Life to Live)* (Random House, 2019).

22: The Contract

203 **the pervasive and completely bonkers idea:** Interview with Dr. Sophie Brock, motherhood sociologist and researcher, conducted via Zoom between Canada and Australia, 2024.

204 **"We treat men's time like diamonds and women's like sand":** Eve Rodsky, *Fair Play: A Game-Changing Solution for When You Have Too Much to Do (and More Life to Live)* (Random House, 2019).

23: Gardening

222 **"True belonging is the spiritual practice of believing":** Brené Brown, *Braving the Wilderness: The Quest for True Belonging and the Courage to Stand Alone* (Random House, 2017).

24: Safety

235 **Experiencing repetitive safety, security, and belonging:** Bessel van der Kolk, *The Body Keeps the Score: Brain, Mind, and Body in the Healing of Trauma* (Penguin Books, 2015).

25: Human

238 **housewives and mothers who felt like they were:** Betty Friedan, *The Feminine Mystique* (W.W. Norton & Company, 1963).

239 **tranquilizers were being prescribed by the millions:** Michel Foucault, *Discipline and Punish* (Pantheon Books, 1977).

ABOUT THE AUTHOR

Libby Ward is a writer, speaker, and advocate redefining the motherhood narrative. Through her social media platforms (@libbyward), Libby is known to connect and empower women with honesty, humor, and her relatable voice. She has been featured on the BBC and on *Good Morning America* and is a member of Reese Witherspoon's inaugural Hello Sunshine Collective. She lives in Ontario, Canada, with her husband and two children.